Rea
M

C000271189

The Walking Worried

Aron Bennett

chipmunkapublishing
the mental health publisher

All rights reserved, no part of this publication may be reproduced by any means, electronic, mechanical photocopying, documentary, film or in any other format without prior written permission of the publisher.

Published by
Chipmunkapublishing
United Kingdom

http://www.chipmunkapublishing.com

Copyright © 2015 Aron Bennett

ISBN 978-1-78382-158-7

Chipmunkapublishing gratefully acknowledge the support of Arts Council England.

Introduction
'WALK A LONELY ROAD'

*"The road of life twists and turns and no two directions are ever the same.
Yet our lessons come from the journey, not the destination."*
- Don Williams, Jr.

I used to write a diary. Then I stopped. I didn't stop so much out of choice but out of being railroaded into stopping. I had, up until that point, always treasured writing in my custom printed, spiral-bound, A5 journal – before that, a black Rustico pocket diary. Partaking in this quiet, unassuming recreation had been somewhat of a comfort to me, a cathartic pastime if you will. I had not predicted its demise, nor did I believe that my anxiety would compromise my pursuit of this essentially harmless hobby on such unforgiving terms. But back then, I had not heard of the devastating condition known as *OCD*. Nor had I any idea of the distressing impact it would have on my life.

For me, obsessive compulsive disorder - or OCD as it is more commonly known - has been single-handedly the greatest block to happiness that I have known. It is a ubiquitous disorder characterised by both inimical anxiety and unyielding shame. It is a disorder at odds with well-being, peace-of-mind, freedom and happiness. It is, as many psychologists describe it, an *egodystonic* disorder. That is, a disorder at odds, or at variance, with a person's true beliefs and core values – or even their very *identity*.

At its worst, I could not function, at least not in a useful or acceptable way. Someone once asked me what it actually felt like having OCD. I told them that having OCD was like walking home at night alone with danger, perceived or otherwise, lurking in every corner; places and things once deemed safe during the hours of daylight, no longer a sure fire bet.

In 2008 it had finally affected my writing. My ten year hobby of keeping a diary had finally grown to become this full-blown risk inside my own head, preventable only by stopping or, in OCD parlance, *'avoiding'*. And so I avoided - I dismantled my journal, tore up old entries and prepared myself for a new sort of life without a journal for company. It was a major surrender and it had cost me my freedom.

The main reason for deeming my diary a threat was based primarily on the fear that it risked making me a *bad* person, a theme that, as you will see, runs through this book like a gushing stream, connecting otherwise isolated fragments of mania together into one unified preoccupation. This was only one manifestation of my illness, though as with all forms, it had become a debilitating affair.

Each night I would tie myself in knots, strangely preoccupied with the idea that my diary might no longer be *pure,* that, at some point in the future, something horrible might happen to someone I knew or loved and that I might derive some sort of perverse satisfaction from writing about it. Illness, death and other mini-tragedies should surely not be a source of enjoyment, even for a diarist. After all, this was real life, not a soap opera. Yet, the thought of an exciting new 'story line' seemingly pleased the little scamp inside of me no end. It was enough to make me question myself in an almost unprecedented manner; perhaps I was a secret psychopath? Maybe I didn't really love my family? Maybe, given the choice, I would sooner witness the gruesome murder of a friend than have nothing to write about?

My mum would often try to convince me that my thirst for drama was entirely natural, that I was a perfectly 'normal' individual in that respect and that *all* people had, as she put it, 'a touch of the macabre' in the way they contemplated life, but that there was a world of difference between *thinking* whatever you liked and actually doing something. Yet I remained unconvinced. Writing in a diary was *doing* something.

Eventually, the thought of putting pen to paper, of scribbling down a new entry, of *tragedizing* yet another life event, however circadian, made me feel positively nauseous. The guilt, the shame, the illusory threat of damnation - it had hit me like a ton of bricks and I knew then that I would have my work cut out coming back to any point of meaningful lucidity.

As I have learned, OCD is very good at feeding you half truths and issuing malign falsities. Over the years, it has convinced me of almost everything from being responsible for spreading HIV, to causing people cancer by having my phone on, to being capable even of rape. A great majority of my OCD stayed within the confines of my own head - sometimes referred to as Pure O or primarily obsessional OCD. A significant amount of my OCD has been sexual in nature and based on a fear of my own sexual thoughts, ideas and fantasies. Most of my OCD, as I have already mentioned, pivoted on a fear of being a bad person.

Giving up my diary was only one of many different 'control strategies' I would later have to adopt in order to neutralise the devastating effects of my anxiety. My compulsions, though most of them remained in my head, affected me in small, yet significant, ways every single day. Of course, there were good days. But it would be incredibly rare to have a totally OCD-free day. I certainly do not remember any.

It is perhaps one of the more curious signature features of OCD that it is *daily* life which gets so readily altered in observance of such bizarre compulsions and rituals whilst other, often more important, life choices tend to get rather glibly passed over. Something as trivial as accidently brushing passed a woman on a crowded train station (how do I know for sure I didn't do it *on purpose* for sexual pleasure??) would keep me up all night, sick with worry. Not kicking a piece glass into the curb and off the pavement (where some child could fall on it, cut themselves and contract TB) was enough to render me borderline asthmatic. Yet, my decision to move away to university, to fall in love, even to pursue a career centred on helping the guilty evade prison (more on all of that later), caused little inner conflict.

Below is a good example of how such immensely trivial, day-to-day events could spark such disproportionate levels of fear:

It was an afternoon in February and I was walking home from the city of Norwich (where I still live with my mum and dad in our family home) and was drawn to an attractive twenty-something year-old in the window of Anne Summers, feeling up one of those deeply alluring monochrome silk bras with black floral lace embroidery. Absorbedly, I gazed at the attractive silhouette shopping serenely for sexy underwear before remembering a rule I had made on the matter only a month prior which stated that staring at an 'attractive' woman for five seconds or more would render the perpetrator of such an act a pervert and hence a 'bad' person.

In my pruriently torpid state, I had no doubt been staring for *at least* five seconds and so in fear of transgressing my own rules any further, and thereby becoming a 'bad' person, I looked away instantly. But alas, I was too late. Something, I am not sure what, had made her look up and she scoured over in my direction just in time to catch me in the act. And in fear that she was now about to phone the police to report me, I bolted across the road like lightening, narrowly avoiding the oncoming traffic, and continued walking on the wrong side of the street until the coast was clear.

That evening, I worried until the early hours about the way I had looked at her. In particular, I worried that I had caused her distress by staring for so long. That by so guiltily flinching away, I had merely galvanised her apprehension that I was up to no good, that something furtively underhand was taking place right under her nose. Maybe she had thought that I was 'stalking' her in secret or even planning on physically attacking her? I thought over and over about all the distress I might have caused her. I had caused distress. I was a bad person.

Living with OCD on a day-to-day basis is like, each day, going off on your own private journey. Such a journey is long, at times distressing, often very time consuming and nearly always utterly unfathomable to those on the outside looking in. However, for the most part, it is a journey that will go unnoticed by most of the rest of the world. Most OCDers are extremely careful to do whatever it takes to keep their symptoms hidden from view. So much so that it is currently estimated that the average lag time between the onset of OCD symptoms and being diagnosed is as many as nine years. Yet nonetheless, millions of these hidden journeys go on each day the world over.

Look at it like this: can you really be sure that the woman walking around the supermarket with her shopping trolley full to the brim is simply there to pick up a week's worth of food for her family or could it be that she is there, on her own, in order to replace every last food item in her single-bedroom flat because the other day she had rather carelessly sprayed some air freshener into the kitchen, thereby contaminating all the food inside her cupboards, causing her to have to discard over a month's worth of food and replace it all immediately the next day?

Living with OCD is like living in your own peculiar 'story line'. Yet, for most people with OCD, the journey goes untold. More to the point, the story tends to be long and arduous and can result in years of needless suffering. I am fortunate that I was able to get a handle on my symptoms relatively soon after my diagnosis. And it is precisely for that reason that I now find myself sitting back at the PC, not writing a diary, but constructing a full blown memoire. After all, writing is what I enjoy doing the most. Far from making me a bad person, I hope that by writing this book, I will be able to reach out to all those experiencing the same thing, maybe even offer some useful advice when and where I can.

In many ways, I am one of the lucky ones. I have not experienced the shame that many people with OCD, particularly from older generations, have had to endure nor have I been shunned by family and friends who have all listened to my stories and offered me nothing but support. In that regard, I have had the confidence to put this manuscript together and the backing to help see it through. It is perhaps only fair that I take advantage of my good fortune and at least attempt to help lift the lid of this rather abject disorder, to end some of the generational shame surrounding the affliction and to expose my own peculiar journey of OCD using the familiar medium of confessional writing.

Unlike many other mental illnesses, the symptoms and secret rituals involved with OCD are willingly absorbed and camouflaged into everyday life by the sufferer, thereby ensuring that a rather tough and debilitating journey goes on for years unnoticed and without disruption. There are often no 'breakdowns' or grounds for committal (at least not typically) and therefore no clear indicator to the outside world that someone even has OCD. Yet these stories of suffering, albeit non-life-threatening or climactic, must be shared if we, as a society, are ever to get a grip on a disorder which affects around twelve in every thousand people in the UK.

Where I can, I try not to put too serious a tone on my writing or to become morbidly fixated on the suffering involved. Due to the outlandish nature of OCD, there is a funny side to most people's journeys. Where one of my own symptoms makes for a humorous anecdote I make no apology in making light of it. To take one's own symptoms of OCD too seriously is as disastrous to recovery as giving into the wretched compulsions in the first place.

There is of course one other very important journey I want to talk about in the book and that, of course, is the journey I made to getting better through therapy and various other invaluable techniques I managed to pick up along the way. Just as one does not get hit with OCD like a bolt out of the blue, nor can recovery be an immediate transmutation. Living with OCD means that one must *un-live* it in order to get better. And so getting better becomes a journey all by itself.

I hope that the various chapters which follow on from here will resonate with anybody who is either suffering or has suffered with OCD together with anyone out there who may know or love someone who now lives with such a debilitating illness. I also hope that this will be informative and interesting to anyone reading from a more general perspective.

As is the case, and has been for some months, my own OCD has largely now attenuated into levity, even impertinence. I am, to an extent, free. But I have not forgotten my battle with OCD and have not taken for granted what it means to gain a large part of my life back. Here is *my* journey...

Chapter 1
OCD AND ME

"I'm a person who also happens to have OCD"
- Patricia Perkins-Doyle

This book is not about me, it's about OCD. And whilst it is sometimes considered good therapy to consciously recognise the distinction – *'it's not me it's my OCD'* - my illness does not exist in isolation. So I take this opportunity to give away a little about myself if, for no other reason, than to give my disorder a context; to give it human qualities by which we may more easily dissect its true nature.

I am 25 years old at the time of writing this chapter and, at present, I am still living at home with both my parents. I have no real plans to move out any time soon. My favourite films are *'Annie Hall'* and '*The Green Mile'* and my favourite dish is my mum's own homemade chicken pilaf, which we tend to have at least once a week. My favourite musical is Les Mis (a firm family favourite ever since my parents went to see it in 1996, who, upon hearing its dulcet tones for the very first time, had brought back its melancholic air into the family home by means of pirated compact cassette) and my all-time favourite bands are *The smiths*, *Mumford and Sons* and *The Magnetic Fields*.

I was born in Southend-on-Sea, a small seaside town in Essex, around forty miles east of Central London where I lived right up until the age of sixteen. We moved to Norwich in 2002 (following the completion of my GCSEs) because my dad had retired and Norfolk was *'a much slower pace of life'*. The choice to move was a good one; I have had some of my best years here and feel privileged to still be able to call this my home.

In 2004 I went off to university in Lancaster to study Law. I did not enjoy living up north. Indeed my time at university saw my mental health suffer an all time low. Understandably, I was pleased when it was eventually all over in 2006 whereupon I graduated with a 2:1.

Currently I am employed to do a non-legal related office job out in a small Norfolk town called Diss where I commute each day on the train. It isn't as glamorous as a job in law but I certainly enjoy it. Before that, I worked as a check-out operator in Morrisons which I did for five years during my A-level and degree study.

Sandwiched briefly in between stacking shelves and commuting to Diss was a short stint as a paralegal for a criminal law firm back in Southend. The job offered me the transom opportunity to witness life as a trainee solicitor. It also meant moving back to Essex. Perhaps unsurprisingly, it did not take me long to conclude that a life away from my family, of courtrooms and prison cells, of opting out of The Working Time Regulations, would not be the career choice for me and I returned after only three months of being away.

I am not an only child. I have a younger brother called Joe. He is creative, intelligent and, like me, can become quite fixated at times. Unlike me, he has long since flown the nest. In fact, whilst I am busy writing this book, he is even busier renovating his first house with his girlfriend Emma which they bought together at the young age of 21. Thankfully, and I pray this remains the case, my brother does not suffer with OCD.

My mum and dad also do not suffer with OCD – or at least hadn't suffered with it by the time I had been diagnosed in 2008 – but have always been incredibly understanding about the way it has affected me. They have provided me with a stress-free family environment as well as a fantastic childhood. And whilst OCD is not *caused* by a dysfunctional family environment, the stability that I have been provided has given me the support and focus I have needed to get myself through.

Other pivotal people in my life have, of course, been my friends. My best friend, Jake, whom I met at sixth form, has been my closest friend now for over eight years. Like me, he is far too analytical for his own good. Unlike me, he does not have OCD. And this I use to my advantage. I trust him more than most to talk me out of my OCD, to journey propitiously into my somewhat *screwy* mindset and drag me kicking and screaming to the shores of sanity.

I have also learned when and where *not* to rely on those around me. I have learned to stand on my own two feet when and where I can; to be 'mindful' of my descent into irrational discourse. In particular, I try not to allow myself to embroil family members into my pursuit for *reassurance* nor do I respond well to reassurance being provided in abundance by well-meaning friends and relatives. Reassurance is OCD *enabling*. It provides sufferers with relief from their obsessive concerns rather than encouraging rational debate. In my house, reassurance in response to OCD is provided only sparingly.

In 2008, I joined an OCD support group and have not looked back since. It has been an excellent source of both education and understanding. It is also one of the few places where I have had the privilege of meeting some extraordinarily like-minded people. As one of my fellow OCDers has testified, "One of the most important supportive elements of the group is the feeling of not being alone with this devastating condition."

And so I have continued to attend group regularly for over four years now. I have seen it transform from a relatively small gathering of downtrodden faces to becoming a publicly funded *organisation* with its own written constitution and offering 'a pscho-educational approach' to OCD. As our organisation founder, Margo, likes to say, "We are not a group based on 'tea and sympathy'."

With such an abundance of support and understanding, it is no wonder I have been able to focus so well on my recovery. Others are not so lucky. Many suffer alone. Many do not have understanding loved ones in their lives. Many do not know that support groups exist up and down the country or even that there is no *shame* in seeking help.

Where I have perhaps not been so lucky, if this is indeed relevant, has been *in love*. OCD is a lonely experience. Sometimes, I cannot help but feel that the intimate and unconditional support from the right person – *a girlfriend* - would perhaps have made a difference to my suffering. How much of a difference, I cannot say.

How much of a difference my *personality* has made both in terms of fuelling my OCD and in exacerbating the symptoms is also difficult to quantify. If I am a product of my OCD, then I am perhaps also the trigger. Though I try not to delve too deeply into this aspect of my illness; the answer is possibly of very little consequence. If there's one thing that I have learned, OCD can affect *anyone*.

OCD is also not a *personality* disorder nor is it linked to a particular type of background or upbringing. Like many illnesses, it is an affliction often pre-existing outside of our control. Though, that is not to say that attitude and lifestyle do not play a part.

Quite crucially, they can be instrumental in recovery.

I did not cause my OCD but I can choose to end it. It is a comforting appraisal. It is also an empowering one. It took me a long time to realise that my OCD was not my fault. It took me even longer to learn that I had it in me to reverse the symptoms of it.

Whenever I am feeling down or struggling with obsessive thoughts, I will always refer to one particular book on OCD that had changed my whole perception of the disorder: *'Brain Lock'* by Dr Jeffrey Schwartz M.D. This defying work impressed upon me the efficacy of self-directed behavioural therapy. It explained, quite neatly, how OCD was nothing more than a genetic disposition, a set of false messages from the brain. But that these could nearly always be overcome by reference to six tiny little words.

"It's not me, it's my OCD."

The phrase was actually coined by one of Schwartz's very own patients and could not, to my mind anyway, sum up the position more perfectly. These inspirational words have given me great comfort over the years. I have learned, through such new appraisals, to tame the voice of doubt that exists conterminously, yet distinctly, within my head as well as to accept the dichotomous nature of life with OCD.

I am me. I am also my OCD. It is this contradiction which defines me. And yet it is this contradiction which has also best lent itself to recovery; a journey which, through blood, sweat and tears, has enabled me to triumph, at least in part, over what might otherwise have been an entirely unconquerable enemy.

If there's one piece of advice above all else that I can offer then it is this: keep on fighting. Never stop trying to be well. However many times you might fall off the wagon or relapse, it is never too late to change or to start chipping away again.

It is never too late to quieten the voice of that pesky, unwanted travel companion we all know as OCD.

Chapter 2
THE SEED OF DOUBT

"Check all the closets and cupboards, look under all the beds, 'cause you never can tell there just might be a gremlin in your house."

- Randall Peltzer, *Gremlins* the movie

Mum passes me the book full of pictures of babies in the womb. "Aron," she says, "take a look at this. This is called a foetus."

I look down with total disinterest at this amazingly crisp image of a 24 week-old embryo, which appears to be frowning back at me. This is apparently what happens in the womb at around this stage in the infancy – they can grimace and stick their tongues out and all sorts. Or so my mum is telling me. I am ten years old and the time is around 11 p.m. It's way passed my normal bed time. My mum and dad have brought me down because they can hear the restless pitter-patter of feet across the upstairs landing and can sense I need distraction.

For a few weeks now I have been getting up out of my bed each night, nine or ten times, to check I have turned the bathroom taps off. It has become a bit of an obsession and my mum and dad want to nip it in the bud.

"And this..." my mum continues, "is an embryo clinging to the lining of the uterus." She hasn't shown me the whole book. I think she may have skipped the very first pages showing the sperm and egg on purpose. This is a diversionary tactic after all, not a full blown seminar on the birds and bees.

Though it would hardly have made a difference; I am far too preoccupied with the taps to care. I look at the page being presented to me with mild stupefaction. Learning about 'the facts of life' for the very first time should be something utterly amazing, breathtaking, awe-inspiring. But for me, the knowledge is ill-timed. When you have so many other gargantuan thoughts floating around, I guess there's just no more room left in your tiny, little head. Besides, I am tired. It's now 11.20 p.m. I desperately need some sleep.

The 'facts of life' for me, unfortunately, were that in 1996, at the age of only ten years old, I had already started displaying some of the classic symptoms of childhood OCD. As well as an unhealthy preoccupation with running taps (which I imagined, if left unchecked, might flood the whole world (a bit like in that Robinson's fruit juice advert where you see through a child's eye a giant silver tap filling up the entire ocean)), I had also become obsessed by *germs*. I feared these invisible, microscopic viruses and bacteria because I could not see them. Nor could I predict their effects. *Better to be safe than sorry,* I thought to myself each time I made my way sheepishly to the nearest basin. And so it went on, washing my hands fifteen, twenty, perhaps even as many as thirty times a day just to stay clean. Or should that be, *safe*.

The results of course were that my hands would become red raw; like a lobster's chelae. In fact, my hands would get so badly chapped that in the winter, they would start to crack and form a sort of rubescent scaly rash, an obscene desquamation that would last for weeks, even months on end. Though no matter how sore they got, no matter how ugly they appeared, my washing continued.

Some nights, I would be up so many times to the bathroom either checking the taps or washing my hands that I would get next to no sleep at all. I would go to school in a sort of sleep-deprived trance; barely being able to stay awake even for the register. Eventually, this behaviour caught the attention of both my parents who tried everything they could to correct or distract me from this seemingly bizarre conduct; everything from taking me out and treating me to curry (my favourite food ever since we had first gone for one in Bognor Regis when I was around four years old and, apparently, had gotten it all round my chops) to showing me endless high definition pictures of unformed foetuses. None of it seemed to work. Certainly none of it put me off of worrying.

One afternoon, my dad, noticing how religiously I washed my hands after each trip to the toilet, had even tried *ordering* me not to wash them – "If you wash your hands once more today," he barked, albeit only semi-seriously, "I'll send you to bed without any dinner for a week!" Though, unfortunately, even this rather drastic intervention – and bribing me with food was certainly drastic – wouldn't do the trick. For me, no authority, not even my dad's, was enough to break such a powerful cycle of anxiety; the perceived eternal threat emanating from my own precocious little brain always far graver than any corporeal punishment a mere *parent* could dish out.

In many ways (and with particular consideration to my experiences as a child), I have cause to liken my OCD to a form of bullying dictator; at first beguiling and sweet-talking and then later corrupting and enslaving, reducing you to nothing but a mere agent of its twisted will. For a child, with little capacity for what is known in the field as *meta-analysis* (that is, 'thinking about thinking' or as American developmental psychologist John Flavell might have it, *knowledge about cognition*), this experience is nearly always far more distressful and confusing. A child, as you can appreciate, has far less powers of *reason* at their disposal, not to mention far less an opportunity to discuss their mental experiences in detail with someone - say a doctor or a counsellor - who may be in a position to help them through it. For some very young children, still unable to articulate their suffering in words, I can imagine that all that bottled-up anguish and bewilderment, all that discombobulation, must be very frightening indeed (ironically, such inability to articulate can often be the *cause* of child-hood OCD: a way of controlling one's own environment in the absence of good communication skills and adult resources).

I am of course by far and away the only one who has suffered with this devastating affliction during infancy. It is generally estimated that up to one pre-adolescent child in two hundred has OCD. Some studies even suggest figures of closer to three or four percent. According to the *'Obsessive Compulsive Disorder (OCD) in Children and Adolescents'* website produced by South London and Maudsley NHS Trust, there are enough young people with OCD in the UK to literally fill the entire Millennium Stadium in Cardiff.

With that in mind, it is, perhaps now more than ever, of vital importance that a surfeit of information is out there; that suffering does not get ignored or brushed aside. That parents seek help for their children the moment they suspect that something is wrong.

Though back in 1996, during the time I had first started to exhibit signs of obsessive behaviour, the message had been altogether different. At that time, most professionals were still keen not to use the 'O' word for fear of creating a *label*. The advice to parents and doctors was to be careful not to brand or delimit behaviour or even to hint at unsafe conjecture; it could be dangerous for development to plant such seeds.

That is not to say that my symptoms did not bring about genuine concern. In fact, the opposite could not have been truer. My mum often tells me that when she first noticed that I was engaging in ritualistic behaviour - checking taps, washing hands etc. - and that this was causing me great distress, she wanted, quite desperately, to get help for me but, at the same time, feared creating a problem where none existed; "I wanted to help," she tells me now I am older. "I just didn't want to make things a whole lot worse."

Eventually, my ever-despairing parents (having already tried absolutely everything they could think of to rid me of my suffering - and getting me quite hooked on chicken dopiaza in the process) finally came up with a plan to see our family GP, Dr Gull, by themselves and without yours truly. They turned up to the local surgery one afternoon while my brother and I were in school and proceeded to describe in great detail my symptoms and experiences to Dr Gull, who, without committing to a firm diagnosis, referred me straightaway to be seen by a local psychologist and family therapist. Possibly today, a doctor would have insisted on seeing any patient face to face before coming to such a venturesome prognosis but back then, Dr Gull had taken my parent's view entirely.

"We must be very careful," Dr Gull said to my parents, "not to plant *seeds*."

Following this intervention, I remember receiving weekly therapy from a psychologist called Mr Khanna and an accompanying family therapist which went on for a number of weeks. During that time, the term OCD was never used. No one so much as even hinted at it in my presence.

I do not remember much of my time in therapy. It is all rather hazy. There are a few mentions of it in my diary - "*Today we went to family therapy and I said I washed my hands too much, sometimes even thirty or forty-something times a day I think*" - but other than these crude snippets my mind is pretty blank. Well, *almost* blank that is. I do of course remember just one session, the first session, in which, rather curiously, Mr Khanna had got me to play a game of chess with him. I do not remember much about the actual playing of the game only that I had been quite fretful over my scarce knowledge of the rules; randomly shuffling chess pieces around the board for seemingly no apparent purpose at all.

And for years, I did not know why we had performed this exercise. It was actually only very recently - during the writing of this book in fact - that I have since come up with a supposable theory behind this particular strategy. I was trawling the internet not so long ago for OCD treatment programmes for a friend of mine at group when I stumbled across a website on OCD 'skills for life'. The website was adeptly wrought with clip-art style images alongside motivational slogans and it was here that it all sort of fell quite neatly into place:

"How much of your mind have you spent thinking?" read one slogan, together with an image of an hour-glass.
"Do you wonder how everybody else can get on with their life?" read another, sitting beside a picture of a traffic light; the lights on green.
"How long does it take you to make the smallest move?" read the final war cry, flanking duly alongside a picture of a chess board and chess pieces.

And suddenly, like a eureka moment, I understood what Mr Khanna had been trying to do all those years ago, how he had been testing to see how long it took me to take the *smaller* decisions. OCD is a debilitating, time consuming and pathological doubting mechanism. It tends to create mountains where only molehills exist. Presumably, the length of time spent over each arbitrary move on a chessboard was one sure indicator of the scale and prevalence of my tendency to overanalyse. As well as in highlighting my fixation, as it would later transpire, with living my life according to arbitrary but nonetheless intricate *rules*.

Although I do not remember any more of my sessions with Mr Khanna (and on this, my diary is most unhelpfully vague), I do not now doubt the efficacy of such tacit and subtle game playing tactics. Therapy tends not to be like this these days. Or at least this has tended to be my experience. Everything seems to be so linear and textbook and woefully ineffectual. By contrast, Dr Khanna had somehow finely and expertly transformed my thinking without my even noticing.

Needless to say, two months after my first session with Mr Khanna and my washing and checking rituals had all but gone. It was a miracle. Or at least, that's how it must have seemed at the time. All of a sudden, I no longer cared if the taps were running. Nor did I care about germs or washing my hands. Slowly, my red raw hands returned to normal and, for a good many years, my OCD remained totally at bay.

It is difficult to say now, looking back, how such a decision not to mention my OCD at the time had impacted on my life. Or even on my future suffering. When I look back on it, I do not regret having had a label-free childhood (though perhaps it might have lead to less confusion in later life). Nor do I think it was wrong to have been kept out of the loop. Whatever suffering I might have experienced for those few very brief months as a ten year old, such an ephemeral splutter in my thinking had seemingly cleared away almost as quickly as it had first appeared. My childhood, certainly in the main, was one of profound cheerfulness – not to mention near-weekly helpings of Southeast Asian cuisine! - and, as such, has left me with nothing but good memories. To all intents and purposes, the OCD I had experienced for only those few months had been nothing but a blip, a nodule in a continuum of ecstasy.

Though, unfortunately for me, the OCD did return once I reached early adulthood. By that point, there was no evading the truth; I was sick. I needed help. I needed a prognosis. I needed a *label*.

*

It is fairly well documented that OCD tends to start in childhood which then persists into adulthood. One study published by the British Journal of Psychiatry in 2010 concludes that paediatric OCD left untreated is the primary predictor for persistence into adulthood. Though this is by no means the kiss of death. The study concludes that early recognition and treatment might be one very useful way of preventing a full clinical diagnosis of the disorder in later life. Indeed, the findings of the study suggest that over sixty percent of the child patients who were assessed or treated at the National and Specialist Paediatric OCD Clinic in London no longer showed signs of having fully blown OCD by the time the follow-up study was concluded nine years later.

The results seem promising. They show us that the more help that is given early on in the onset of this chronic disorder, the more likely it is that one may be able to fend it off in later life.

Unfortunately for me, as is perhaps already quite clear, my OCD *did* come back again. This, despite early intervention and an extremely supportive framework at home. Yet, I am not the only one for who this is true. Far from it in fact. Whenever I talk to fellow adult sufferers, their experiences tend nearly to be always the same: that they all managed to rid themselves of their OCD in childhood only for their demons to return, albeit in a slightly altered manifestation, years later.

According to the Child Development Institute in the US, at least one-third of all cases of adult OCD started out in childhood meaning that OCD in childhood, despite the effects of early intervention, is still perhaps the biggest indicator that we may indeed go on to present symptoms of OCD in adulthood. Moreover, according to a study in 2009 which compared OCD symptoms in children, adolescents and adults whom had all reported juvenile-onset OCD, the phenomenology of OCD, both the experience of obsessions and compulsions, was found to be exceptionally similar across the lifespan. In other words, symptoms and severity appear relatively similar for *all* OCD age groups with little difference in sub-types and themes. The age of onset does not seem to affect the clinical phenotype (although, there have been findings to suggest that there are differences in sex ratios, triggers and comorbidities such as tics between early and late onset OCD).

In my case, perhaps atypically, my OCD *had* changed quite dramatically over the years. The OCD I experienced during my preadolescence - concerns over general hygiene, germs and running taps - seem now to be so remarkably unschooled, so refreshingly incomplex by comparison to the much more nuanced versions I had suffered as a young adult. As one grows older, so the intellect becomes livelier; the capacity for analysis and introspection always far greater. In a way, my OCD had grown with me. Almost like an unwanted best friend or annoying younger sibling. And as I had slowly become more analytical, more socially and philosophically aware, so my OCD had become also more convoluted and labyrinthine.

Though for a very long time there had been nothing at all; a hiatus that had spanned almost a whole decade. For years following my treatment with Dr Khanna, my OCD had gone away almost entirely. Apart from the odd spell of low self-esteem (my teachers would often write in my school reports how I lacked confidence in all my subjects even though I had no reason at all to doubt myself) I remained almost completely unaffected by the mild *hiccups* that had so inflicted me in childhood. Yet by the time I had entered early adulthood and, in particular, following my travels up to university during the Autumn of 2003, the suffering and the grief had returned like never before. Unexpectedly. Without warning. Only this time, the symptoms were much more prolific and the subject matter often far darker and ignominious.

In many ways, my suffering as a child was almost like a 'dummy run'; a veritable taste of things to come. Though even that could not have prepared me for the horrors, the self-butchering and martyrdom that lay ahead.

Following the commencement of my second bout of OCD, it would take almost a decade to regain control from those inner voices inside my head; the fast growing gastriloquism of doubt that would ebb and flow at various stages in my illness. Who could have predicted that those spawning new mogwais, those cutesy little (self-contained) worries, might ultimately transform into fully blown adult-sized *gremlins.* "Tell me," says Sheriff Frank in the 1984 hit of the same title, "how come a cute little guy like this can turn into a thousand ugly monsters?"

Indeed, it would be a question I would ask myself on an almost daily basis for the next two decades.

Chapter 3
A DIRTY WORD

"Whenever a taboo is broken, something good happens, something vitalizing.
Taboos after all are only hangovers, the product of diseased minds."
- Henry Miller

September 2008. I turn up for my hospital appointment twenty minutes too early. The Grove Clinic Department of Genito Urinary Medicine had been much easier to find than I thought - simply straight into the west ward, through the in-patient discharge lounge and up to the third floor.

I am not ordinarily so punctual. Often bathroom rituals and copious checking of taps, doors, windows and locks (although these do not, by any means, tend to form the bulk of my obsessional behaviour), mean that I am invariably late; late for work, late for meetings, late for social events, late for dates, late even, dare I say it, for hospital appointments. This morning's appointment, however, is different. Not least because, like my checking of the taps, this is actually just another *ritual*; perhaps my most elaborate to date...

The receptionist, a meek thirty-something year-old with mousy brown hair books me in and points me to the waiting room where I slink over and take a seat opposite a man in an old British army style field jacket and ill-matching, Goretex trousers. He smells like a unique blend of marijuana and body odour but, unfortunately for me, there are no other free seats available and so I hold my nose and resolve just to grin and bear it. Of late, I am rather used to suffering in stealth. I have learnt it through necessity. They say that tolerance is a virtue. Though for me it is fast becoming a wearisome guise.

I lay my coat on my lap and pull out my mobile phone from my inside pocket which I am unsurprised to learn is still off and hasn't magically switched itself back on since last checking only two minutes ago outside the Jenny Lind's Children's Department upon my entrance into the hospital building. The phone, in actual fact, has been off since catching the number 25 Bus outside the Co-op on St Stephen's Street but I'm having trouble accepting this fact. Or at least, my anxiety is preventing me from accepting it. Exposure to RF fields can apparently cause everything from headaches to epigenetic changes to our very DNA. Not to mention, disrupt some of the extremely expensive and much essential hospital equipment.

Not surprisingly, I put my phone back into my coat pocket for about the fifth time this morning and resolve I will not look at it again.

Instead, breathing deeply in and out (largely in order to calm down), I shuffle back in my seat and let my eyes wander around the room. The malodorous chap in the khaki attire sitting opposite - let's call him George - briefly looks over in my direction and I smile back at him politely, though with what can only be described as eremitic reservedness. After all, I certainly do not want to be giving him the impression that I actually want to, you know, *talk* to him.

Nevertheless, I cannot at the same time help but feel sorry for poor old George. He looks withered and rumpled; like he hasn't washed or shaved in weeks. *Poor old George;* I know perhaps only too well how it feels to be so preoccupied with the woes of life that you forget even to wash. During the worst of my tremendous anxiety whilst still at university, I once had gone a staggering eight days without so much as a shower.

Though all this makes me wonder why George is looking so lost and bedraggled in the first place? Why is he here? Is this just a routine check-up, a quick once-over, or is he dying of some horrible, unmentionable disease? Judging by the look of him, I fear it may be the latter though I hope desperately for his sake it is not.

And perhaps just as concernedly, though rather more selfishly, I also hope that whatever is wrong with him, it isn't *communicable*. But just in case, I decide against my initial leaning to pick up the magazine I have my eye on which is sitting on the table between us both. After all, he might be here with something highly infectious like herpes or syphilis. And so, I choose instead to pick up a 'H

ow to avoid MRSA' booklet which is sat on the other table, adjacent to where I am sitting.

In my haste for distraction, I scan the pages of the booklet fixedly though half-heartedly. I am not particularly interested in the content of it but I resolve that it must be far better than just aimlessly sitting, staring silently into space, twiddling my thumbs or thinking too much. The melodramatic pamphlet belabours considerably the importance of keeping hands clean at all times, in particular, after coming into contact with another person. It mentions that hands should be washed regularly, ideally using alcohol gel or sanitary wipes. Soap and water are OK but apparently not entirely dependable. I find that, very quickly, the booklet is starting to stir up some mild but nonetheless palpable anxiety over contamination and so I put it down. I certainly don't need any *more* things to worry about this morning.

Eventually, after a further ten minutes or so of sitting in the waiting room looking up at the ceiling, trying desperately not to make eye contact with anybody - a mutual shame and dishonour pullulating between all those awaiting whatever dreadful scenario lies ahead - I am, at last, called in.

"Aron Bennett," announces the nurse frostily, "the doctor is ready to see you now."

I am so humiliated to be here that I cringe at the sound of my own name. Though for the life of me I don't know what I have to feel ashamed about.

For one thing, I haven't had sex.

It is perhaps a less well known fact that approximately a quarter of all those suffering with OCD will experience or have experienced sexual obsessions at some point in their illness. Though often it this manifestation that is left out of the literature. In many ways, sexual OCD is a bit like the final no-go zone, the last taboo; the North Korea of the mental health world. It is one thing admitting to being *a bit OCD* (and thereby admitting that, in a world still uncertain of mental illness, you are, in fact, one of the minority (or perhaps that should be *majority*) struggling mentally) but it is quite another to come clean to, say,. worrying about one day *raping* someone or questioning yourself over whether or not you are aroused by children. Notwithstanding the more generalised stigma surrounding this disorder, sexual OCD is, in many ways, one of the very hardest manifestations to *come out* with.

And yet, according to William M. Gordan, there are a whole host of common or day-to-day OCD symptoms typically involved with *sexual* OCD, far more than most people even realise. He explains that:

"The range of content in sexual obsessions is limited only by the imagination of the afflicted individual. Common themes deal with homosexuality, AIDs, infidelity, sexual perversions, incest and blasphemous thought combining religion and sex. The obsession can concern the self (e.g. 'I must be immoral to notice that woman's breasts'), a significant other (e.g. 'What if my wife is a whore?'), or a relationship (e.g. 'Is Diane the one to marry?). These examples also illustrate that the content of sexual obsessions can be mundane and ordinary. Many people might have unfounded doubts about their spouse of experience guilt about certain sexual thoughts. For the obsessive, though, the high frequency, intrusiveness, and perceived perverseness of the thought distinguish it from similar thoughts of a person without OCD."

Moreover, it has also been suggested that symptoms of sexual OCD tend to come on significantly earlier than other forms of OCD. According to a study conducted by J.E Grant et al in 2006, taboo obsessions such as sex usually begin during puberty, an average of four years earlier than most other adult OCD sub-types and tend to elicit longer durations of treatment. The study goes on to conclude that:

"Social understanding and comprehension emerge during puberty, and the taboo content of these pubertal obsessions may reflect the anxiety associated with social concerns commonly seen in this age group."

For me, the first stirrings of sexual discomfort had possibly emerged as far back as thirteen years old. During sex education lessons at high school, I remember I would quite literally cower in fear at the mere notion of intercourse. For me, it had always felt so *dirty*. I hated both the idea of penetration as well as the rather scarier prospect that, from such an occurrence, a baby or even a slow and painful death might arise.

"Sex is something we should all enjoy," I remember the PSE teacher telling us one lesson rather clumsily, a cucumber in one hand and a freshly opened condom in the other. "But there are tremendous risks involved."

Somehow, it was the latter that had fixed itself most firmly in my mind.

And yet back during my high school days, when sex was nothing more than a hollow digression, my real focus on school work and comic books, the fears surrounding one day *making love* seemed, in many ways, about as far away as owning my own house or scientists mastering the art of time travel. I cared not for girls my own age - instead getting my thrills from the late night German soft-porn channels like Sat1 and RTL when my parents had gone to bed - and certainly lacked the skills required to ever get one to actually go out with me (mainly as a result of being educated at a purely all boy's grammar school; my 'reward' for passing the rather arcane Eleven-plus).

Indeed, it wasn't really until I had reached my very late teens and early twenties, and following my migration to a mixed sixth form up in Norwich, that the gravity of my situation really started to hit home. Sex was now something I was expected to *do* and not simply something I could continue cowering away from like a frightened mouse at the sight of a ravenous bobcat. Not surprisingly, the prospects filled me with dread.

So much so in fact that, whether consciously or reflexively (probably both), I made it my mission to avoid sex for as long as possible. And, for many years, I had managed to defer the issue quite successfully. Fortunately for me (if indeed *fortune* is the best way to describe it), my luck with girls had been, at best, abysmal and my three year unrequited obsession with a girl at sixth form had led to nothing but a sexless game of cat and mouse (not to mention a rather bitter and heavy-duty heartbreak from which it would take many months, years even, to recover - though more on that later).

Nevertheless, as the years flew quickly by - my virginity flashing above my head like a neon sign - I knew I could not avoid sex forever and in 2008 I met an attractive girl called Isabel who would become my first, as it were, 'proper' girlfriend. The timing, in many ways, was far from ideal. Having suffered with sexual obsessions all through university (again, much more on that later), sex was perhaps the last thing I wanted to be thinking about, let alone engaging in. Though, at the very same time, I knew I could no longer remain caught in this vestal snare of my own making. Certainly not if I wanted to retain any credibility in the real world; a world where sex is a staple part of any healthy relationship and certainly an activity no one would dream of waiting until love (or indeed marriage) to partake in.

Isabel, to all intents and purposes, was my first real taste of intimacy. She was my first attempt at being a *man*. Unfortunately for me, she was also the beginning of a wave of obsessions with my sexual health that would eventually see me attend countless treatment sessions and therapy rooms for years to come.

It would perhaps be my final descent before finally getting the help I so very badly needed.

From the GUM waiting area, I follow the nurse into a small consulting room and it is here that I am introduced straightaway to an Asian doctor, Dr Cherupara, who smiles at me with unnecessary exuberance as he offers me a seat by the small, single casement window in the corner of the room.

"How can I help you today?" Dr Cherupara asks airily, as if there is quite simply nothing on earth to be worried about. In his own rather clumsy way I know he just wants to make me feel as relaxed as possible. Though, his mollifying attempts, I cannot help feel, are wasted on me. The fact that I could be sitting here right now with anything from hepatitis B to fully blown HIV AIDS is enough to keep me more than suitably anxious.

"I'm afraid I'm here to take, you know...*the test*," I reply. The unease is clear in my voice, embarrassment oozing out of every affricate. "I'm worried that I might have picked up a...you know...an *STI* from my ex-girlfriend." I actually wince when I say STI. It forms an uncomfortable ellipse as I attempt to stretch my lips wide and pronounce each miserable letter one after the other through closed teeth. It is, in point of fact, one of the few words I know that even in its abbreviated form still sounds so tarnished, so maligned.

OCD is perhaps the only other.

"I see." Dr Cherupara picks up a pen and paper as if to start taking notes. "Well...do you have any unpleasant symptoms Mr Bennett?" he asks me concernedly. "A stinging sensation when you urinate; irregular sore patches...a curious discharge?"

Dr Cherupara looks down at his piece of paper, waiting patiently but uprightly for my reply so he can commence scribbling. I scratch my head.

"No to all of that," I reply, instantly feeling like I am now in some way unworthy of being treated. "But most STIs are, you know, symptomless...right?"

Of course I *am* right. Certainly in theory. Though for whatever reason Dr Cherupara seems unwilling to give me that reassurance. Instead he simply looks down again at his clipboard of notes, purposefully it would seem not giving me an indication either way and, in a soft yet down-to-business tone asks me why I think I might have something wrong in the first place. The question immediately triggers an imposition of terror which rises in the pit of my stomach and settles in my chest, arms and legs. Undoubtedly, this is the question I have been dreading the most. How do you tell someone you may or may not have engaged in sexual activity of the nature proscribed by health professionals but that, in reality, you are completely unsure? After a small pause, Dr Cherupara asks me if I have recently engaged in sex without wearing a condom. I tell him I am still a virgin.

Isabel and I had first met actually as far back as 2004. We had both started at Morrisons at roughly the same time (she in the cafe and I, for my sins, on checkouts), staying on through school and then university just to earn some extra money. We never really spoke much, particularly in those early years, but I remember how I would always try to catch her eye, passing her a semi-flirtatious smile whenever we were about to cross on the stairs or walk past each other in the staffroom.

As it happened, Isabel was extremely attractive and certainly someone who might more objectively have been regarded as way, way *out of my league*. Isabel had long, lustrous hair and a body that was perhaps the envy of all the other girls. I recall now how I would so often just stop and stare at her as she glided round the cafe, her black Morrison's pencil skirt always down passed her knees like she had just stepped out of Edwardian Britain. She was eccentrically sexual though with a certain calmly defiant grace that meant that she always received copious male attention from both young and old, work colleagues and customers alike. It was perhaps more by luck than anything else that one afternoon, after literally three years of watching her absorbedly from afar, I had my first chance to talk to her properly when I got to cover a miscellaneous shift in the cafe. We got chatting, I made her laugh (accidently: I tripped over a potato bunker) and the rest, so they say, was history.

A few weeks later, Isabel and I were officially boyfriend and girlfriend. It had all happened so fast. The relationship seemed to gain momentum with almost effortless participation from me. She called me 'Checkout Boy'; I called her 'Cafe Girl.' It was a done deal. Or so I had thought, perhaps rather naively, at the time.

Over the course of our relationship, I found out that Isabel had a strange variation of OCD about recycling: each night, after her shift, she would be compelled to collect up all the empty plastic bottles from the cafe, load it into the boot of her car and take it down to the local recycling bin. This, I found to be an endearing quality. And although I never mentioned my own more lascivious obsessions to her (which, by that time, had started to rear up like spear thistles on a roadside verge), it was a talking point of sorts, a topic of conversation about which I had plenty of experience and therefore input. She was a fellow worrier; a person who cared as much for consequence as she did for immoderate merriment. In my eyes this made her almost sacrosanct.

Other qualities, however, I found less endearing.

Isabel had what I would later go on to describe in my diary, a 'manipulative streak'. She would lie, goad, hoax and tease. She would often think nothing of fibbing about her life and about her past, even about her intentions and aspirations for the future. At times, she would be so implausibly conniving that I would frequently be left questioning whether our whole relationship wasn't just one big joke to her or, worse still, that she was simply leading me on for the fun of it.

"I like you," she had told me on more than one occasion, "but you're far too short to be marriage material."

Then one warm summer's evening, after the two of us had been going out for almost four whole weeks, Isabel invited me back to hers for the very first time. Her parents were away on holiday and this had been the perfect opportunity for us to spend some quality time alone together. Isabel lived in a small Norfolk village off the A140 Cromer Road called Aylsham, around a 35 minute drive from Norwich. I had been there a few times before but always had to catch the Sanders Coach from Castle Meadow which would take an absolute age as it meandered in and out of every pointless, sleepy village along the North Norfolk Coast. Tonight was a cool summer's evening and we drove back to hers with the windows of her white Nissan Micra rolled right the way down. Her hair blew around like the dance of the whirling dervishes in the crosswind.

That evening, following an *Old El Paso Healthy Fiesta for Tea* which Isabel rustled up in a hurry, the two of us ended up in bed together. In fact, it had not been planned this way. At least, not on my part it hadn't. Nor indeed had I expected such a hurried apogee. For the month or so that the two of us had been seeing each other, Isabel had always insisted that we would not be *consummating* the relationship for a good long while. "I'll sleep with on your birthday," she had promised teasingly on only our second date. As it was, my birthday wasn't until February.

It was now only August.

Nevertheless, that evening, in her large, copacetic room, underneath the bedclothes of her Middleton pink coloured polycotton deluxe duvet, Isabel instructed me, quite casually, to take off my boxers.

"Why?" I said, with genuine guilelessness, having expected no more than perhaps a quick fumble and a few kisses.

"*You'll see,*" she said as she removed the last of her remaining garments.

In fact, I did not see. Fortunately - or should that really be, *unfortunately*- the embrace had ended before I had been given a chance to know what might otherwise have been in store for me. Following a small amount of kissing and cuddling underneath the bed sheets, and with absolutely no warning at all, Isabel had somehow rolled over on top of me, her now naked body pressing firmly against my own and, in a fit of sheer panic, I had literally flung her off me like a beanbag in a game of *Hot Potato*.

"What's wrong?" she exclaimed, half in shock, half in quite bitter outrage.

"What were you doing?" I said, counter-accusation in my tone.

"What do you *think*?

"Oh."

"Yeah...*Oh.*"

And so it was, perhaps in many ways unsurprisingly, my relationship with Isabel did not last too much longer than that disastrous evening round hers. The next morning, as she drove us both sullenly to work, we barely said a word to each other. From my point of view, she had lied to me about her intentions; about wanting to keep me waiting until my birthday. She had caught me off-guard, put me on the spot, pressurised me when I simply wasn't ready. From her point of view - and the point of view of possibly most other people - I had refused the kind of sexual intimacy that a modern relationship such as ours more typically necessitated. I had proven to be as futile in the bedroom department as I had been a Morrison's checkout operator (my packing skills were diabolical and I would constantly forget to offer cashback).

And so, a few days later, she dumped me by text; “We've lost our spark,” she wrote rather matter-of-factly one evening. “I'm sorry.” Of course my first reaction had been to cry my eyes out on my bedroom floor and to drink neat vodka straight from the bottle. Though a day or so later and the crocodile tears had all but dried up, replaced by feelings of what can only be described as profound anxiety. The kind of gut-wrenching feeling you get before taking an exam or jumping out of a plane. Isabel and I had very nearly had full-blown intercourse. And I couldn't help thinking about the ramifications for my sexual health.

When I later read up online that some STIs could spread simply through contact with the penis, vagina, mouth or anus of an infected person (the teachers at school had only ever warned against *penetrative* sex), I almost passed out with fear. Apparently, gonorrhoea and Chlamydia were particularly nasty *bacterium* which tended to grow and spread in warm, moist areas of the body. No intercourse was required. My bedroom encounter with Isabel, which might have involved brief contact between our genitalia, may well have been enough to pass on something unpleasant. Maybe she had had skin sores, or swollen, irritated eyes and I just hadn't noticed? I remembered how she had complained of a sore throat, and how she had also said something about a pain in her lower abdomen. Or was that just the *Old El Paso* repeating on her?

The prospects were almost too much to bear.

And so, a few weeks later, after much turmoil and many sleepless nights, of being too afraid to leave the house for fear of passing on an STI, I eventually called up *NHS Direct* to book an appointment. Getting *tested* it seemed might be the only way to alleviate such tormenting anxiety.

"That'll be tomorrow at 3 p.m. Mr Bennett," said the woman at the other end of the phone quite coldly. "Please arrive promptly."

“No worries,” I replied, as if there really were none. But, of course, there definitely were. And not only worry, but *shame* too; a striking and pervasive sense of ignominy that cut through me, through my self-worth like a razor sharp knife through *pate de mulo*.

And yet, at the same time, I just couldn't help but quietly wonder to myself: *Why?* What did I have to be so ashamed about? For one thing, I hadn't had sex!

Dr Cherupara again looks up at me with a mixture of what appears to be both shock and sympathy. I have explained absolutely everything to him, not merely the physical incidents leading to my coming here but all the mental symptoms too; the anxiety, the shame, the constant ruminations. Quite surprisingly, it is this aspect of my disclosure, this part of my neurotic tale of woe that Dr Cherupara seems to be most taken with. Or at the very least, the piece of the puzzle which seems, in his eyes anyway, to make the most amount of sense.

"You do realise," announces Dr Cherupara finally with aplomb, "that the chances of contracting anything serious like HIV are almost non-existent."

"Really?" I say, actually quite surprised.

"Yes...really."

"But..."

I look down at my feet. I am loathed to believe him. Is he saying all this just to make me feel better? Is he simply trying to *reassure* me? Blustered and rather bewildered, I tell Dr Cherupara that I am surely quite right to be concerned. That, despite perhaps coming across this afternoon as a bit *highly strung*, my lines of reasoning are, in point of fact, still quite sound. "There is still a risk," I tell him with the conviction of anyone who had done as much research on a topic as I had. "Surely you must agree, there is still a risk?"

"There is a smidgen of truth in what you are saying," Dr Cherupara patiently concedes. "But, nonetheless, you are still probably fine."

"*Probably*?"

"Yes, probably."

"But not definitely?"

"No."

"So do you think I need to take the test then?"

"Probably not."

"But you cannot say for definite?"

"No."

"I See."

Eventually, after much jousting backwards and forwards, advice proffered, the same advice ignored, I decide, perhaps rather heedlessly (especially in light of everything that has been said), to take the test anyway. I had been told many times prior to this afternoon's appointment by friends far more experienced than myself in matters of this kind that the swab test hurts only very briefly but is, in fact, nothing at all to worry about and, to my relief, I soon find that they are right. Dr Cherupara ushers me exhaustedly into the adjoining room where I am handed over to a nurse who, after a small introduction, speedily inserts a cotton swab precisely into my otherwise most intimate and impassable orifice which stings like an absolute mother fucker but in microseconds it is over. Following the swab is a urine test before it is finally back in with Dr Cherupara for a round-up. There is apparently the matter of my next appointment to discuss.

"A new appointment!?" I am somewhat taken aback by the news."You mean, there's more?"

"Yes, I'm afraid so," says Dr Cherupara, as I seat myself back down in the consultation room. "That is...if you still really want to pursue all this?"

"Well...what's got to happen next?"

"The blood test."

"The blood test?"

"Yes...the blood test."

Dr Cherupara explains that it has only been a month or so since my sexual encounter with Isabel and that this is apparently only enough time to test for the more common STIs like Chlamydia. According to the 'HIV TEST, Information & Advice' pamphlet, a copy of which Dr Cherupara has given to me by way of further reading, it can take up to three months for HIV to be detectable in the blood after someone has acquired the infection – this is also known as a window period.

My window period for HIV has yet to elapse.

"So I guess I'll see you in a few months' time." Dr Cherupara closes his note book and passes me a stiff, diplomatic smile. He has given me as much information as he possibly can this morning and is quite noticeably fatigued. In fact, he could probably do with a large single malt whiskey or whatever else doctors drink to get themselves through a stressful day.

"I guess so," I say, acquiescently. "Thank you doctor."

I leave the consultation room, somewhat deflated, and make my way over to the patient registration desk where the receptionist books me a new appointment, writes my clinic number into a new appointment booklet and informs me that I will receive a text message in a week's time with my results contained therein. I thank her and then switch my phone back on.

I had hoped more than anything to come away this morning feeling somewhat reassured, allayed, unburdened.

Instead, I am feeling shot-down and crestfallen. So many questions that needed answering have seemingly been met only with more questions. And, of course, more waiting. Plenty of waiting.

I walk passed the radiology department on my out, and, as I do, my phone lets out this long, high pitched bleep; one new message. *Shit!* I look around me; doctors in white coats are to-ing and fro-ing out of spring-hinged doors behind which lie thousands of pounds of mammography equipment, a special ultrasound room and millions of electronically stored images and X-rays. Suddenly I come over in a cold, anxious sweat as I question whether the electromagnetic waves from the incoming text might have disrupted all the equipment and, thereby, ruined all the highly delicate readings.

I walk briskly out of the exit by the Jenny Lind Children's Department and cannot get out of my mind how many people may now die as a result of my recklessness; how many lives I will no doubt have ruined. And of course, how many lives I will no doubt ruin now that I am walking around with a dangerous STI.

I get outside and look at my text message; "Fancy a few drinks tonight mate," reads the short, upbeat message from a friend from work. "There will be some single girls going ;-) "

There is a final surge of anxiety. I read the message a few times over, my palms sweating, my thumb hovering nervously over 'reply'.

No...I think...I wish...but...no...I just...*delete*.

Chapter 4
"THE DEVIL YOU KNOW"

"When the disease is known it is half cured."
- Erasmus Colloquies

The good news when it comes to OCD is that it isn't usually too difficult to spot. Whilst the *causes* of OCD are not so clearly identified (though there are some extremely plausible theories out there), the symptoms are both prominent and universally acknowledged. As Bruce M.Hyman and Cherry Pedrick, authors of *'The OCD Work Book'*, point out, "The style and manner of the thoughts and behaviours presented by people with the disorder are remarkably and unmistakably consistent."

Regardless of the type of OCD we are talking about – whether it be washing, checking, hoarding or even something far more elaborate like getting check-ups for STIs - the pattern always seems to be the same. And for me, this idea of a *universal blueprint* for what may otherwise appear on the surface a complicated and abstruse disorder has always been an empowering notion. It has given me the inner strength to stay glued to the path of recovery. The idea that you really may *know your enemy*, and therefore have an upper-hand, strategically, in the war against it, is, without doubt, a most enlivening prospect.

It took me a long time to attribute the internal confusion I experienced on a daily basis with some of the more documented symptoms referred to in books and articles. In hindsight, I would have familiarised myself much sooner with the various characteristics of my disorder. For it is only through an understanding of the pathognomonic qualities of an illness that one may stand any chance at all of effectively combating it.

According to the Diagnostic and Statistical Manual of Mental Disorders, Fourth edition (DSM-IV-R), a document published by the American Psychiatric Association which provides standard criteria for the classification of mental disorders, the essential features of OCD are summed up as follows: "recurrent obsessions or compulsions that are severe enough to be time-consuming (i.e., they take more than one hour a day) or cause marked distress or significant impairment." (DSM-IV-R, p.417)

This common language and standard criteria for the classification of OCD is used by clinicians and researchers alike to effectively diagnose and treat people suffering at the hands of such an outwardly bewildering condition. For me, it has often been useful for the classification to be broken down further into its two core components: *obsessions* and *compulsions*. It is my belief that without an understanding of both these fundamental processes and the interplay between the two, one cannot hope to unravel a disorder that even Sigmund Freud, in his relative ignorance on the subject, had termed *zwangsneuroses*. Let's begin firstly with *obsessions*.

An obsession is defined as 'persistent, often irrational, and seemingly uncontrollable thoughts'. Obsessions are, in effect, the result of what is known in psychological circles as automatic negative thinking or *NATs* as it is often abbreviated. This type of thinking tends to be elicited almost exclusively by those with anxiety disorders and manifests as a peculiar, self-destructive voice that always looks for the danger, the negative consequence in everything: *"What if I don't get checked out at the hospital and consequently pass on an STI to a loved one?"; "What if I fail to look away and thereby make a woman feel uncomfortable?"; "What if the door still isn't locked (despite checking twenty times) and a burglar manages to enter in, rape my wife and kill the kids?"* The content of the thoughts will vary from person to person but will tend to affect the sufferer in much the same way every time. The word obsession actually comes from the Latin meaning "action of besieging" and, in my opinion, sums up perfectly the way in which an obsession will, quite literally, overcome its sufferer, so ubiquitously and so forcibly that one is almost left entirely defenceless, bereft of their own self-determination. An obsessive thought is an uninvited thought. And, by virtue of its unwelcomed and interposing nature, will often produce high levels of both stress and anxiety. In most cases, a person suffering an obsessive thought will know just how unrealistic the content of their obsessions are but simply feel powerless to rid themselves of them or to control them.

This is where *compulsions* come in. Compulsions are defined as 'actions which are used to neutralize the obsessions'. They exist to alleviate the anxiety brought on by an obsession as well as to help regain an element of *control*. In essence, they are safety-seeking measures gone partly, if not wholly, awry. As we always like to say in group: "OCD has a logic; just not a truth." The aphorism could not be truer. Often people with OCD will engage in compulsive activities even though they know deep down that what they are doing is merely perpetuating or giving credence to their unfounded obsessions. But they just can't help it. They are a slave to their thoughts.

Together, obsessions and compulsions form like this unholy alliance, the two processes often working in treacherous syncopation, which can leave a sufferer quite literally locked in torment.

For me, like so many of the millions of people the world over living with the wretched disorder, my OCD has been both time-consuming and distressing. Very often, I would feel enslaved, burdened, held literally at gun point by my OCD. All the time convinced that if I didn't engage with it, that if I didn't give in to its demands then something truly terrible would happen.

During the worst of it, I would act almost entirely without temerity; make choices which would leave me feeling completely alienated from my own decision-making processes. I was a stranger to myself, a shadow lurking in the dark. When things were particularly bad, I actually did not even feel human but rather, a mere agent of mental aberration.

I recall an afternoon whilst still at university in Lancaster. I had been on my way back from the Ruskin Library and Research Centre on campus to my student accommodation in the city when I happened upon a rogue plastic carrier bag which had blown into the front garden of one of the houses along the M6. The bag had seemingly become entangled in overgrown shrubbery and was now flailing helplessly, upside down, over a triumvirate of *common toadflax*. I am not sure even now what it was that had drawn my attention to such a prosaic, run-of-the-mill spectacle but, for whatever reason, the sight of this supermarket branded plastic carrier ensconcing these three rather ugly looking yellow flower heads had triggered this bizarre sense of unease that I could not shake off.

I walked on further down a small cobbled street, passed the local chippy, all the while consumed with grief. Desperately I tried to recalibrate my mind onto something else. Though, as I continued to pound the cobbles of Hope Street and then Prospect Street, I found that my anxiety began only to worsen. With each step, my fear seemed to grow almost exponentially, my legs becoming as heavy as cemented artillery bunkers; *What happens if there are insects, or even a bird, stuck underneath the offending carrier bag,* I thought to myself at random? *What if it is suffocating all the wildlife and I am the only one able to save them?* My stomach began doing somersaults at the mere notion that I could bring about such suffering or, perhaps worse still, that I would do nothing to attempt to end it. And then almost out of nowhere at all, there came this overriding urge to go back; to return to the overgrown garden and remove the bag from over the flower heads.

And so I did. No longer able to fight the tractor beam inside my head, this resounding voice beckoning me to return to the scene of the crime, I marched all the way back down to the main road. It was ludicrous, wacky, *insane* and yet, at the same time, I knew I had precious little choice. I was *compelled.*

For me, it was always issues of morality (usually sexual, though not always) which kept my mind churning and my insides voltaic. It was not so much that I wanted, by reason of some virtuosic gusto, to be a good person but rather, I yearned desperately to feel safe from being a bad one. By nature I am no saint. I am not even always all that nice. Like all of us, I have said and done things I am not proud of. Quite ironically, some of the worst things I have said and done, I have not suffered any retroactive OCD at all.

And yet it is that same incongruous distinction that applies to all types of OCD. A compulsive cleaner doesn't scrub the kitchen, disinfect the shelves, steam clean the carpets for the love of cleanliness, but for the fear of dirt and germs or for making others sick. They want to feel safe from contagion and from being responsible for contaminating others. People with OCD are *not* perfectionists or enthusiasts. They are not fanatical or zealous. They are simply ill. In many cases, they are very ill indeed.

Depending on the severity of one's condition, a person suffering with OCD may go to unbelievable lengths to feel safe. They will do or say things that, from any outside perspective, would seem inexplicably bizarre. For the majority of sufferers, their versions of OCD can be as intricate and far-reaching as their own imaginations permit. There is no limit. OCD can be made up of anything on the planet. With this in mind, one can perhaps appreciate why it is so often remarked that intelligence is a curse. Or why analytical people especially tend to see danger in every crease and fold.

When I eventually arrived back at the house that wintry afternoon after a long day at university, I was somewhat surprised to discover that the bag that had caused me such grief had seemingly vanished completely. Either it had been blown away by a violent gust of wind or the house owner, noticing that this rogue plastic carrier bag was clearly suffocating some of his flowers, had removed it as a matter of urgency and placed it dutifully in the bin. Either way, the relief was immense. I returned home that afternoon ecstatic, overwhelmed with the extrication that all was well with the world again. I had done my duty. I was still a good person.

Over the years, the type of OCD I have suffered has changed. Though in reality, the various faces of my OCD have only ever been two sides of the same coin. As my best friend Jake (also a PHD student of computer science at the University of East Anglia) liked to tell me, they were no more than a "single sequential flow within the context of a full-blown system of OCD". In their various manifestations, they were no more than a set of wayward processes running independently but cooperatively within the same unhelpful OCD program.

For Jake, his main problem with my OCD, aside for the suffering it caused me, was how arbitrary it all seemed. If my selective experience of OCD was, in computer terminology, like only one small subtask, a single thread of execution, then why did I knowingly and wilfully focus on such a small area of living to the exclusion of all else. Why should OCD about morals or *sex* take up all of my time whilst obsessions relating to checking, hoarding and washing be almost wholly inconsequential? And why did some subsets of morals feature much more highly than others? Worrying about looking too long at an attractive girl in case she felt uneasy might have made me feel incredibly guilty whereas, on the odd occasion, refusing to help my dad in the garden or not giving my mum a hand laying the table because I was in the middle of my favourite programme on TV, didn't even register as slightly unkind.

It was a selective process. Logically and objectively, it didn't make sense. Though to the sufferer, it makes perfect sense. When one undergoes an episode of OCD they are, at the very same time, looking at life down the lens of a rather powerful microscope. They are concentrating on the minutiae to the exclusion of the rest of the world. And whilst this kind of thinking can, invariably, lead to ingenious breakthroughs the likes of which the world has never seen - breakthroughs such as that of Marie Curie who discovered radium or Charles Darwin, the English naturalist who first proposed the concepts of *natural selection* (they both incidentally had OCD) - it can just as easily lead to a narrow and discontented existence. It can lead to melancholy, depression, and even out-and-out insanity.

Nikola Tesla, a mechanical engineer and important contributor to the birth of commercial electricity, is a brilliant example of the above. Nikola Tesla is famously purported to have said the following: "I do not think there is any thrill that can go through the human heart like that felt by the inventor as he sees some creation of the brain unfolding." And yet it was perhaps the unintended consequences of his ever unfolding mind that had lead to a number of debilitating obsessions that Tesla suffered throughout his life; namely, a fixation with the number three, a physical aversion to jewellery and a pathological fear of contamination and germs. In addition, Nikola Tesla was celibate for much of his life and did not have, by all accounts, much time at all for socialising, preferring to spend his time in isolation from others.

Tesla spent the last of his days in a hotel room in New York, alone and senile.

Unfortunately, as I have learned through my own experiences, once stuck down the rabbit hole, it can be very difficult to come back up for air, to engage with the world again, to re-inject context back into otherwise irrational dialogue.

In the beginning, I did not even know that my suffering had been symptomatic of OCD at all, believing instead that my symptoms were merely creations of my own peculiar brand of balkiness and malignity. Had I known then what I know now in abundance, perhaps I might have been able to prevent the disorder from taking so much of a hold. At the very least, had I been more informed, I might have recognised the glaring hallmarks of OCD much sooner and vetoed future transmutations. But such is the nature of the disorder, to the 'untrained mind' the symptoms can initially be incredibly difficult to single out and contain. Relabeling your own thoughts - often ideas and beliefs you have valued and lived by for many years - can be a tough and complicated process. At least to start with.

The good news when it comes to OCD is that, despite an often complex array of obsessions and compulsions, the disorder is always the same. And this has some very positive implications for treatment.

My journey through OCD as with my journey *away* from it is not indistinct but rather, a journey which is taken every day by OCD sufferers committed to getting better. Certain treatments may indeed be more effective for some than others and, of course, there are pitfalls. I should know, I have fallen down a fair few of them on more than one occasion. Yet, for those looking for a way out, there is a suitable treatment out there waiting to be utilised. The best advice ever given to me was to 'chip away' at the disorder. It is not something that can shift overnight, nor can you hope to practice treatment a couple of times and expect to be 'cured'. But with time and effort, there is hope for anyone suffering with OCD.

As I have discovered, OCD has only one real pattern, however obscure and perplexing it may seem on the surface. It is a bit like a Sudoku puzzle. It can appear, at first, to be difficult to solve, almost impossible. But, as with all puzzles, once you have become practiced enough at doing them, there is no level of difficulty, no level of involvedness that can stump, baffle or confuse you.

It would take me a number of years to realise the pattern. As you will see, I engaged in numerous rituals throughout my OCD career. Such is the nature of the disorder, it would be a long while before the penny eventually dropped and the truth came out.

Though, it needn't be that way. With hindsight, my journey with OCD might have been that much shorter.

In December 2009, I went back to the hospital for an HIV blood test. Jake, being my best friend, had urged me not to bother with yet more testing, that the whole thing was just a waste of time and for goodness sake should I not just be getting on with my life. But, in the face of near-apocalyptic anxiety, not even those friends or family whose advice I trusted often without question, would be able to desist or dissuade me.

"You really haven't got to do this to yourself you know," said the male nurse on duty that afternoon at the hospital as he plunged a 21-guage needle into my arm. "You're such a low risk you probably have more chance of being hit by lightening than having HIV."

A few weeks after the blood test, I received the results by text. 'You're results are fine,' read the electronic bulletin, thrusting itself jubilantly at my phone screen. I feigned relief. None of this was really *news* to me. Indeed, I had not taken the test to ease any genuine doubt that I was sick but rather, I had done it merely to appease the uncontrollable urge in my brain to eliminate all risk; to purge any chance of being or doing something 'bad'. Unfortunately, the plan had back-fired. I *did* feel bad. I felt bad for allowing myself to give in so easily and for getting caught up, yet again, in a torrent of pathological behaviour.

I felt bad for being so weak.

Chapter 5
"PERSISTENCE & PROGNOSIS"

"A crack on the head is what you get for not asking, and a crack on the head is what you get for asking" - The Smiths, *Barbarism Begins at Home*

OCD is many things: it is a control mechanism, an anxiety disorder, a chemical imbalance and a brain dysfunction. In my opinion it is also an *addiction*. Of course, this is not how you will see it described in most text books or by psychologists. Most professionals draw a line under OCD, claiming that the lack of *pleasure* involved in compulsions (the want of pleasure being the main motivation in addiction), renders it an entirely separate mental process. Yet there are a number of parallels between OCD and addiction which simply cannot be ignored. Most strikingly, is the tendency of both not to know when to quit. As with alcoholism or even anorexia (which some scientists have described as *'an addiction to starvation'*), OCD is a condition that seemingly defies logic and rebukes the evidence; it takes hold and keeps hold even at the cost of our own physical and mental well-being. OCD, as with any addiction left to its own devices, is staunchly and devastatingly *persistent*.

Back in 2009 and following the all-clear from my various visits to the hospital for swabs and blood tests, I found, quite to my surprise, that my obsession with STIs did not go away. Instead, the ruminations actually began steadily to worsen, at first gradually and then abruptly. Each day I would catch myself spending ever-increasing periods of time attempting to 'solve' the next up-and-coming hypothetical moral question such as: "If I have unprotected sex with one girl, should I get tested before having 'safe' sex with another?" or, "Is multiple unprotected oral sex permissible without a check-up in between?" or even, "Am I a bad person if I fail to divulge the full extent of my sexual history to a new partner? Whose duty is it to take the necessary precautions in seeking disclosure, the giver or the receiver, the inciter or the *incitee*?"

As the days went by, the worry rose almost exponentially. If someone could have constructed a line graph to illustrate the rise in apprehension, the sudden, sharp abruptness in gradient that represented the dire thoughts and rituals in my head then it would no doubt have resembled the semi-'U' shaped growth rate in the world's population or, even, the steep augmented rise in global emissions of CO_2. And the more I did my best to curb the anxiety by creating rules or working my way through the ever-ludicrous future-scenarios conjured up by my ailing mind, the steeper the rise in anxiety; the steeper the rise in anxiety, of course, the greater the mental rituals.

Do you notice a pattern here? Of course you do. Unfortunately, when you're stuck in those deeply addictive concentric circles, it is often almost impossible to see the wood through the trees; to see the world for how it really is. When the anxiety rises so high it resembles the feeling of drowning in a rather large vat of quicksand, it becomes perhaps no less detrimental to perspicuity and lucidity than an over-salted meal is to just about every other flavour on the plate.

During my latter blood test at the GUM Clinic, I had been given the opportunity to express most of my concerns over passing on STIs to the duty nurse who had listened both patiently and tenderly and who had sat me down and explained as carefully as he could how the risks of contracting an STI might best be minimised. He explained, for example, that by undertaking regular check-ups (ideally between each new partner or, at the very least, twice a year) as well as employing various methods of contraception such as dental dams or condoms, the chances of contracting an STI were incredibly low.

Low but not negligible.

"It is still possible to pass on an STI even if you take all reasonable precautions," said the nurse finally that afternoon. "Short of abstention, there are simply no guarantees. But if you do the things I suggest, then the risks are minimal."

Minimal risk? It seemed almost unfathomable to me then. Like a *tiny* heart attack or a *minor* brain tumour. Unfortunately, as is the age-old story of the misguided OCDer, where there is a silver lining there is nearly always a looming, great cinereal cloud. A dark and stormy nebulosity, ready just to thunder and pour at almost a moment's notice. In the world of an OCDer, there is simply just no such thing as a *minimal* risk. That there was no one hundred percent totally foolproof way of avoiding passing on an STI made me sick to my very stomach. Check-ups, contraception, they all perhaps helped but they still could not prevent completely the emergence of life-long conditions such as herpes or genital warts. Nor could they even always guarantee protection against the more well known (and treatable) diseases such as Chlamydia or gonorrhoea. And as I continued to ruminate over and over in search of a more comprehensive and fail-safe way of staying out of harm's way (whilst trying not to resort to a life of celibacy), so I found myself coming up only with more questions. I wrote them down in my diary so as not to forget:

Is multiple unprotected oral sex allowed providing you get checked out twice a year? Must you always use condoms when undergoing oral sex? Can you have unprotected oral sex with one partner followed by safe sex with another without getting checked? Is there a risk of catching gonorrhoea or Chlamydia just from cuddling someone naked? Is it permitted to have multiple unprotected cuddles with different partners without getting checked? Is there a chance of catching herpes from kissing a stranger in a nightclub? What are the chances of contracting hepatitis from anal sex? If I only ever have protected sex, is there still an onus to get checked out between each and every sexual partner?

Without answers to these burning questions, I felt both helpless and afraid. I avoided contact with the opposite sex and spent hours at a time on my PC, researching online, looking up the same STIs over and over again and the risks involved with each different type of coital (and even non-coital) activity. Some nights I would get less than two hours sleep as I trailed hopelessly through website after website in search of anything at all that might assuage my abounding anxiety and thus provide me with the answers I so desperately sought.

As you might expect, the articles I did find, on the whole, were remarkably unaccommodating. Some of them were darn right scary. Ultimately, after what amounted to weeks, even months of frenetic scurrying, it felt like I had read pretty much everything there was out there to read; everything from circumcision as a means of preventing HIV to the rise of the herpes simplex virus in the USA (down, primarily, to an overall rise in the practice of oral sex). Most of it had seemed pretty irrelevant. Worse still, some of it was actually dangerously misleading. For example, one religious article I had read, produced by the Catholic Church and proscribing both fornication and contraception, actually dared to argue that even *protected* sex posed a massive health risk as the latex in condoms contained pores through which the Aids virus, four millionths of an inch in size, could pass through without difficulty. The article, rather than anxious, had at once made me furious. It had surely been hard enough working out right from wrong, discerning that which was safe from that which teetered on dangerous, without the warped campaigns and hazardous proselytization of the Catholic Church. "Contemptible! Utterly *contemptible!*" I spat out aloud to myself in my bedroom. Though, theocratical misconstructions aside, I knew deep down that I had perhaps no one else but myself to blame for wasting so much of my time trawling through crackpot sites; for clicking so hysterically and so heedlessly through absolutely anything I could come by regardless of its authenticity or credibility.

And yet, I simply could not stop. Or at least, it felt like I couldn't. "Insanity," goes the infamous quote from Albert Einstein, "is doing the same thing over and over again and expecting different results." In OCD it is not so much the expectation over outcome that is misguided so much as the compulsive drive to engage in and then to repeat over and over again totally unhelpful behaviour. The French perhaps had it sized up the best when they referred to OCD as *la folie de doubt* - the madness of doubt. In other words, the madness lies not in the person but in the alien intruder, the bacillus of uncertainty. In my case, I was not mad, or even slightly delusional. I was ill. Or, perhaps more aptly, I was addicted. Addicted to answers, addicted to 'working out' the problem (albeit imagined), addicted to *control*.

As the late night Google searches and further check-ups continued (going back to the hospital as many as five times for unnecessary tests), I eventually began to accept that what had started out as perhaps a prudent undertaking, an ultimately selfless and dutiful assignation, had now gotten way out of hand. Indeed, what had simply begun as a means by which I might keep myself (and thereby other people) safe, had, quite ironically, become a mechanism only for my own continued torture and enduring suffering.

And perhaps worst of all, it was a dependence, an *idée fixe* I could not now kick to the curb.

Sometimes when we are so blinded by our behaviour, so frightened by a world that no longer makes sense, we must allow others close to us to step in; to stage some sort of an intervention; a *coup d'état*. Fortunately for me, about a month or so after my very last check-up at the hospital, my behaviour, my dark moods and long silences, the protracted periods out of sight performing some ritual or another (usually research or rule-making), aroused the suspicion of both my parents. They could see something wasn't right. That, although they knew not of the particulars of my ruminations, it was clear something rather major was on my mind.

"Your mother and I are worried," said my dad one evening, with a sombre tone. "We have noticed that you are acting rather odd; you seem morose and withdrawn almost all the time. We think you may need to get some professional help."

As with the careful averting implemented by Dr Gull and Dr Khanna back in the late nineties, my parents didn't use the word OCD though I could tell my mum was thinking along those lines. After all, it didn't take a brain surgeon to work out that the condition I now found myself in, although not entirely the same, bore more than just a degree of semblance to my ritualistic washing days as a young boy. It was certainly, if nothing else, causing very similar levels of distress. And so, that very evening, feeling like I had perhaps come to the very end of my own secret little road, I told my parents absolutely everything about my current unease. I told them about my rituals, my need for certainty, and the endless fear of being a bad person. I explained to them how many times I had been to see doctors and nurses and the hours spent trudging through website after website in a desperate but ultimately vain attempt to find the answers. Crucially, I told them how my life was now becoming a living misery.

"I knew it," they both said. "Then it's settled. You are definitely going to get help."

Shortly after this unanimous proclamation, yet another appointment was booked to see my local GP. Though this time it was not for blood tests and swabs but to discuss my declining mental state. Far greater than the physical threat of HIV or Chlamydia was the much more imminent threat to my very sanity. "You need to give this some real attention," my mum told me seriously one evening. "You can't neglect yourself like this any longer." She, of course, was right. Despite still not being convinced I was safe from passing on some rather horrific sexual disease, I knew that the consequence of me losing my mind might be far worse; might be far more dangerous to me and to those around me.

More importantly, I knew I would not be able to successfully go about 'solving' this rather long and discommoding STI issue if I didn't have my sanity intact. Then and only then I considered, might I have everything I needed to finally find the *answers...*

There are possibly two main reasons why people with OCD do not in fact seek help the moment they suspect that something is wrong. One is pure fear; the fear that a coping mechanism (albeit dysfunctional) may be taken away, leaving the OCDer exposed and vulnerable. (After all, if OCD, to some extent resembles addiction, it is only understandable that it will not be a process an OCDer will want to let go of.) The other is the shame involved. Will my symptoms be taken seriously or even understood correctly? Will I be told I am a pervert or *sick in the head*? Will I be locked up in some form of mental asylum for my own and others' safety?

Luckily for me, I suffered no such fear or shame. Or at least, fairly little. I had done a lot of reading on the subject of OCD, knowing it to be a fairly common-place and benign (at least to others) disorder. Moreover, I had also spent the last three years studying law. I knew about the Mental Health Act 1983, amended in 2007. I knew its clauses and its provisions. I knew of its many safeguards and the difficulty in getting someone committed. I knew that OCD definitely *wasn't* madness and that most people with OCD knew full well how irrational their behaviour was and seemed to other people. Finally, I knew just how far removed current legislation was from previous enactments such as The Madhouse Act 1774, The Lunacy Act 1845 and even the Mental Deficiency Act 1913 which had first proposed the concept of separate institutionalisation for "moral defectives".

For me, telling my parents had been the very hardest part of my illness. My symptoms were embarrassing and not really the sort of things you typically discuss with *parents*. I have since learned that there should be no taboos when it comes to mental wellbeing. That, in many ways, it is those taboos and expectations over so-called polite and 'socially acceptable' conversation that perpetuate symptoms of OCD just as fixations with appearance and dieting in wider society help to fuel symptoms of anorexia and bulimia nervosa.

Once I had told my parents what was wrong, explaining to them the inner-workings of my neurotic mind, I felt almost totally at ease about talking it through with strangers. Perhaps I am alone here in saying this but I do not think I am: My OCD, as misguided as it is, has only ever been interested in unearthing the 'real' cracks. It has no time for cosmetic indentations; no place for mere *appearances*. If a stranger thinks I am bad or even mad, it is a judgement that has far less significance and impact than if *I* or even those around me whom I trust implicitly (like close friends and family) think that I am bad.

And so, as I walked to my local GP surgery for my first appointment that mildly sunny October afternoon with Dr Okoro, I couldn't help but feel, if not optimistic, then certainly very slightly relieved. At last, I was going to be looked at by a truly qualified professional. At last, it looked as if something really was actually going to be *done*.

In point of fact Dr Okoro was one of a fairly large handful of doctors at the surgery - long gone are the days that people can see the *same* doctor each time (remember good old Dr Gull) - though he was no stranger either. I had actually visited him once before when I was seventeen about a mole I had found near my belly button. It was a large unsightly thing with irregular edging and a pebbly surface. I had not seen one like it before. On that occasion, Dr Okoro was able to put my mind at rest in mere seconds; a *dysplastic nervus* he called it, nothing at all to worry about. "If it changes colour or starts to itch," he told me unconcernedly, "then come back and see me then."

This time, however, Dr Okoro passed me a lost expression. Seemingly, he did not know much about OCD or the effects it could have on daily life. Nor, as it transpired, was he able to treat me then and there as he had done over four years ago.

"I will have to take down some more notes," he told me, scratching his head and playing with the chest piece of his black single-head stethoscope.

The symptoms of mental illness are often far more progonostically challenging than the otherwise distinguishable manifestations of physical sickness. At what point does a negative internal experience or a simple quibble or *quirk* become a true indication of feeble or deteriorating mental health? At what point do we apply a medical label for the abounding misery and insecurity we are feeling inside? For a doctor, whose profession relies on a paint-by-numbers understanding of the inner workings of the human body, the haziness, the wholly indistinct nature of a disorder that remains both outwardly invisible as well as disquietingly subjective, is possibly at odds with everything they have ever come to know or learn.

Nevertheless, Dr Okoro listened to what I told him with keen interest and, having heard me out patiently, decided it best to refer me straight away to be seen by a professional.

"I am going to refer you to see the link worker."

A link worker, I repeated back to myself; it sounded like something to do with credit cards or the tram system up in Lancashire that I would often have to catch to visit my grandparents who lived, as we often jibed, up *t' north* in Bury. It certainly didn't sound like someone who might be able to instruct on mental well-being; to issue advice pertaining to the numerous and intricate frailties of the mind. As it transpired, I couldn't have been more wrong. Dr Okoro went on to explain that the link workers were kind of like the 'go-to people' of the mental health world. "As their name suggests," he continued informatively, "they provide a *link* between the local GP surgery and community mental health teams, ensuring patients receive the fastest route possible into the best available treatment."

It made a sort of sense.

And so it was, a few weeks later, at the same surgery, I met my link worker for the first and only time in Dr Okoro's office. There, I told her what was wrong with me, how I found it difficult to cope both at home and at work, how rituals and the fear of passing on STIs had seemingly taken over my whole life and she at once whipped out her notebook and started scribbling furiously.

"That sounds like OCD down to a tee," said this scruffy though discernibly middle-class woman in her late forties, a slovenly nest of grey hair sat upon her corrugated brow. "I tell you what...how would you feel if I put you straight on the waiting list for treatment?"

"That would be brilliant," I said enthusiastically, not quite being able to believe how quickly and easily steps were being put into place.

Indeed, I had heard prior to that morning's session, a number of horror stories about people going to the doctors with things like depression and stress and simply being fobbed off with the option of medication or sleeping tablets. In the so-called *Macdonald's culture* of health care, where the aim of the game is simply to process patients as quickly as possible, this had perhaps been all I had expected. As it transpired (and quite contrary to my initial presumptions) I couldn't have been more thrilled that my own complaint was being taken that much more seriously. That the broken circuitry in my head was going to be looked at properly and corrected over a course of prolonged and suitably instructive treatment. For the first time in a long while, I actually started to feel somewhat *hopeful* over my otherwise outwardly intractable and somewhat bewildering predicament.

And if all that wasn't good enough, there would be yet more good news to follow. As it turned out, putting me on a waiting list for therapy was actually the very least the link worker would be able to do for me that morning. As the session went on, I was provided with a whole list of interim counselling services to make use of while I waited for NHS treatment - the link worker told me that sometimes the NHS waiting list for treatment could take up to six months - as well as given information on books, library schemes and all sorts of other handy tip-bits to aid my recovery. In many ways, had it not been for the link worker and the help she had given me so early on, I probably would not have ever managed to get back on my feet. To a large extent, I owe her my freedom.

"Walking worried."

"I beg your pardon."

"Walking worried; that's what they call people like you," said the link worker, after she had finished giving me all my options for therapy. She was, as I like to describe such, a real *'jolly hockey sticks'* sort; staunch, effusive, boisterously enthusiastic.

I looked at her curiously: "Why is that?" I said.

"Because you have an anxiety disorder which makes life difficult, sometimes dreadfully so, but you cannot die from it nor do you need to be locked away for your own or others' safety. You can get up in the morning, live your life and then do the same all over again the next day."

I looked up thoughtfully. I had perhaps never considered my illness in those terms before (in reality, I had barely even considered my symptoms as an *illness* full stop). Yet, the link worker had possibly hit the nail right on the head. Although it felt like I couldn't cope most of the time, actually, I *was* coping. Or at the very least, I was still able to function within the norms of society. And in that light, it was perhaps not difficult to fathom why waiting lists for treatment were in fact so long: I might have been suffering every day but at least I was *getting up* every day. I wasn't considered dangerous (except perhaps in my own mind) nor, as I had already established prior to my GP's appointment, was there a risk of me losing the plot and doing harm to someone.

I was *sane*. Although at times it didn't feel like I was.

I guess, though, in many ways, this is what makes having OCD often all the more unbearable. You *don't* lose control. There is no obvious cry for help, a point of collapse that will see friends and loved ones - and indeed professionals - flock to your aid; to pick you up when you haven't the energy left to go on. OCD is a silent disorder, shrouded in shame and secrecy with no emotional tipping point, but rather a continuous, frustrating struggle through endless routine and rituals. Sometimes, I think I would have loved to have been able to just...*fall*. Maybe it was the dramatist or the writer in me that made me want to implode, to hit some sort of emotional breakdown, a point of no return, but I think what perhaps appealed to me more was the idea that somewhere down the line there would be this breath-taking emancipation, of finally being able to let go and relinquishing all that crushing responsibility. After all, what makes OCD so intolerable is the way in which it causes the sufferer to seek ever excessive ways to maintain control.

Unfortunately - or perhaps *fortunately* - I have had to accept that no such lifeline existed for me. Nor does it exist for the great majority of those suffering with OCD. I would have to *fight* if I wanted to get through this. Though, unlike before, I would not have to do it alone. Now, I had help on the way.

A month or so after my appointment with the link worker, I started my first bout of counselling. It was daunting, even a tad humiliating, but I knew that I was doing the right thing; taking the first steps on the road towards recovery. And if nothing else, I was sure, surer than I had ever been about anything else, that I wanted to be well again.

*

The Norwich centre was my first port of call: a person-centred counselling service established in Norwich as far back as 1908. It was number one on my list from the link worker and had, by comparison anyway, a really short waiting list. The building itself was situated on the stretch of road between the city centre and the ring road and was tucked discretely - perhaps intentionally so - from the wayside with a large rusty iron gate covered in plants and shrubbery. An old wooden welcome sign hung cordially at the front entrance.

I remember well my first appointment. The receptionist that afternoon had introduced me straightaway to my counsellor James, a fairly young man in his thirties, tall, with a short haircut wearing smart jeans and a baggy blue jumper who smiled at me warmly as he took me upstairs to the room where, for the duration of my sessions, I would have my person-centred therapy.

"Please take a seat," he said as he pointed over to a dark blue TULLSTER arm chair in the far left of the room. Indeed I had expected a therapy couch or a *chaise lounge* or perhaps even one of those Barcelona chairs you see in all those American films. Unfortunately, as with most aspects of therapy, it is never as glamorous as one supposes it to be. It is certainly never as it appears on the telly.

James settled into an Indonesian styled woven wicker chair and doughtily yet tenderly enough asked me to tell him, in my own time, what, generally speaking, the matter was. I took a deep breath in and out and told him that I had recently been diagnosed with OCD. I told him that I no longer felt safe and that, even though I desperately wanted to remain a good person, I feared how easy it might be to cause suffering or, worse still, to catch myself doing something *'bad'*. I told him that I no longer felt I could trust myself.

"I find it almost impossible to go about my life. I feel like something awful could happen at any time and that I might be responsible for it. And the more I think, the more I lose perspective and eventually I'm sitting here and I'm not sure I know right from wrong anymore or even what I'm capable of."

James looked at me and smiled: "It sounds to me like you probably have a better idea than you think. After all, if you really were such a *bad* or reckless person, you would surely not be sitting here so worried about it now..."

He fixed me a sort of dialectic squint; a look indicating that, contrary to my own misgivings, there really was light at the end of the tunnel. I looked down at my feet. I hadn't before been met with such abounding optimism. It was different to the types of *reassurance* I had received previously from friends and loved ones (as well as from doctors and nurses) which only ever seemed to provide ephemeral relief at best. This time, a more panglossian portrait hung in the galleries of my psyche, one which promised even the smallest slice of that often taken for granted commodity we call freedom.

Over the course of our sessions together, I found James to be a most sincere character and I warmed to him quickly. He never seemed to throw at me hackneyed sound-bites or to misunderstand the point I was trying to make. He listened well and seemed even to understand the rudimentary nature of my OCD:

- "But *how* do I know that cuddling a girl naked won't give me an STI? Surely I should get checked out afterwards before engaging sexually with somebody else?"

- "You don't know. Nobody knows. Life is uncertain. You take 'reasonable' precautions and trust in your gut instincts. Remember, it's as much *their* responsibility as it is yours to keep safe. Your concerns are not completely implausible Aron, they are just grossly out of perspective."

In many ways, James spoke a lot of sense and it wasn't long before the severity and the frequency of my obsessions, particularly those regarding STIs, began gradually to decrease. Though, always at the back of my mind, was the knowledge that James was not in fact a trained psychologist (nor was he any sort of medical expert). Nor did he have much in the way of experience with the various treatment protocols for anxiety disorders. To a large extent, James relied on his instincts and intuition.

One night, sometime after my second session with James, I was sitting around the dinner table with my family. We sat in silence; a prickly, deathlike quietude that had come to signify a particularly rampageous bout of OCD. That evening, my dad, rather impatient with my sporadic engagement in family life (due primarily to my OCD symptoms), had decided to probe further into how my counselling with James was going:

"So is this bloke you're seeing doing the trick?" he asked with mild chagrin and whilst I still had my mouth full of Mum's chicken pilaff to ingest.

"How do you mean?" I said waspishly, swallowing down abortively the last remaining morsels of masticated chicken.

"Well...you know...is he *qualified*?"

"Not to any great extent," I answered, honestly.

My dad was not a particularly patient person and, like me, was one of life's worriers. In those heightened states, he liked to know things were being done; that a solution was imminent. When it came to my OCD, I sometimes couldn't help but think he wanted it solved as much, if not more, than I did. Indeed, a while after our initial suspicions of my having OCD, both my parents had offered to pay for me to "go private". They wanted me to get the very best treatment. But I had declined; *I had got myself into this mess and I should be the one to get myself out.* Or so my thinking went.

Yet I could not now help but wonder whether I had been perhaps too hasty in asserting my independence or in dismissing the option for private medical care. I also started to wonder whether any amount of personal experience that James had acquired in treating patients with anxiety could indeed atone for a nonexistent qualification in essential interviewing skills or cognitive therapy. Could James, who had no real basis in psychotherapy, who had obtained no more than the very basic qualifications in psychology, be as proficient in handling such an abstruse disorder as a fully trained *expert*?

"I think it's like with everything," my mum interjected. "It depends on the individual and how in touch they are. I'm not sure that the qualification is actually all that important. It's all about creating that *connection*."

James and I had certainly made a connection. Of that, I was sure. In fact, it is possibly true to say that of all the mental health professionals I would later encounter (or, in many cases, *endure*), it was James, in his relative sciolism, who had made the most positive impact on me. It was also James who had taught me the most about my disorder and what it was doing to me; how it messed with my head and skewed my judgement.

Nevertheless, it was not a quick or easy awakening and my progress with James was slow. I argued with him often, selectively incorporating his counsel only so long as it fitted in with my own pre-established apetheosis. I am a malapert at the best of times. Sometimes, this caused unnecessary strain on our patient-therapist relationship. At other times it frustrated significantly the road to recovery. The problem when it comes to therapy, or advice in general, is that the patient or listener must be one hundred percent receptive to what is being said in order for it to truly work. They must be willing to take on new ideas and leave old, ingrained beliefs - often beliefs they have held for many years - by the wayside. If not, the guidance will simply fall on deaf ears.

I was not one to listen. I am the patient that always knows best. It took a while for me to appreciate that I was not always right. It took even longer to learn that a conclusion derived at through relentless analysis did not, by virtue of sheer bloody endeavour, equate to the kind of exactness and veracity that my illness demanded. Like I say, "OCD has a logic, just not a truth." Often it was the *truth* that had conflicted most abrasively with my beliefs, an almost rasping inconsonance that would invariably see a hasty abandonment of reality in favour of my own rather more crippling and miscalculated logic. It would be a mindset I would need to alter significantly if I were to ever truly stand a chance of getting better.

"So where do you think your OCD *came* from?" James asked me one particular session. It was late on a Tuesday afternoon and we had just finished discussing how my anxiety caused me to feel constantly on alert for danger and how I felt overwhelmingly that, at any moment, something really terrible would happen and that this would all be my fault for not taking the appropriate precautions or taking the time to get things one hundred percent *right*.

"Why do you need to know that?" I asked defensively.

"I think it could really help us here."

I looked at him with a sort of murmuring disdain. *How would this help me?* I thought, grumpily, arrogantly, to myself.

According to pretty much all of the books I had read on treatments for OCD, the more controversial method of Freudian psychoanalysis, or other such insight-oriented therapy designed to encourage patients to discover hidden meanings behind their disorder, had largely proven to be unhelpful in providing a 'cure' for the affliction. Much more effectual was the utilisation of cognitive behavioural therapy - or CBT - which focused primarily on the present interrelationship between thoughts, emotions and behaviour.

And on that basis I told James that I did not think that looking back in time would help us get to the bottom of anything.

"I think we should just concentrate on the here and now," I told him, rather patronisingly. I was doing it again: clinging to my own beliefs and ideas like an Australian koala bear to a eucalyptus tree and resisting any new information that might potentially prove me wrong and cause me to have to re-evaluate.

James looked at me querulously and told me that he did not want me to focus on the past at all. "This is not an exercise in regression," he told me. "I simply wanted you to recognise that your OCD had very probably been *triggered* at a point in time. Sometimes it can be very useful to view your OCD as a sort of control mechanism gone wrong."

"*Control mechanism*?" I said, fixing him a hard, invasive stare. I had not heard the term before and it, at once, caught my interest.

"Yes, a control mechanism," James repeated.

"I see," I said, stroking the bottom of my chin with my thumb and forefinger, pretending to be quite au fait with his words now they had been repeated.

He began to explain: "OCD is often caused by a trauma or set of mini-traumas in someone's past. This can cause a person to be on constant alert for danger, going to excessive lengths to keep safe or to prevent themselves from experiencing any further trauma. At first this is useful. But the OCD will often not know when to stop, prompting the sufferer to go on to engage in so-called rituals to reduce the risk of something bad ever happening again in the future. The manifestations of the OCD may or may not bear semblance to the triggering event but will undoubtedly exist to keep danger at bay. Trying to keep safe at all costs soon becomes an unwanted agenda, causing much disruption to a person's day-to-day living."

"Ah I see..." it started to make sense, "*Like a control mechanism gone wrong*?" I jumped in, as if somehow transforming all of this now into my own idea.

"Precisely."

I hadn't really thought about the origins of my OCD before my session that morning with James. I knew I had had it as a child (my parents told me of my bizarre behaviour as a ten year-old as well as my various trips to see child psychologist, Dr Khanna), but it had gone for some years, only to re-emerge quite unexpectedly during university. I hadn't explored *why* it had come back or even when exactly it had started taking hold. I had simply come to accept that I had re-developed my OCD out of thin air at around the same time I darted off to university and now, as if getting better from a sudden yet transitory cold virus, needed to get myself 'sorted out'. But OCD isn't like that. It had clearly existed inside of me, potentially, my whole life. More to the point, it had been 'triggered'.

After my session that afternoon with James, I decided that it would be perhaps only prudent (not to mention, a bloody good idea) to re-visit my adolescence in order to obtain some clue as to why and how I ended up re-developing such a debilitating disorder. This was to be the first part of my journey towards getting better and I felt hopeful that I would be able to find what I was looking for. I went home that night and looked through my diary scurrilously to see what I could dig up. I also spoke at great length with my mum about my early childhood. I needed to know exactly what had happened to me; to find the missing parts of the jigsaw so I could understand where my OCD had come from and, most crucially, why it had returned.

What was thrown up would be a surprise even to me.

Chapter 6
CAUSES

"Fate is the endless chain of causation, whereby things are; the reason or formula by which the world goes on."
- Citium Zeno

What causes OCD is, as yet, undetermined by medical science. Some argue that the basis of OCD lies in psychodynamics and life events, whilst others look more to chemical and brain dysfunction as the most likely cause. Some scientists even point to a genetic link, though this is by no means conclusive.

My own personal hunch is that all the theories have at least some relevance in solving the mystery that is OCD. Even the psychodynamic explanation - which argues, in my view, rather dangerously, that OCD has something to do with our need to separate delinquent subconscious desires from rational appraisal (we check the taps are off because we secretly want to flood the house) - has something useful to say in terms of the role of guilt.

However, with the exception of maybe the latter account, all theories make one thing very clear: "OCD is not a hidden wish fulfilment". People do ***not*** have OCD because they would otherwise be dangerous individuals.

In fact, the opposite tends to be true. According to Bruce M. Hyman, PH.D and Cherry Pedrick, RN in their guide to breaking free from OCD, *'The OCD Workbook':*

"People with pure obsessions are not in danger of acting out these unwanted horrific thoughts. People who *do* act on such thoughts may have what is known as antisocial personality disorder. They are people lacking a conscience. Unlike people with OCD, they tend not to worry much about their bad thoughts."(p.126)

Most psychologists will agree - and, indeed, my own personal experience of meeting so many people with the disorder backs this up - OCD tends to be an affliction reserved primarily for *nice* people. The reason we OCDers give ourselves such a hard time is surely indicative of our good nature. We don't want something bad to happen or be responsible for causing suffering, however small. That is why we go to such extraordinary lengths to avoid these things from happening.

But there is a danger here of glamorising the disorder, of justifying it on the grounds that having it means you're naturally a *good* person. Despite certain personal characteristics of the sufferer, OCD itself is arbitrary and needless. It has nothing to do with good or bad.

This is probably why I like so much the biochemical model for OCD which states that OCD is simply a medical condition that is related to a biochemical imbalance in the brain. No more, no less than that.

In the book *'Brain Lock'*, written by Jeffrey M.Schwartz, M.D, OCD is characterised simply by a malfunction in the brain's circuitry. Schwartz tells us:

"Our research on people with OCD at UCLA led us to find that, without question, OCD is a neuropsychiatric illness resulting from a malfunction in the circuitry of the brain."

Over the years living with OCD, I have learned a lot about the brain. I have used it as a form of therapy; a way of being able to distinguish *me* from my OCD. I have found it to be, on the whole, most enlightening. Here is what I know:

The OCD loop starts with the caudate nucleus, based in the primitive part of the brain (the part we share with our reptilian ancestry). From there, messages (often *false* messages) are sent up to the orbital cortex, a prefrontal cortex region in the frontal lobes, where thoughts and emotion combine and where cognitive decision making occurs. In response to these (false) messages from the basal ganglia, the orbital cortex, which is also part of what is known as the 'error-detection' circuit, goes off like a car alarm inside the head, putting the OCD patient on heightened alert for danger and forcing them into taking some form of *action*. Compounding this process is then finally the cingulate cortex (also part of the error-detection circuit) whose job it is to keep attention resolutely fixed on the feeling of unease and in turn forcing the patient to carry out *compulsions,* sometimes over and over again, until, ultimately, the problem is gone or until their anxiety is abated.

It is unclear what causes this circuitry to become so awfully awry in people with OCD. Some argue that it is down primarily to structural abnormalities in the cortical-basal ganglia; a 'fluctuating' caudate nucleus is how it is sometimes referred which, ordinarily, acts like a brake pedal, filtering out 'worry' signals and preventing hyperactivity in the neuronal loop, but which fails woefully to do so in those suffering with symptoms of OCD. Others contend that an imbalance or *lack* of the neurotransmitter serotonin (the neurotransmitter responsible for carrying messages between nerve cells) might also play a crucial part. It would certainly make a great deal of sense. In OCD, it is often reported that there is this sort of heart-head lag whereby the OCDer *knows* one thing but *feels* something very different.

One thing that is abundantly clear from all my research on the matter of the brain is that the circuit primarily involved with OCD is firmly rooted in *survival*. In other words, the behaviours involved in OCD are deeply entrenched in our human makeup and tend to constitute the basis of our continued endurance as a species. Only, it would seem that people with OCD tend to experience the effects of *their* circuits at seemingly irregular or inappropriate times. Or, at the very least, during periods where there is in fact no real danger and thus no need to carry out such safety-ensuring behaviours. As Rita Carter points out in her book *'Mapping the Mind':*

"The instinct to keep clean, to check the environment constantly for signs of anything untoward; the need to keep order and balance - all these things have a basis in survival. In OCD they have simply come adrift from the survival superstructure and appear as isolated, inappropriate and exaggerated habits." (p.92)

Looking at the brain is perhaps one way of looking at the causes of OCD but, despite some extremely sophisticated explanations for the disorder, it still doesn't provide us with everything we might wish to know about what brings OCD on. It doesn't tell us why it all starts when it starts or indeed what will determine the content of the obsessions. Why some people wash, whilst others hoard has not been answered by brain science.

This is where 'life events' become an important factor in looking at the causes of OCD. As I have already mentioned, OCD is often said to be 'triggered' by trauma or even a series of min-traumas. In actual fact, it can be brought about by any sort of *change*. Major life transitions such as leaving home, bereavement and child birth all seem to play a part in the onset of OCD. Again, according to Bruce M. Hyman, PH.D and Cherry Pedrick, RN:

"Environmental factors [leading to OCD] include psychological and physical trauma, childhood neglect, abuse, family stress, illness, death, and divorce, plus major life transitions, such as adolescence, moving out, marriage, parenthood, and retirement." (p.25)

In my case, it was my move up to Lancaster to study law at university. At least, this is what I have since concluded with a great deal of analysis. Before then, everything had been ticking along just fine. Dr Khanna had done a good job with me whilst we had been living in Southend and I had remained functioning well for over eight healthy years. But the upheaval of living by myself and away from home, of leaving all my friends behind, of starting again in a brand new city, had triggered a *change* in my brain. The result would be a relapse that would take me to the depths of despair and see me enter into a new type of living where happiness would and could no longer be taken for granted.

If going to see the doctor and link worker in 2009 had been the start of my journey towards recovery, my journey up to Lancaster University had most certainly been the beginning of my journey *away*; away from wellness, away from inner unity, away from *living*. It would be a trip, as they often say, *to hell and back*.

* * *

I remember well the day I packed my bags and drove almost two hundred miles to my new accommodation up in Lancaster. Having lived in relative opulence, in a four bedroom detached home in Norfolk for the last three years, I couldn't help but wonder what sort of life awaited me up north, *in digs*. Of course this was not the first time I had moved away to somewhere totally new, to a place where I didn't know a single other person, but it was the first time I had moved anywhere without my family by my side. Unsurprisingly, as we drove tenebrously down the M6 towards Lancaster that cold, overcast morning in September, I couldn't help but feel somewhat nervous of my new dwelling.

The college block I lived in up in Lancaster actually no longer exists. County West was knocked down a year after I graduated. Though for one whole year it had served as my home. It was, if you like, my home away from home. The college itself was part of one of the eight colleges, seven of which named after regions of the traditional county of Lancashire. County College was always the odd one out; named after Lancashire County Council itself and being erected as late as 1978, adding to the already-established County Main building opened by HM The Queen in 1969. But by 2007 was no more. I had been resident there in 2005 and so was possibly the last swathe of students to experience life on those narrow corridors. I am not sad to know that the building has since been demolished.

That first evening, having spent the day perusing the campus, prolonging the inevitable long goodbye, my parents eventually left me at my college dorm to return home to Norwich. Had I not been trying my hardest to affect an air of stoicism, I could have cried my eyes out. Not only was I saying goodbye to my family for the first time in my life but my new accommodation had quite literally shocked me to the core.

"It's not *that* bad," my dad had said, before leaving with Mum with a tear in his eye. Though, his facial expression told an altogether different story.

My room in County West was bare-bricked, painted an almost incandescent shade of yellow and contained a bed narrower than my single bed back home. The floor was dirty and the curtains, colourless and ragged. Someone later told me - I'm not sure how true this actually is - that the reason the walls were not plastered in the rooms was due to the extra layer contravening EU regulations regarding the size of non-prison accommodation. In other words, had the room been any smaller, it would have been classed, legally, as a prison cell and would have breached my very human rights. Like I say, I do not know how true this is but, back then, nothing would have much surprised me.

In addition to the shocking accommodation were the even more shocking amenities. On County West B floor, the water ran orange from the taps and the toilet paper was crisp and shiny; the kind of stuff I couldn't help think MSFC must have used to coat the Hubble Space Telescope. The carpet was old and stained, the toilets were separated from the showers only by a partial divide in the wall which didn't even reach the floor (meaning urine and faeces were free to flow in from one chamber to the next) and week-old black bin bags littered the kitchen and stunk out the corridors; 'Like a scene from Beirut' I think I once described it to my poor old parents down the phone, close to tears and trying my best not to break down between sentences.

As one might expect, none of this did much good for my mental well-being. In fact, it had frequently left me feeling ripped and crestfallen. Friends back at home, often with great relish I regrettably hasten to add, had told me as far back as my UCAS application that Lancaster might indeed have been an inappropriate choice for someone of my undoubtedly gloomy and recusant nature. "No one in their right mind would go there," they had smugly told me. "It has the highest suicide rate of any university in the whole of the UK." Though being somewhat obsequious and self-assured, I had taken such comments as mere repartee and shrugged them off without a further thought. Though now, looking around the place, examining the filth and the dereliction, it no longer felt like such a joke. It also did not take a rocket scientist - in light of said fifth and dereliction - to work out why such a high suicide rate did exist. (The fact that I was afraid of heights had probably saved my life; sky diving off of Bowland Tower, around fourteen stories high, being the seemingly preferred choice of termination here.)

It did not help of course that it took me a while to make friends. The other people on my corridor were neither like-minded nor melodramatic. Instead they followed the football religiously, drank lots (and lots and lots and lots) of alcohol and had frequent bouts of casual sex. For them, university was a chance to let their hair down in ways that perhaps not even they had dared imagine. Here, people ate what they felt like (*meal* time was almost unheard of), woke up when they fancied (happily skipping the odd inconvenient morning lecture or two) and fitted in their course around recreation and partying. Being a stickler for routine and rules (not to mention still battling with a rather debilitating fear of having sex), I found the fetid, almost scatological atmosphere to be both improper and discomforting.

"It's like a Club 18-30 holiday," I told Jake one evening down the phone during Fresher's week. "I really don't know if I can stick this out."

And when it came to the cultural aspect of life on campus, I was perhaps not too wide of the mark in my censure. Unlike how I imagined the atmosphere at Oxford's prestigious Oxford Union or Cambridge's infamous 'Festival of Ideas', stirring, intellectual debate at County College seemed to be the very last thing anyone wanted to be bothering themselves with (I did have just one friend on the corridor from Germany, a mature student called Eckbert, who had studied social science at Humboldt university of Berlin and who shared my enthusiasm for both philosophy and political history - but that was about all). As each week passed, I spent more and more of my time missing my old best friends, the juvenile yet over-intellectual conversations about girls that seemingly demarked our formative years; not to mention the various funny nights out to Norwich, trying but failing dismally to initiate even one good chat up line with an attractive female counterpart. By contrast, nights out in Lancaster City had simply meant doing my best to avoid lofty, inebriated young *scallies* whom always appeared to have a violent glint in their eyes and (somewhat undeservingly I couldn't help but feel) a fit *lass* on their arms.

Lancaster City has in fact been described by Alan Bennett as “sullen, tight-fisted and at night raw and violent". The description could not have felt more apt. Each night out, I would feel the threat of having my head caved in or my face glassed with great coruscating premonition. And although I never did end up getting attacked (I view this more as luck or good fortune than of any kind of prejudicial misjudgement on my part) I had certainly felt endangered on numerous occasions. Some of my contemporaries were less lucky; one lad from Fylde College, mindlessly assaulted by a local yob, had ended up in the university hospital of

Morecambe and needing over twenty stitches. Yet the violence I felt at sure risk of befalling was contrary to everything that I had experienced to be true back home; Norwich being such a vibrant and cultured city and surely much safer than any mangy municipality up north.

And so I spent much of my time indoors, away from the crowds, away from the so-called *detritus*. It was around this time that I also became quite fanatical about writing in my diary. I wrote about my experiences living on campus, about my hellish subsistence in Lancashire and my longing to be back home in Nelson's County. The misery made for great material, the continual wretchedness keeping my creative juices flowing like the great and vigorous Colorado River. As the writer and playwright Graham Greene once famously remarked:

Writing is a form of therapy; sometimes I wonder how all those who do not write, compose or paint manage to escape the madness, melancholia, the panic and fear which is inherent in a human situation.

And so I would write cathartically, a page every day, almost without fail. It kept me going through tough times. It helped me to make sense of my growing fear and anxiety. Though it happens that it was not just my own melancholia I was interested with immersing myself in. I enjoyed reading about other people's miserable lives also: *'The Bell Jar'* by Sylvia Plath, *'Experience'* by Martin Amis, even a small memoire by Harry Mount entitled *'My Brief Career'* which despairingly chronicles Harry's less than happy experience as a Pupil in Chambers had been an interesting read (this book especially would come to have special significance in the years that followed).

Perhaps most cogent of all, had been the influence of Alan Bennett, whose own diary entries, running from 1996 to 2004, can be found neatly intermingled in his 2005 memoire, 'Untold Stories'. (It had been a Christmas present from my parents because they knew I liked reading 'complicated' books – or at any rate, books with big words in.) By the time my second year at university had started, I had read the book almost cover to cover and found it to be most transfixing. I had been particularly taken with Alan Bennett's gripping narrative on his own *Mam* whom had suffered severely with mental illness and had been admitted to the Lancaster Moore Hospital up here in Lancaster. Reading it had made me feel restless and agitated; something I had not felt before just by the mere act of imbibing words on a page. Despite my own dispiriting and somewhat painful mental deterioration, my diary (which I now wrote in daily) had always remained peppy and roseate; a naive hopefulness pervading each lengthy entry. Now, I felt my writing taking on newer, *darker* styles.

Aside from life on campus, my weekend job at Morrisons of Morecambe had proven also to be a source of dark and wretched material (I had been transferred up there during term time and then back down in Norwich during the holidays). I hated profoundly this run-down little seaside catch basin with its dilapidated buildings and needle-strewn pavements. I hated the location of the store, sat facing the section of Warton Sands where 21 cockle pickers tragically drowned by the incoming tide. I hated the northern trogs, the ignorant soccer hooligans that comprised the majority of the staff; the boring, inane conversations about football and the awful jibing I received on a constant basis for being, as they saw it, of *blue-blood.*

Though perhaps above all else, I hated the travelling up on bus. Each Saturday and Sunday morning, I would drive nervously passed the Lancaster Royal Infirmary and, for a reason unknown to me at the time, would become stricken with terror; a paranoia that forced me, again and again, to ask myself the same old (or should that be *new*) question: *How long did I have left on the* outside? The thought of being institutionalised - perhaps in a similar way Alan's *Mam* had been locked away in the psychiatric ward at Lancaster Moore - petrified me. Had I still been back home in Norwich, we would possibly have been talking about Hellesdon Hospital on the Drayton High Road as opposed to The Royal Infirmary up here in Lancaster. Somehow, I think I would have coped with that a lot better.

What bought on these profound feelings of unease was unclear. I blamed my new life living up in the brutal North, living amongst such abounding decadence and ruin, away from all civility and reason, but, looking back, it was possibly as much to do with *loss* as anything that Lancashire could have dished out. For despite many things I hated about living, working and studying in Lancaster, it would also be equally true to say that I was missing home, missing my friends, missing my family, missing my house, missing every part of my old life in Norwich.

I was also missing Loretta.

I eluded very briefly earlier on in the book that I had been infatuated with a girl at sixth form before leaving for university. In fact, I had been truly, and dare I say it, *madly* in love with Loretta. She was, at least to my sex-starved and adolescent mind, the most beautiful girl I had ever seen and I had all but fallen head over heels for her from the very moment I had first laid eyes on her. She would often be the first thing I thought of when I awoke in the morning and would, inimitably, be the last thing I repined as I drifted off to sleep at night. And portentously for me, nothing at all had changed by the time I was ready to start up my new life in Lancaster. Other than, of course, I knew I would no longer be able to see her every day. And the prospect of her absence killed me.

Here is a brief extract from my diary dated back in September 2003 (the beginning of sixth form):

Loretta has the most beautifully burnished red hair which she has, at all times, tied back into this long, shimmering tress. I often wonder why she has it like this; why she never seems to wear it down like the other girls. Sometimes I like to daydream about seeing her hair down. I know that if I do ever see it in its natural, flowing state, I will have no doubt succeeded in winning her heart. And then what of her beautiful coffee eyes and her delightful, small, upturned nose? These too are demarcations of her undue exquisiteness, another collection of features that I cannot help but find so downright irresistible. Every minute I am not with her is another day I must spend torturing myself and watching from a distance. I must ask her out and fast. Sooner rather than later. If I do not, I fear I may lose my mind.

And so I asked her out. Twice. Both times I failed dismally.

The first time I propositioned her had been, admittedly, rather childish, involving a pretty lame and artless declaration of my undying love just outside the school gates. The two of us had been walking back from the local pub, the *Maid Marion*, at the time and we had both just skipped a double session of General Studies (which we had both despised and reckoned totally unnecessary). By this time, Loretta and I had started becoming quite close and I had even managed to convince her to go to the school prom with me, you know, *just as friends*. As we walked along the empty path towards the school gates, the last of the afternoon sunshine splashing across her pale face, I could not resist the urge to tell her how much she meant to me.

"I love you," I told her, just as we were drawing close to the school entrance. A minute or so before my revelation, my mates had driven passed in the Vauxhall Astra and honked the horn (as if to say, *get in there my son*) and I had taken great inspiration from the fact that she had gone slightly red but had, at no point, started wincing.

"I don't know what to say," Loretta started to wince.

"Well...do you feel anything for me?"

"*I'm fond of you,*" she replied.

Silence. No more was said. She gave me a look intimating sorrow but I could tell she was not mournful. I, on the other hand, was utterly grief-stricken; my hopes and dreams had literally been demobilized in the course of one sentence from her melon salved lips. She was fond of me. I was fond of my goldfish.

Then a few months later, I asked her out for a second time. It was but a day before I was due to start university and, this time, I had been far more hopeful. Over that summer, Loretta and I had become remarkably close; a relationship etching itself slowly and unsuspectingly out of the crumbs of abstention. Though frustratingly, the liaison had remained enduringly platonic and, as a result, I'd been perhaps understandably rather desperate to move things on from their fluid, rather indeterminate state.

That afternoon, we had decided to go out for the day in her car to Great Yarmouth. It was the first time we had ever done anything, just us two, *alone*, and I had been literally overjoyed by the prospects. It was not a date - at least neither of us had called it such - but it was nonetheless pretty darn special. The two of us went to the sea life centre together, took a gentle walk down the Britannia Pier and even had a key ring made at one of the amusement arcades; a sketch of the two of us sitting in front of the Eiffel Tower with the words *'forget me not'* inscribed across the bottom. That evening, once home from possibly one of the best afternoons of my life (and I don't say that flippantly), I decided, with more than just a hint of liquid courage - or *potvaliancy* - to send Loretta one final text elucidating on my feelings towards her and asking, just one last time, whether she would consider ever being my girlfriend. Indeed, I had been so utterly overwhelmed by her that splendid afternoon that I simply could not stand the thought of not at least giving it one last try.

I pressed my finger firmly on 'send' and then waited nervously but expectantly for her reply. A few minutes later and an answer that I had not hoped for (but half expected) popped up on my display: "I'm so sorry," read the rather succinct response back, "I had no idea."

And so I went to university with the pangs of dejection to deal with. I loved her. She did not feel the same about me.

Over the weeks at university, I found each day hard without her. Two hundred miles away from home and with no one really around to confide in, I felt, at times, almost nihilistic. Not to mention darn right lonely. Nevertheless, and despite her rejection of me, Loretta and I continued to text each other daily. And as days turned into weeks and weeks into months, I came to rely on Loretta's messages as a crutch to get me through. They were the only thing that provided any happiness at all and I longed always for the next communication.

Eventually, being so far away from Loretta made me resent my new dwelling with a brutish unreason that, for many years, in fact until only quite recently, I mistook for faults in my physical environment. Now I am forced to question whether Lancaster really was so awful, so cold and so destitute. Was it really so "raw and violent"? Or did it merely represent an almost unbearable absence, a cold and deathlike paucity that ate away at me, at my physical surroundings, like an attack perhaps not dissimilar to Stephen King's *Langoliers*.

Even now, I am not sure how to decipher it all. I am not sure I will ever know. Heartbreak as with isolation has a funny way of skewing just about everything. As American Author Louise Erdrich warns us through her novel *The Painted Drum*, "Life will break you. Nobody can protect you from that, and living alone won't either, for solitude will also break you with its yearning."

It is perhaps no wonder, against a context of being removed and rejected, sexless and alone that I felt so raw and so unsettled. For better or worse, my life up north was poles apart from the life I had experienced back home. Whilst the others on my corridor were out enjoying themselves and having indiscriminate sex all over the place (the sorts of liaisons that I still feared bitterly for the chance they had of leading to illness and pregnancy), I was locked away for most of my first term in my room, licking my wounds, thinking of Loretta, refusing to go out and, in turn, developing a mild self-disdain which would linger for many weeks and months.

Little did I realise at the time how bad things for me were about to become. That in the months to follow, I would become stricken with the onset of what I now know to be full blown OCD; a disorder which would, over the years, cause tireless disruption and chaos in my life. And now, having raked it all up again with James all those years later, having finally pin-pointed the 'trigger' of this second wave of OCD, I could not now help but feel a sense of relief that I had at last unearthed how it had all begun.

But alas, the story does not end here. This was only the very beginning.

Chapter 7
'APOCALYPTIC LOVE'

"Love keeps you up at night, fills your mind at school, and obsesses with your soul."
- Jeanie Wilding

Prior to meeting Loretta, I had never before been *in love*. Of course, I had developed numerous crushes on girls over the years - most of them little more realistic than a Surrealist painting by, say, Max Ernst or Leonora Carrington - but never before had I been subject to that ubiquitous ache, that heavy gasping inside my chest, of not knowing whether I was coming or going. This new feeling, which started at sixth form and continued rabidly through to university, was different to anything I had encountered previously. I was overwhelmed on a daily basis, no longer free to think and feel as I pleased. Was it something wrong with me, something askew with the way I had come to view and process the world around me, or was it all down to her own grand magnificence?

In his book, *'Love Sick'*, Frank Tallis, clinical psychologist and lecturer at King's College London, highlights a number of strong correlations between obsessive love and OCD. "The most obvious similarity", he tells us, "is that patients with OCD and people who have fallen in love seem unable to govern the contents of their own minds." In other words, once an intrusive idea has entered the mind of someone in love or suffering from OCD, it is often extremely difficult to get rid of it again. Back in 2002, I had not heard of OCD. Nor of the disruptive nature of obsessional thinking (bar some of those *hiccups* in childhood). And yet, it is also true that I could get Loretta out of my head no more easily than the obsessive thought in years to come that I was a sexual deviant or some other form of grave malefactor.

Nor had I ever really considered how my behaviour towards Loretta might well be viewed by some as *compulsive*. Now of course I am only too aware.

In so many ways, my persistence in trying to attain the girl that would never fully love me in return is perhaps the strongest example, the greatest indicator, of my penchant for or my inclination towards compulsive behaviour. According to Tallis, "Of the many compulsions associated with obsession, the compulsion to follow is perhaps the most strong." And as with the OCD that ensued, my unwillingness to move on from Loretta - our coalescence having long ceased to be a viable proposition -

became, ultimately, a thankless pursuit which would lead not only to suffering and angst but to total extirpation, like a collapse of an otherwise bourgeoning universe into totally dimensionless singularity. My second rejection from Loretta, occurring the very day before moving away, should have been the end of such an unpromising infatuation; the end of my longing and solicitude. Yet, unable to let go or move on, the violences to my heart and mind persisted.

It is perhaps no wonder, in light of this so-called "compulsive following", such bloody-minded persistence, that the whole thing would eventually come crashing down around me in my third year of university. And just as with the feeling associated with falling foul of an OCD ruling, my devastation during this time would prove almost too grand to comprehend.

Even now, after eight years, I am still, at times, stumped by the series of events as played out in my mind. How had I ever become so entangled? How had another human being, a mere fleshly ethological mammal, managed to cause such utter carnage; to hold over me that much power; to cause me to ponder and weep so recurrently and for so long.

The ultimate rejection from the girl I loved so rapturously has tainted my experiences ever since. It has also, I hasten to add, taught me more about myself and my OCD than potentially any other formative experience to date. And so I re-live some rather profound and emotional feelings in order to shed some serious light on my disorder as well as to see what tell-tale signs may have lurked in the background of what is, even without analysis, a stirring chronicle of love, loss and 'moving on'.

* * *

Following my rather painful rejection from Loretta just days before starting at university, it was, quite surprisingly, only a few weeks later, during a cold October evening in Fresher's Week, when my fortunes looked finally like they might change for the better. I remember it clearly even today not least because, following two years of obsession and just as many failed attempts at asking her out, such a turnabout must have seemed like something of a miracle. It was, as I recall, as late as 10 p.m., absolutely freezing cold (far too cold for the time of year) and I had been queuing outside our college block for what had literally felt like hours on end for a coach destined for some glitzy yet equally tacky night club in Blackpool when the text message from Loretta eventually came through.

"I miss you so much," read the unexpected transcript. "I'm sorry but I do. I'm sitting at home right now and all I can think about is how much I want you to be here." The words were enough to send me instantly spinning out of the car park, away from all the hoards of screaming, hedonistic freshers underneath and orbiting somewhere deep into outer space. I couldn't believe what I was reading. Immediately, as if awoken all over to the potentials of life itself, I decided once and for all to abandon my journey to Blackpool and retire to my bare-bricked, bright yellow room to ponder further. She was missing me. I had been gone literally only a few weeks and she was missing me. I lay on my bed that cold October evening whilst everyone else was out getting impetuously smashed and scrolled through the message over and over. She was missing me.

I couldn't have been more thrilled.

When one is subject to obsessional love, every incident, every communication is ridden with significance. It is what the obsessive clings on to. Jake and I have often made each other laugh at just how much significance we had placed on the various interactions (or *non*-interactions as was more often the case) between ourselves and the objects of our unseemly affections. Every pithy exchange, every extra kiss at the end of a text message, even a smile in our general direction, had given us great cause to dissect and analyse.

Loretta was, to all intents and purposes, a difficult one to 'crack'. Kind, sensitive and deep, she was also, at various other times, quite unsettled and dramatic. Though not in the sense girls are dramatic these days. On no, Loretta was never in any hurry to publicise her mood in the way that schoolgirls today operating on social media sites seem hungry to plaster their affairs to internet audiences of hundreds of thousands. Hers was a hushed agitation, an undisclosed depth of character that made her almost uniquely fathomless. So fathomless in fact that all these years on and I am in no doubt that it was that sense of mystery, that portrait of outward inaccessibility, which had caused me to fall for her so abruptly and so hardily. My analytical tendencies - which by that time had already started burbling violently away at the surface - meant that my desire to dissect Loretta in totally microscopic detail would eventually become something of an unhealthy fixation. Often, I would find myself doing my level best to "work out" Loretta, gathering and decrypting what little information I could lay my hands on as if a top-rate code-breaker working at Bletchley Park. In reality, I had probably as much chance of working out Loretta as I did winning the lottery or becoming the next Pope. Loretta, in all her mystifying allure, was deep on a much more sophisticated emotional level than my own rather more callow and bookish discernment and I lacked the insight and maturity, the sensitivity and assuredness, required to ever truly *understand* her. I certainly lacked the maturity to ever actually go out with her:

"I wonder if she will ever go out with me," I wrote one night in my, by now, rather hyperbolic diary. *"She is so beautiful. She looked at me briefly this morning during history and then, this afternoon, she began, again, to ignore me. I think she may be leading me on."*

Yet following my departure to university almost two years on from those early and rather adolescent days at sixth form, it seemed finally like the tables might well have turned. Purblind and obtuse as indeed it must have seemed to those around me, the text message that I received from Loretta during that Fresher's Week had provided me my first real glimmer of hope, keeping me going, quite literally, through the whole first term of university. I clung to it like small town Americans cling to guns and religion. When the Christmas holiday eventually came around a few months later, I simply could not wait to see Loretta again. And to my elation, she, likewise, seemed excited about seeing me too. That magical December, just as I had hoped and daydreamed, the two of us spent pretty much all of our free time in each other's company; trips out to random Norfolk villages like Banningham and Saxilingham Green during the day and outings to the cinema at night, sometimes watching two films consecutively and staying out right until gone midnight. We frequently went out for lunch together and, on one occasion, even went to Lowestoft to walk along the seafront with an ice cream in the bitter cold.

Then one beautiful, crisp, sunny afternoon, while the two of us were out driving together - I believe we were on our way to Ranworth Tower - Loretta and I both received a text message from a mutual friend. "I think I've got a message" said Loretta, looking perplexed at her vibrating handbag.

"Yeah me too," I responded, smiling puckishly before looking down curiously at my own purring handset. The message, generically constructed, was an invitation to a sixth form reunion party over in Tasburgh, a small Norfolk village just south of Norwich where Loretta, at the time, still just happened to live in a bungalow with her folks. For her, the venue was perfectly contiguous. For me, however, living at least eight miles away, the locale would prove rather trickier to get to and, perhaps more significantly, back from; a detail which, as luck would have it, did not go unnoticed by Loretta.

"Maybe you could stay round mine afterwards," Loretta offered sheepishly. The invite had caught me off guard and I almost choked on the butter bonbon I happened to be sucking on at the time.

"Yes," I said, "that would be great."

"Then it's a date," she said, smiling.

"Yes," I said. "I guess it is."

In truth, the term 'date' had not been meant as a romantic tryst nor indeed as an invitation for some opportune rollick. Rather it was a platonic arrangement, borne perhaps from no more than mere convenience, between two loyal and trusting *friends*; *Tu es mon meilleur ami*. Nevertheless, that being the case, it did not stop me from being profoundly excited at the prospects. So thrilled in fact that for the two weeks leading up to the party, I thought of little else but the impending night at Loretta's. This would be the first time I would get to see the inside of her bungalow; the place where she grew up, where she ate her meals, where she slept, where she no doubt would parade around in her purple Jacquard Rose dressing gown and curl up on her mocha couch watching Coronation Street. I couldn't believe I was finally being invited into her home, into her family, into her *life*.

When the party eventually came around a few weeks later I had resolved to play it cool for the duration of the evening. I spoke to old school friends and female acquaintances alike. I also got stupidly drunk. By the time Loretta had arrived by herself almost two hours later, I had knocked back precisely four double vodka and cokes and had already thrown up in the bathroom. *Twice*. Dutch courage, you see.

That night, as usual, I did my best to ignore Loretta and she, likewise, tentatively avoided me. We always did this when other people were around. For me, I never wanted to appear too eager. For her, I guess it was more the exposal she found difficult. Loretta was a private individual who invariably liked to keep her business her own; a preference I am now shamed to say I tended to bulldoze straight over by virtue of my enormous great gob. By the time the New Year's Eve party had come around only a few weeks later, there was perhaps not one single mutual friend who did not know of my infatuation with Loretta nor about the text message she had sent me privately during my first term at university.

Like I say, I regret those indiscretions now.

As the evening progressed, Loretta and I folded up, backsliding ever closer towards each other until, finally, the two of us were sitting conterminously on a three seater large black leather couch, our knees touching, her right shoulder overlaying my own. We said nothing to each other the whole time but I knew, just by our being so physically close, that we were as hermetic now as we had ever been.

We would get much closer in the hours to follow.

Later that evening, a friend kindly agreed to drop us off back at hers. We were both, by this stage, pretty squiffy. Or at least, we were certainly a lot more oblique and frivolous than we might normally have been. And yet, what came next, I remember in almost photographic detail. As if it were as significant as my own wedding day or as other-worldly as the afternoon the two Boeing 747's flew so pitilessly into the twin towers (they reckon that almost everyone remembers exactly what they were doing and where they were on that fateful day). At last I was going to be spending the night with the girl of my dreams and the excitement, the sheer hormonal overdrive, had been almost enough to make me pass out.

Almost that is. Fortunately for me, and indeed for the memories that followed, I would remain, at all times, fully cognizant:

Loretta and I stepped quietly out of the car so as not to make a sound. It was now around 2 a.m. and most of the villagers in her quiet, leafy suburb were fast asleep. Loretta let us in via the back door into the kitchen where we snuck a couple of drinks from the fridge into the lounge, before, once again, finding ourselves lying together on a couch. Though this time on her own box bordered, contemporary mocha settee that I had, up until that point, only dreamed about resting on. Together, we snuggled up cosily under a soft mink purple blanket that just so happened to be close at hand as I laid down my head slowly and steadily onto her left breast. I looked up and, for no apparent reason, we both started to giggle. Of course, we had to be quiet so as not to wake her parents (who were both fast asleep in the adjoining room) but this was a small price to pay. This had been my first opportunity to get so physically close to Loretta, our bodies intertwined like ribbon around the maypole, and I couldn't have been happier.

"Shall we watch a film?" Loretta suggested, jumping up like a Mexican jumping bean from the couch almost immediately having settled down next to me.

"Yeah sure," I replied.

After a small amount of umming and arrring on genre, we eventually decided on 'Along Came Polly' which I had incorrectly referred to as 'When Sally met Polly' and which had made Loretta chuckle. (Incidentally, I was always able to make Loretta laugh by being silly (often intentionally). In fact it was the one thing I seemed always able to do with the most minimal of effort. If only, I often thought to myself, I could make her laugh so hard that she fell head over heels in love with me. Now wouldn't that be something.)

Having set the video, Loretta darted back to the couch and nestled up next to me. I was so overwhelmed by my closeness to her, her smell, the softness of her body that I could happily have died in her arms that night. Perhaps a part of me did die; the same part that would no doubt later find room for my OCD.

"You have R-tex ceilings," I told her as I laid the back of my head back onto her chest, my eyes looking straight upwards. By this time, we had both grown disinterested in the film.

"*What?*" Loretta started laughing, gazing down at me interrogatively.

"Well...I didn't want to say anything but...did you know an R-tex ceiling can devalue a property by as much as fifty percent." Loretta laughed some more, giggling inveterately as she often did when her guard was down and was enjoying herself.

"Oh I see," she said. "And what other interesting little facts have you got for me?" She looked at me expectantly.

"I love you." There was a small pause.

"I really care about you too." And with that, she closed her eyes and squeezed my hand tight. It was now about three-thirty in the morning. I could barely keep my eyes open. We drifted off holding hands.

Nothing more was said as her parents tip-toed nervously around our steaming carcasses the next morning in the lounge. We had a bite of breakfast, Loretta drove me home and that was pretty much that. Except for me, it was far from over. The revelation that she at least shared a smattering of reciprocal feeling for me, albeit far less intensely felt, was not something that I could simply walk away from. Nor was it something I could shake off like a colubrid snake's skin or a bout of mild but acute coryza. It was a vital revelation, the first real glimmer of hope since I had first laid eyes on her back during my very first few days at sixth form and I wasn't about to let the trail go cold now.

That evening, keyed up and feeling somewhat valiant, I decided to ring up Loretta. We needed to talk:

"Loz," I said, in a serious tone down the phone, "we need to talk."

"Oh," she said demurely. "What about?" She seemed rather bemused. And distant. Like she was stuck inside one of those large, steel shipping units. It reminded me somewhat of Rob Brydon's *man in a box* routine and I almost wanted to laugh out loud. But this was no time for jocoseness.

"Last night," I said, "I want to talk about last night."

"*Last night?*"

"Yes. Last night. We got...well...you know...we got *close*."

"I know." She sounded guilty, her voice now so quiet you could probably have heard a pin drop over the top of it.

"I want you to be my girlfriend," I said boldly.

"You're *girlfriend*?"

"Yes."

Silence.

"Loretta...you there?"

"Yes."

"I was saying I want you to be my *gir...*"

"I can't!"

"Why?"

"It's just...I don't know."

"It's just *what*?"

"I just can't."

The call ended and I sat on the edge of my bed; my head dangling uselessly, lifelessly between my legs, like a bulky, loose fitting cowl. Dry tears ensued. Followed by demented, lachrymose, squalling. I went down to make myself a cup of tea.

She didn't want to go out with me. She would *never* go out with me. I could have cried forever.

* * *

My relationship with Loretta - and I use that word quite flaccidly-continued right on through the first year at university and well into the second. We went out, mostly alone, and texted each other daily. And whilst the two of us were always never more than 'just friends', I clung turbulently to what affection I could get. Sometimes, when the two of us were having so much fun, the mood just right and the surroundings idyllic, I would pretend that we were far more than simply bosom buddies. That we were in fact hopelessly, fiercely in love and that nothing, *nothing* would ever be able to form a wedge between us or stop us from being, as it were, *together*.

Summer times were always the best. During the summer holidays, Loretta and I would have three whole months to spend together, mostly at the seaside (Norwich being prohibitively inland meant that we would have to travel at least twenty miles (she drove) to Great Yarmouth, Lowestoft and even as far afield as *Hemsby*). We loved the sea air, the freedom it excited. For me, the seaside served as a reminder of our first ever assignation on Britannia Pier, eating fresh sugary doughnuts down Marine Parade, prodding and poking each other, pretending, rather coquettishly, to push the other over the railings and into the North sea.

A prod here, a pinch there: this form of physical touching (as well as the odd grope once I got a bit braver) began to form the lion share of the *goings-on* between us. We never kissed or embraced publicly. Nor did we ever come any way close to *making love*. Being somewhat nervous of full-blown sexual intercourse, I guess I never really pushed for it. Though that is not to say I did not act persistently towards her as the months went on and we became more familiar. One summer, I remember we had been watching the new Superman film at the cinema in Norwich and my touching had, quite literally, driven her to distraction:

"Move your hand," she had said sternly on account of it being half way up her brassiere. Hard done by, partly because I had long since tired of the film and partly because she had let me fondle her breasts on so many occasions previously, I refused outright; "Move it *now*", her tone indicating that she now meant business; *move it or else* being the obvious adumbration. And so, afraid of angering her further and thus blowing my chances completely, I did as I was told. It went without saying that this would mark the end of pretty much all of the physical interaction for that afternoon.

If memory serves correctly, this particular cinema trip had actually been one of the very last times I had seen Loretta. At that point, things between us had, rather irrevocably, started to steadily wilt and deteriorate. She had been living in Reading for almost a whole year (she had gone up there, a year after my departure to Lancaster, to study psychology) and had gotten into the swing of things considerably, becoming more and more absorbed into university life by the second. Her new best friend, a Norwegian girl called Elísabet (without the *th*), who we agreed had been 'the female version of me' on account of her ironic wit and slightly neurotic humour, had soon taken my role as her primary confidante. More disturbingly, Loretta's corridor had consisted mainly of lads, all of whom, I couldn't help notice, a great deal taller and better looking than me; qualities which had made them all nauseatingly endearing and which masked my own more faint and delicate virtues. Each night, up in Lancaster, face down into my pillow, I would pray to some form of higher power that Loretta should not move on or fall for another lad; that for the three years she was down in Reading, she should remain single, allowing for the possibility of the two of us reuniting at some point in the future.

My adjurations had, ultimately, fallen on deaf ears.

...But I digress. We were talking about beaches and frivolous trips to the Suffolk coast. For the time being at least, there were no signs of her moving on. Nor were there any real doubts that Loretta and I would indeed remain friends for life. Even, that we might someday become more than 'just friends'.

Following on from our first 'date' to Great Yarmouth, the next momentous seaside trip had been our day out to Lowestoft almost a whole year later. It was during the summer of my first year at university (Loretta had not yet started up in Reading) and we hadn't seen each other for almost four months solid. "Where shall we go this time?" I turned to Loretta from the passenger seat of her white Vauxhall Corsa.

"How about Lowestoft?" she responded, a certain *joie de vivre* in her tone; it was a sprightliness and enthusiasm that I had never before experienced from a female counterpart and certainly not from a girl for whom I had no doubt harboured such plethoric lust.

"Sounds good to me," I replied. In truth, I never really minded *where* we went so long as we were together. And, of course, that it remained sufficiently drawn out. A short trip out was always a disaster; I would get moody and irritable from the outset, hard done by that our time together was being cut short or, worse still, that she had elected to limit our time so readily. By contrast, beach trips were always long and fulfilling and Lowestoft, being even further afield than Yarmouth - a whole three miles to be exact - promised a whole day of fun, sea and frolics.

And so we ventured off to the Suffolk coast. The sun shone brightly that day and I remember contemplating how perfect everything had seemed. When I was with Loretta, nothing ever looked greyish or dull, damp or dingy; there was no scum on the streets and every building looked tall and splendid. It was almost as if Loretta could manipulate the very physical matter of my surroundings. I am certain, even now, that she could have made even such a place as Lancaster seem appealing (or, as it turned out, made it look bleak in her absence).

There is a wonderful line from Wordsworth's *Immortality Ode* which has always resonated with me, particularly in light of my ongoing liaison with Loretta: "There was a time when meadow, grove and stream, The earth, and every common sight, To me did seem, Apparelled in celestial light."

Now, of course, Lowestoft is one of my very favourite places to visit. Not so long ago, I went back there with my parents where the three of us walked along the Blue Flag-award-winning seafront, went on the two-penny machines, mooched around a few of the shops and had a 99 by the sea. In the sun, everything had been as it was. Just by Claremont Pier is the 'Royal Plain Fountains', a lattice of 74 individual water jets, each one autonomous yet beautifully synchronised. My parents and I couldn't help but to stop in front of it and sing along in wonderment as the water spurted to the tune of *The William Tell Overture* by Gioachino Rossini.

Several years earlier and Loretta and I had pushed each other into those very same jets, splashing and fumbling and having not a care in the world.

That afternoon, as I recall, we had spent mainly lying on the beach together, fully clothed, neither of us brave enough to venture into the North Sea, instead running up periodically to the fountains for a refreshing interlude. Upon arrival on Lowestoft's wide, sandy littoral a few hours earlier, Loretta had noticed a fat boy, a few metres away from us on the sand with no top on, dripping wet still from the interactive jets.

"That boy's got tits," she remarked. She didn't mean it to sound so cruel. In her Norfolk accent, I imagined this to be something her dad might have come out with; *co ter heck thas a rummun* or something equally as contumelious. For Loretta, it had simply been an observation.

Nevertheless, it made me laugh and I grabbed hold of her tightly. "They're almost as big as yours," I said, going in for yet another feel and kissing her passionately on the neck.

That night, after a long and pleasurable day at the seafront, Loretta, as she always did, dropped me off back at mine and we said our final goodbyes for the season. As one might imagine, I always hated the dénouement of a day trip, of saying goodbye, especially when I knew it would be so long before seeing each other again; it was like ripping off an old plaster or eating the last bit of steak fat that you'd been saving right up until the very end of the meal. Each time we arrived at mine, we would park just around the corner from the house and I would do my level best to eke out the last remaining moments we had left together. There we would lie, cuddling, sometimes even for whole hours at a time. One time, I remember, it was almost one o'clock in the morning and we had been in the car for nearly three hours with the battery running. When Loretta had gone to drive away, unsurprisingly, the car would not start which meant that, rather embarrassingly, I had to go all the way up to the house and get my dad to come out with the jump leads to help start it up again.

That evening, as with most, we lay in the car, seats rolled down, talking, cuddling:

"I'll miss you when I'm away," I tell her, expecting similar back.
"I'll miss you too."

"Do you love me?" I ask. I have not asked this question before. Secretly, I know the answer and so have avoided the asking of it. Though now, it seems only pertinent that I ask, particularly in light of such an impeccable day.
"No Aron... I don't love you."

In 2007, Loretta and I, unbeknown to me at the time, met up for the very last time. It perhaps upsets me slightly to say that I have not seen nor spoken to her since. I still, in many ways, miss her quite dearly. Though I no longer love her and do not spend much time thinking of her (save for the writing of this chapter and the profound analysis that resulted from our parting).

Ironically, the choice of venue that day had been the beach. A fitting end in many ways; Loretta herself had dubbed it 'the perfect day'. And, in every way that made our relationship so special, it perhaps was the *perfect* end.

That morning, as I recall, we had met quite early. Loretta picked me up (as she always did) outside Norwich station, we fumbled briefly and then made our way down the A1064 towards Hemsby beach. Hemsby, for the majority of you who probably have never witnessed first-hand its magic and charm, is a beautiful, secluded little seaside resort some seven-and-a-half miles north of Great Yarmouth. In August 1999, just before we had moved up to Norfolk permanently, my family and I had come to Hemsby with its great, stretching skies to get a good look of the sun being eclipsed by the black disk of the moon which had truly been spectacular and, perhaps even better, had meant a free lunch on Dad at the local cafe in Gouleston.

The beach at Hemsby is vast and empty. The sand is pure and white and like silk to tread on. Loretta and I, having arrived and parked in the local village, immediately set up our blanket on a patch of sand not far from an old anti-tank block left over from the Second World War (which Loretta later used to change behind, away from my *pervy* glare) and we unpacked the food and drinks onto the blanket. "I'll race you to the water," dared Loretta after she had finished setting everything out. And with that, we both ran as fast as we could down into the water, shedding our outer garments as we reached the shoreline.

As a quick aside (and relevant in many ways to my OCD), it is perhaps worth noting that I have never been all that comfortable with exposing my body in public. I am not nor have I ever been proud of my figure, even though I have no real reason to be overly discomforted by it either; I am hardly Quasimodo, more a Jason Biggs or Adam Sandler. And yet, I have remained ill at ease over my shape, over my perceived maculations and deformities ever since high school. Back then I had what my parents had quite affectionately designated 'puppy fat'. In fact, by all accounts, I had been quite the little chubby chops. There is a picture of me, aged twelve, eating dinner round the dinner table with my top off, gravy dripping down my walloping chins and a jouncing tyre of fat covering, like a stapler in jelly, my ribs and abdomen. It was quite the spectacle. Though by the time I was in my mid-to-late teens, the so called puppy fat was gone. Unfortunately, the negative self image remained.

To this day, I have issues surrounding my weight. I weigh myself daily, my happiness often pivoting on the readings of my mum and dad's white, Speedometer dial mechanical bathroom scales which can be found in the en suite of their master bedroom (I sneak in to use them when I think no one will catch me). And whilst I would not say I have full blown body dysmorphia (BDD) I am sure, at various times in my life, I have come pretty close.

And yet, splashing around in the water with Loretta almost a decade on from those darkened high school days in Southend, I would hardly have seemed bothered by such matters. My focus was not on my own passable yet toneless body but on the firm, magnificent one which lay before me. I had not seen Loretta in all her bikini-clad beauty before and, being anything but effete on such occasions, I pressed myself against her in the water, throwing her, dunking her and trying desperately to sneak my hands into her bikini top. Surprisingly, I was met with little resistance.

Finally, we ran out of the water and, dripping wet, I chased her around the beach bare-footed in the pure silk-like sand. I eventually managed to catch up with her at our blanket and pinned her playfully down whilst I kissed her neck and tried, once more, to undo her bikini top. Eventually, tired out, enervated, I put my arm around her and together the two of us drifted off to sleep.

Loretta, without a doubt, had been the girl of my dreams; beautiful, intelligent and sensitive. I have met no one like her since and can only hope to find her moral and Apician equivalent at some point in my future. That night, after Loretta had dropped me off, we said or final goodbyes for the summer; I was off to start my final year at university, she, her second year down in Reading. Little did I know at the time that, unlike all the other short-lived dénouements, this time would be the very last either of us would lay eyes on each other ever again.

Had I known this to be the case, I might just have held on that little bit tighter.

*

It was about three months later when I received the call from Jake. I was at home at the time (or rather, I was suppurating in the lounge of our student house in Lancaster) watching TV, pretending to peruse my legal text books, when all of a sudden my phone let out an unexpected, old-school style *brrrring brrrring brrrring*. The time was roughly 11.30 p.m.

"Hello?" I say circumspectly, slightly bemused by the time of the call. It is unlike Jake to phone me so late. Not unless he is drunk or upset. Or both.

"Hello Aron," Jake says rather timorously. "I... errr...I don't really know how to say this, so I'm just going to come out and say it..." There is an awkward pause.

"What is it?" I say, nervously.

A further silence. Then: "Are you and Loretta now in a relationship?" I frown extemporaneously.

"No?" I say, confused. "Why?"

"I think she might be in a relationship. Her online profile has changed to 'in a relationship'."

Immediately I become frozen in horror; the room going deathly silent but for this gushing, rather brimful rivulet; a violent throbbing in my ears resembling a pretty awful attack of pulsatile tinnitus. As the news sinks partially in, I end abruptly my call with Jake and begin furiously typing out a message to Loretta asking her if what had just so nervously and awkwardly been relayed to me was indeed an accurate account. That the girl unto whom I had declared my undying love only months beforehand and who had declared having 'feelings' for me too had met someone else in the short time that we had spent barely corresponding. I cannot text the words out fast enough; it is like being trapped in a dream where you are trying as hard as you can to throw a punch, each blow, each attempt at composing a forceful wallop as ineffectual as the last.

"Yes, it's true," reads her rather terse response back. "I am so sorry."

The hurt beggars description. Immediately, I smash up my room; kicking at my wardrobe and lobbing my bedside lamp as hard as I can at the far wall; the bulb smashing into a thousand pieces on impact and a deluge of glass raining down on my bedroom carpet.

Depleted, I fall in a heap on the floor and sob. And sob and sob and sob.

"The sunshine is a glorious birth; But yet I know, where'er I go, That there hath pass'd away a glory from the earth."

Chapter 8
'STORY OF O'

"There are moments when hideous possibilities besiege us like a throng of furies and break down the doors of our brain."
- Victor Hugo, *Les Miserables*

Loss, so they say, is nothing else but change. Unfortunately, *change* in any of its expressions is without doubt one of the biggest triggers of OCD. The more impactful the change, the more likely it is to trigger an emotional overreaction. A chain of neuroses which then needs to be tended to by some form or another of *control mechanism*.

As you can possibly imagine, losing Loretta had, quite literally, knocked me for six. It had hit me harder even than moving away to university. For weeks, months in fact, following the news from Jake, I trembled and shook like a man whose very soul had been ripped out and then trampled on with rather heavy size twelve metal boots. I had not expected her to give up on us. I had not accepted that, in reality, there was no *us*.

For a good few days succeeding these rather uncomfortable revelations, angrily and no doubt quite unreasonably, I sent Loretta a steady flow of abusive text messages; short, embittered disquisitions blaming her for *leading me on* and telling her in no uncertain terms how little she now meant to me:

"I guess you never gave two shit covered twigs about me. Well that's fine! It hardly matters to me now anyway. It's just a shame I couldn't have got what I really *wanted from you before you left - you know what I mean!!! PS - I've thrown away our key ring. I saw little point in keeping it. :-) "*

Of course, I regret those rather galling attacks now. I regretted them at the time. "OCDers do not do anger well," says Margo now. "We tend to prefer beating *ourselves* up before we will try and attack others. We are, in many ways, our own oversized punch bags."

"I don't get angry okay," says Izzy in Woody Allen's 1979 romantic comedy drama *Manhattan*. "I mean, I have a tendency to internalize. I can't express anger. That's one of the problems I have. I...I grow a tumour instead."

Thankfully, it was not long before my rapidly incurving conscience, buckling, as it invariably did, under its own tumour-like weightiness, eventually got the better of me and within only a very short period of time (no more than about a week), the text messages, and indeed all forms of communication with Loretta, stopped completely.

Though following the anger, the hurt and the heartbreak, came very swiftly in its place two emotions I had not really experienced fully since early childhood but which now spilled out like the *Ixtox 1*. As with the obsessions and compulsions which underpin the mechanics of OCD, *anxiety* and *guilt* are a bit like the Turner and Hooch of the experiential discomfort generated. The anxiety had been the first emotion to surface. It had come on gradually and at first I had barely even noticed it. Though after only a few months I found I could actually no longer sleep; my mind frequently restless and agitated, my body primed, *wired*. It felt, in many ways, like being a fire lookout on duty atop a large wooden tower, constantly watching, waiting for even the smallest trace of smoke in the surrounding terrain. In truth I did not know what I was scouring so spiritedly for or even what it was that I was so afraid of encountering only that I knew that something forbidding was out there (or perhaps more aptly *in there*; inside my head). Eventually, the constant disquietude, the endless being on alert and regular monitoring started to warp my thinking, invoking a strange and somewhat disruptive paranoia; '*Why had Loretta not wanted to be with me?*' went this new set of thoughts, whirling around like a Bauhaus spinning wheel. *'What had I done to put her off so absolutely?'*

Of particular concern to me was that perhaps I had, in the course of our time together, treated Loretta *badly*. That I had, in some small - or maybe quite significant - way, done wrong by her or caused her somehow to suffer. It was, from any rational perspective at least, a rather peculiar unease. For, whatever reason all this had now become rooted and immotile in my mind, I was perhaps far less worried about how my behaviour had impacted on her decision not to be with me and far more about how it might now somehow have made me a wretched or unforgiveable human being; a *'bad person'*. As it later transpired, this new uneasiness would become my first true taste of that second emotion, guilt, which, over the coming months and years, and with more than just a loose alliance with the preliminary anxiety, would inform so much of the fully blown OCD that followed.

One of my biggest concerns regarding my treatment of Loretta was undoubtedly how I had so frequently and so forcibly badgered and harassed, chased, pestered and plagued her to be my girlfriend. How I had not accepted that her feelings for me held no real hope for a future together and that she did not nor would she ever *love* me. On top of the oft-repeated supplications for her affection, I could not help but to recall how much of my time I had also spent fondling and groping her, pawing at her, lustfully, and not always when she expected or even wanted it. Such loathsome and sybaritic endeavours had surely been indicative of my beastly and wanting nature. Of my inherent depravity.

Over the weeks and months, in almost dire confabulation, I thought back to some of our many outings together; about my time trying to feel her breasts in the cinema or about our last ever trip out to Hemsby in which I kept trying to undo her bikini top. Oh what a persistent little scally wag I had been. Perhaps this alone had qualified me as some sort of *sexual deviant*? Perhaps it had been this quite *sordid* behaviour that had caused Loretta to doubt, seriously, the durability of our affiliation? And then I remembered one night, an evening involving a particularly demonstrative and lustful session which had caused her (indeed both of us) considerable discomfort. Instantly, I felt like curling up into a ball and drowning myself in the nearest available sink such was the devastating *wallop!* of pure solid guilt.

It was during one of our last ever times together and I had gone up to stay with her for a couple of days at her university in Reading. I was, as usual, keyed up and anticipative at the mere prospect of seeing her again. I longed for Loretta in much the same way Jocelyn Wildenstein or Joan Rivers long for the next facelift or the next injection of Botox. That weekend, we did not sleep. Having insisted on sharing the same bed, I spent the entire night touching and caressing her underneath the duvet almost to the point of distraction. In fact, at one point, she had displayed her protest at my unending persistence by getting up out of the bed to sleep on the floor. Though even this would not stop me. I, at once, followed her down onto the ground to resume groping, forcing her to climb back up again onto the bed to escape my clutches. This routine was repeated over and over right up until the early hours of the morning, ceasing only once I had run out of steam and had involuntarily drifted off to sleep.

The next morning when I awoke, Loretta was already sitting upright and dressed.

"Morning Loz." She passed me a brief though decorous smile.

"Did you get much sleep?" I asked.

"I didn't get any."

"Oh... why not?" I said credulously, though with a tinge of guilt.

"Wasn't sure where your hands would go if I wasn't awake to stop you!" Accusation laced her tone.

"I love you Loz. Of course I would have stopped. I... I..." I looked around the room for inspiration on my next sentence, both worry and indignation rising in equal parts. "*Well your mum manages to sleep with your dad in the same bed!*" I eventually managed rather fatuously, not being able to think of anything at all cleverer to say.

Loretta looked at me squarely.

"My mum *trusts* my dad."

Silence.

As my last year of university dragged slowly by like corals through treacle, I thought back to this night over and over again. I felt sickened by my depraved attempts to *cop a feel* or, at any rate, to satisfy my own carnal needs by grabbing hold of her as if simply just a slab of meat for my own filthy enjoyment. Months after seeing Loretta for the very last time, a large part of me could not help but to conclude that my lustfulness had perhaps gone too far. Had her comments that morning in Reading been a tender gibe at my persistence or a full condemnation of the way I had treated her?

Now, in her absence, the guilt was able to swill around inside of me without anyone to dispel my paranoia. Guilt, as with anxiety, is a cognitive or affective emotional state that is apt to weigh down heavily on its victims; like a thick, tropical heat sprawling overhead, pressing down and compressing the air beneath. In my view it is *guilt* that is without doubt the most insidious of mental states and the hardest part of living with OCD. It engulfs and it lingers and, very much like a stink bomb that goes off unexpectedly in a school lavatory, its effects can cause irremediable disruption and havoc.

My university work had been the first thing to suffer. The imbued dread and self-loathing, the fear that I had actually sexually assaulted Loretta (and that, by extension, this might mean I was capable of even worse things, such horrific misdeeds being almost more than I could bear to think about), made it increasingly difficult to concentrate on coursework and assignments. I would often find myself reading the same pages of my textbooks over and over again, unable to resist these new darkened preoccupations which kept me distracted for sometimes hours at a time and meant my productivity resembled something of a Russian metal factory following the fall of the Soviet Union. Nothing would go in. The words had lost all meaning. They had, almost overnight, become as unfathomable as the quirky little Latin phrases we had learned during the first year when much of the legal terminology presented to us by lecturers and associate tutors had been totally and utterly foreign.

Of course, I could have appealed to my law lecturers for concessions. I could have requested extended deadlines for coursework assignments or for exam marks to be moderated in accordance with the severity of my illness. But back then, there was no such thing as an Equality Act (at least not in the more comprehensive format we know it today) nor was there any extended duty to make provisions for those who might be suffering mentally. Back then, I didn't understand my illness or even that I was suffering from an illness at all; half of me even considered that I *deserved* to suffer so profoundly. After all, had I not just spent the last two years sexually assaulting the girl whom I had, up until that point, professed to be madly, deeply, in love with?

And so I muddled through as best I could, all the while ridden with the shame that maybe, just *maybe,* I might be some sort of perverse human being, a *sexual predator.*

"It is now almost too much to bear," I wrote one evening in my diary, "*not knowing whether I am so perverse a human being as to be a write-off to all society. I fear these crystalline thoughts, which plague me now on a daily basis, more than anything I have ever encountered before. Worst of all is that I remain almost totally undecided as to their validity; hoping for the best but preparing myself, like Javert stood over the River Seine, to have to throw myself over the edge, into the abyss."*

In many ways, being so far away from home, away from friends and loved ones did not help my situation. Not having heard of the condition of OCD before and instead attributing all of these rather base thoughts to my own surely depraved moral character, I felt both isolated and scared. I hated the idea that I might be a bad or wicked human being. Even more, I hated the feeling of being so alone. Sometimes, I would try and seek counsel from my parents (parents, of course, being the only people in the world that can truly love us unconditionally and thereby forgive us anything). But this was never easy down the phone:

"*Mum,*" I would say at the end of a long call.

"Yes, what is it?"

"Well…I just wanted to say…"

"Yes, go on…"

"Oh…err…nothing. Speak soon yeah."

"Are you sure sweetheart? You don't sound so good."

"Yep. Sure. Just wanted you to send my love to the family."

"Ok then darling, will do. Bye for now."

"Yeah…bye."

By this time, I had been living off-campus with four others (two of whom girls) in a small terraced house on a cobbled street around a twenty minute bus ride from the campus and I had been almost unsparingly miserable. Portentously for me, none of my housemates were what you might describe as particularly amenable, or even for that matter all that friendly. I found that often I could not tell them what was on my mind regarding Loretta; I certainly could not confide in them my fears (albeit totally bonkers premonitions) that I might someday be capable of things as awful even as *rape*. "Excuse me guys, while I've got you all here, there's something I need to tell you..."

And unlike some of my true friends back home (who I felt understood me sometimes profoundly), my housemates in Lancaster were neither deep, nor analytical nor particularly open-minded. Whilst I pined over Loretta or worried that I was now some form of horrific miscreant, they hankered only for a night in with Match of the Day and a six pack of lager. (The consequence of living and studying up north was that all four of my housemates - including the girls (!) - were passionate Liverpool fans who no doubt found it fundamentally odd that I did not follow the greatly admired team sport as fanatically as they did. They could not understand that I had perhaps much more pressing concerns, that the burden of an obsessive or fervent mind, quite ironically, killed my enthusiasm for most things.)

I remember one cold night in January, I had been particularly upset over Loretta and unable to concentrate on my law essay. That night they had all decided to commandeer the living room to watch the match between Liverpool and Manchester United at Old Trafford which meant that there were banners on the walls, empty beer cans strewn across the floor and popcorn all down the sides of the couch. That evening, I decided to sit with them and not retire to my bedroom to study as I normally did for a bit of peace and quiet in the hope that their uplifted spirits might rub off on me; that a cheery atmosphere downstairs might brighten my ever demulsifying mood. I could not, unfortunately, have been more wrong. After two of possibly the most desultory hours of my life, the game finally drew to a close; one-nil to Manchester United. No big deal to me but, to my housemates, an unrivalled catastrophe, the end of the world as we knew it. To this day, I'm pretty sure there were actual tears in their eyes as their beloved players walked off the pitch, heads down, crestfallen, not to return again to victory until beating Arsenal four-one at Anfield a few weeks later.

But whilst my housemates cried because their team had lost a Premiership match, I was crying because I was losing my mind. Or at least, it felt like I might be. The guilt that perhaps I had physically molested Loretta or that my nagging for her to be my girlfriend had been tantamount to psychological abuse filled me with an almost nauseating fear. These wretched voices in my head, which never really left me alone even in my sleep, were able to sound-out unbidden with little assuagement from those closest to me. Without receptive housemates able to understand or willing even just to listen, I felt myself drifting further and further away from reality; into a cold, companionless turmoil.

It felt like the end of the world. Some nights, shivering alone in my room, I wondered seriously if it really might be.

Though I would perhaps be lying if I said that there was absolutely no one to whom I could pour my heart or unburden my weary soul during my three years away at university. Far from it in fact. There were the friends I had made on my corridor during the first year (in particular, Lauren, Camilla and Lizzy - the three best looking girls in County College I might add) not to mention the guys on my course (Zoe T, Zoe H, and Gez) who had all been a great laugh, especially during our first ever group assignment which had involved negotiating a legal dispute between two make-shift corporate entities.

Though one girl in particular had stood out as a real confidante. Her name was Gemma and we had met one morning, quite by chance, when I sat next to her during a rather tedious second year lecture on ‘Offender Management and Community Reintegration’. That morning, as I recall, we had both been literally bored to tears at the droning voice of the balding, book-learned dullard before us and so had started instead whispering stridently amongst ourselves, doodling effigies of Garfield and Fred Flinstone on each other's notebooks as much to survive the hour lecture without trying to gouge out our own eyes with a blunt spoon as anything else. As it turned out, Gemma and I discovered we had plenty in common; favourite books, TV shows, *The Smiths*. Most importantly, however, was that Gemma seemed to be the first true female friend to *understand* me. After only a few months, I felt I could tell her almost anything. And likewise she would often confide in me (though it was nearly always the first way around). Over time, this sense of *opening up* would go on to include pretty much every last one of the dark, unspeakable thoughts that went round, like Maleficant’s spinning wheel, inside my head. Indeed, this had been the first time I had shared my innermost thoughts with anyone, even my parents, and the unburdening, when it came, not to mention the attendant relief (itself a totally new experience) was almost positively addictive.

One night, during the middle of the final year, whilst at home on my own (the others had all gone to watch the England pre-match between England and Uruguay in one of the local pubs), I had, once more, got myself into a bit of a stew about Loretta. As she was online at the time, I decided to initiate an MSN conversation with Gem; a last-ditch attempt at reassurance:

"Why don't you just stop what you're doing and come round," Gemma typed with almost zero hesitation, having heard all my neuroses a billion times before. "We can talk it through face-to-face."

"Ok," I said, bereft of any better ideas and still feeling inconsolably sickened by my past actions, "I would like that."

Gemma lived near the Ridge Pub off of Slyne Road which was a particularly long trek from our student house in Dale Street. The streets were dimly lit at that time of night and the stench of violence lingered in the air. But it was always worth the effort of going to see her. Gemma, as I think might already be clear, was a good listener and took my neuroses in her stride, patiently, without fuss or protestation, hearing out my latest dilemma in the comfort of the shared kitchen of her self-catering student flat. Sometimes it was difficult for me not to wonder whether all of the frenetic cerebration I subjected her to, all that mental *noise* would someday become too much for her; that she would grow to resent me for the burden I placed on her and on our friendship. But for some reason she loved the manifestations of my neuroses, not the suffering it caused me so much as the endearing way it seemed to affect my demeanour, giving me the look, as she described it, of a rather lost 'puppy dog'. Sometimes with OCD, you tie yourself up in so many knots you don't know who you are any more. Or what you're capable of. Gemma knew who I was, or so she often told me during our many nights out together. "You're a sweet guy Aron," she would say. "Don't ever forget it." And no matter how outrageous the confessions that followed, how depraved the disclosures, none of it seemed to convince Gemma that there might just be a different side to me. That I could ever be a risk to someone or that I had it in me to do *bad*.

"So do you think what I did to Loretta was unforgiveable?" I asked her, nervously. I had barely stepped through her front door. Gemma's housemates were all out at *The Sugar House*, our local student night club, meaning that Gemma and I had the lounge pretty much to ourselves. Nevertheless, she chose to take me to her bedroom. I didn't appreciate it at the time but this was possibly evidence in itself of my particularly benign and unthreatening nature.

"I really don't think you've done anything wrong Aron," said Gemma, drawing her curtains and trying her upmost to engage in my plight.

"But she said no and I carried on."

"Yes but there's no and then there's *no*."

"Well, how do I know it was the latter no and not the former?"

"Because you would just *know* if she had been that upset. The two of you remained close right up until the end *right*?"

"Maybe she was confused?"

"Maybe *you're* confused."

I looked down at my feet; my right leg was crossed compactly over my left thigh, my foot wagging excitably, nervously in the air, in turn vibrating the whole bed up and down like a Wilberforce pendulum.

"You need to get a grip," Gemma told me quite firmly before passing me one of her infamous cavillous glares (a reprehending glower which I am now in no doubt will someday bode extremely well for her in her chosen career as a criminal barrister) and I had no choice at all but to take heed.

Or at least, I took heed for a few hours. Unfortunately, though perhaps all-too-predictably, the doubt slowly crept back in during the weeks that followed my trip to Gemma's. The heteronomy of the inner voices in my head seemed always to be far more gripping, far more compelling than the peccant, often second-rate utterances of a mere fellow human being. Even if that human being did happen to be like my very own make-shift 'guardian angel' (I had referred to Gemma as 'like a guardian angel' in one of my diary entries following my first ever disclosure to her. I had literally been overwhelmed by her compassion and kindness on that occasion).

And so, a month or so following my trip to Gemma's, still unable to gain perspective over any of it, or indeed to govern the content of my own thoughts, I did the only thing I knew for sure might end months of distress and confusion. Foolhardily, perhaps somewhat inappropriately, I decided to contact the one person I felt certain might be able to clear it all up for me once and for all.

I decided to text Loretta...

I had, at the time, been travelling up from Norwich for my second term (or *Lent* term as we called it at our university). It was a crisp, sunny day in late January and we had just passed Nottingham station, next stop *Langley Mill*. I had been listening to *The Smiths* on my MP3 player, trying somewhat doggedly (not to mention oxymoronically), to relax, when, seemingly out of nowhere at all, I was hit with a familiar pang of shame; the same contumacious guilt that had so thoroughly ruined my first few months of university and which had left me totally up-in-the-air as to whether or not I was still a good person; had I sexually assaulted Loretta? Had I been responsible for the ruination of an innocent girl's life? As I stood in the inter-carriage between coach B and C on an over-crowded National Express Service to Liverpool Lime Street, I found I could no longer take the not knowing. Of not being sure whether or not a crime had been committed and, by extension, whether or not I deserved to continue living a care-free life.

In the heat of the moment, ridden with so much guilt and anxiety I thought I would literally drown where I stood, I decided to finally send Loretta a text; to end the inner torment and unending questions once and for all:

"Hey Loz, I know we're not talking much right now. I just want 2 say sorry for everything that I might have done in the past. I truly am sorry."

I stepped back, temporarily disorientated by the magnitude of my grave unburdening. A couple of times I careened into the carriage walls; a combination of nerves and a bumpy train ride (the G-force reading, should one have been conducted, possibly a moderate-to-high turbulence).

Three minutes passed. And as I stood waiting eagerly for a response back, I noticed the battery of my phone was nearly flat out. *Bugger,* I thought to myself, now to starting to panic! *How had I not noticed this before? How had I allowed myself to be so undisciplined, so careless in keeping my one form of communication replenished?* I switched off the Wi-Fi and prayed that my phone would not run out of juice. That I would receive some sort of absolution before the inevitable break in communication. The battery icon on my phone started flashing empty when a text message eventually pushed its way onto my screen:

"You have nothing to be sorry about. Take care. x"

With that, the phone went dead. I was able only to digest the message's content momentarily before the image whizzed away, replaced by the Nokia start-up screen and, ultimately, blackness. It was all so very vague. Was this really the pardon I so desperately sought or merely a flippant dismissal; avoidance on her part to deal with an otherwise difficult subject matter? I suspected the latter and, as a result, remained highly mistrustful. Had I really scarred her so badly that she could not even bring herself to discuss it with me? Caused her that much anguish and despair that she could not bring herself to remember? I felt sick. Yet, surprisingly, still I was unsure that I had actually done anything wrong.

Frustrated, I pressed down hard on my Nokia to turn it back on. Somehow, there was just enough juice left to excavate the worn device from its slumber and I used this window of opportunity to send one final text. Quickly I drafted a new message and banged on the 'send' key:

"Are you sure I have nothing 2 b sorry 4??? I feel really bad that when we were together I may have touched U 2 much? Sometimes U said no and I carried on anyway! I hope U can 4give me??"

The message was so desperate, so frantic that I should not perhaps have expected a response back. Nevertheless, as I quietly suspected, Loretta replied almost instantly in the same cryptically succinct format to which I had become accustomed:

"It's all in the past. It doesn't matter now."

The words sent a chill down my spine. I read the message over and over.

I *had* done something bad.

When I eventually arrived at university that evening, after what had been five hours on an overheated, overcrowded, screeching metal wagon I was, admittedly, feeling a bit better. By which I mean I no longer had thoughts about taking my own life. Admittedly, such thoughts had gone away almost as quickly as they had arisen - I knew that I had, in reality, no choice but to carry on and face the music. My housemates historically had offered little in the way of support and so I found myself walking straight round, bags and everything, to Gemma's house.

No doubt I should have rung through first to check is was OK or, better still, waited until the first day of term, until our first criminology lecture together. But this wouldn't wait. I rang on the door that cold, rainy evening, trembling with grief.

Gemma opened up the Georgian entrance to her rather lacklustre student home and, not wishing to stand on ceremony for a moment longer than necessary (particularly in moments like this), I immediately showed her the text messages: "Gem, look at these!" I said, thrusting my phone into her face. Gemma, who no doubt had been taken totally aback by my presence, gently took the phone from out of my hand, walked over to a nearby stool in the hallway and sat reading through the messages whilst I remained nervously by the front door. In truth, I had expected her to throw me out immediately or, worse still, phone the local *filth*. Eventually, Gemma looked up stricken and censorious and immediately I braced myself for a well-earned *blitzkrieg*. Instead she laughed. She simply just looked at me, chuckled to herself and then offered me a hot chocolate from the kitchen.

I scuttled behind her, gobsmacked by her frivolity, her totally untroubled response to an otherwise devastating and admonitory litany of my transgressions.

"But Gemma this means I definitely did something to her. Look here...she says, '*It's all in the past*'. All in the past means that I *did* something back then. I must have done something terrible for her to be so reluctant to now talk about it."

"She doesn't mean that you did something to her. She thinks you're worrying about the relationship and the reasons she didn't go out with you. She's telling you to forget about it because she wants you to move on with your life."

"Really?"

"*Really*."

"But she didn't say that. Why didn't she say I have done nothing wrong?"

"Because she probably doesn't understand where you're coming from; that you are having these diabolical *obsessions*."

"Maybe I should text her, explain."

"No."

"But maybe..."

"Aron. *No!*"

That night, once home and unpacked and admittedly feeling slightly calmer, I cried gushingly into my pillow. It felt finally like I might be losing my mind for good. My anxiety had seemingly reached a point of no return; I could neither control it nor avoid it. Nor could I rationalise or soften its impact when it did hit. There seemed only to be two logical options for what was happening to me: either I was turning mad or I really was *bad*.

I feared beyond anything in the world that it might be both.

* * *

Perhaps not surprisingly, I did not look forward to coming home again that Easter. Usually, the first thing I would have done upon arriving back into Norwich during the Spring vacation would be to see Loretta. We would meet usually on my very first evening back either to go to the cinema or else get a bite to eat or even, on a few occasions, go bowling; "I feel so guilty," Loretta would say, "stealing you away before you've even had a chance to spend time with your family". Now, however, I had no such melioration. My parents, who always looked forward greatly to my homecoming, were mildly sympathetic with my plight and my heartbreak but seemed much more concerned over my declining mental state (which, although I never made mention of explicitly, was clearly more obvious to them than I had anticipated). By contrast, my infatuation with Loretta, to my parents' way of thinking at least, had been no more than a mere childish phase, an inevitable part of growing up. Certainly it was nothing of any particular *consequence*.

And so, over the few months I was home, I did my level best to adopt the same mantra. I spent more time out with friends, went out to parties and bars and drank away my guilt and heartbreak as if pouring thick, industrial strength bathroom cleaner over the very grimiest of dirt and bacteria. On top of the booze and the partying, I also tried to meet girls. Though this was not always as easy as I would have liked. For one, my confidence around women had never been all that great (certainly this was not helped by the current rejection from Loretta). But also because, by this time, I had seemingly stopped trusting myself around the fairer sex almost entirely. I had lost faith in my own inbuilt moral compass - if such a thing indeed existed - and constantly feared that I might be capable of anything from sexually inappropriate patter to full blown physical or violent assault.

In truth, I was no threat at all. Or at least, no more of a threat than any other of my male contemporaries. Around women or *girls*, I was always kind, funny and gentle; indeed, if any criticism were to have been levelled at me it would have been that I could, at times, come across as a tad *too nice*. By which I mean, I was often seen by the female populous as rather too pliant and keen to impress (as opposed to authoritative and aloof which I was sure, and still am, most women secretly yearn for). Nevertheless, and despite being outwardly *epicene*, I couldn't help but worry that my general lustfulness, my selfishness and my druthers for physical indulgence (as demonstrated by my pursuit of Loretta), might one day mean I would cross the line in the most devastating way imaginable.

"It's always the ones you least expect" is a phrase you'll often hear people band around, often in relation to heinous sexual crimes. I had never really paid much attention to it then but now, in light of my own over-blown fears and misguided premonitions, it had seemingly taken on a whole new meaning. Maybe I, on the surface a nice or decent fellow, was actually capable of far worse than even I had dared imagine. After all, aren't most serial rapists

often on the surface and in their day-to-day lives quite sequestered and shy? The sort of unassuming people that no one ever notices until it is all too late, always an element of complete surprise when next door neighbours are finally met with the truth of the numerous extracurricular activities going on right under their very noses.

The prospects of being some sort of *secret* monster, played on my mind greatly. Indeed, the idea that I could be, or *appear* to be, good on the surface but perfectly rotten underneath without anyone ever noticing was a difficult one to reconcile. Maybe, I began to wonder, the basement or nether portion of my character was so putrid and nefarious that I had simply just blocked it all out? Perhaps living in denial all these years had been the only way I had managed to *cope*? But that with just a little bit of mental digging around, a bit of concentration, a whole repository of evil intentions might somehow emerge.

It was better to find out *now* than to wait until someone got hurt.

And so, during that Easter break, I focused all my attentions on the past. For days, weeks, I tried to 'work out' whether or not I was a bad person; whether or not I had done anything in my past which would provide evidence as to my *propensity* to carry out the sorts of horrific misdeeds my imagination was now prophesying. Portentously for me - and as is *always* the case with OCD experiments of this kind - I could think of many an incident. For example, when I was six at infant school, I recall how I had chased a little girl around the playground for literally weeks on end. Months later, when it finally came to the attention of my teacher Mrs Sutcliffe, she had been most unimpressed. "You're a *beast,*" she told me, quite venomously, spitting out the final word; *you're a beast, you're a beast, you're a beast*. These words have stuck with me ever since. Then there was the time I had told my parents aged nine that the school ceiling had collapsed in on us and that I had pushed another little boy out of the way of falling rubble thus saving his life. The whole thing was of course a lie - the truth of the matter was that one of the school huts had been condemned and the class of year three was forced to relocate into the main school building - but because I was always "such a good little boy" (at least, according to my Nan) my parents had believed fully my dramatic yarn.

Perhaps you're getting the picture here...a nice lad on the surface, academic and respected by adults but a liar and a predator underneath it all. Was all this *proof* of my sexual and devious nature? Evidence that I might naturally be a serial rapist, no different in character and deportment to Fred West or even the infamous local 'Suffolk Strangler'.

Over time, these rather dissident trips down the darkened alleys of memory lane, far from helping to provide comfort or even to reveal the 'truth' of my now questionable moral make-up, simply caused me to question myself and my fleshly urges in ways I did not think were even possible, coming up with all sorts of wild and fanciful indictments and allegations:

Could I be a rapist? Did I get off on the idea *of rape? If a girl said 'no' once sex had been initiated, could I count on myself being able to stop? Does not being one hundred percent sure that I would definitely stop make me a bad person? Am I a reckless (and therefore immoral) human being every time I so much as start talking to a girl, knowing in the back of my mind that there is always a small possibility that I might rape her? Perhaps I am a bad person simply for leaving the house, for even attempting to enter into the outside world where meeting girls will inevitably become a distinct probability?*

When the answers to these questions could not be provided, or at least could not be provided with one hundred percent surety, I felt as if I might already be guilty. "*Stay away!*" these wretched voices inside my head would hiss whenever I was anywhere near a member of the opposite sex. "*Who knows what you might do.*"

The song *'Trouble'* released a few years before I went to university by Coldplay has a line in it which, for whatever reason during my third year at university, had stuck in my head like a positronic brain implant. *"Oh no what's this,"* Chris Martin would croon affectedly, a tinge of both melancholy and fear blended into one stanza. And every time a new obsession would pop into my mind, a new sexual concern or a memory of doing something inappropriate (particularly to Loretta), I wouldn't be able to help just chanting these words chillingly to myself before preparing myself for yet the next painful onslaught; *'Oh no what's this.'*

Unfortunately, as time went on, so these instances and occurrences increased in both frequency and potency. Before long, it had started to affect, quite literally, almost every last encounter with members of the opposite sex.

For example, one evening, towards the end of the Spring break I had decided to go out with a few friends to the new R&B night club that had just opened up by the River Wensum. We were all ridiculously drunk and dancing like morons to some urbane piece or other when a girl - perhaps no older than eighteen - came up behind me and asked if I would kindly move aside to enable her entry to wherever it was I was blocking. Of course, normally in those circumstances, I would have said nothing, moved out of the way graciously and smiled somewhat apologetically. Though, for some reason, drunk and, admittedly quite relaxed, I had instead responded by saying something totally crazy, a comment I would never normally have uttered in a hundred million years:

"Only if I can have a kiss first."

I couldn't believe the words had come out of *my* own mouth. It was like listening to something scripted by Charles Shyer or even *Chevalier de Seingalt* himself. Nonetheless, and to my greater astonishment, the girl who thus far had only appeared annoyed with my hesitance to get out of her way, simply responded by moving her head steadily, intractably, towards my own. In seconds, the two of us were in the throes of a rather vigorous pash on the lips which went on for what felt like forever, our tongues entwined, lapping earnestly in a sort of fervid, inveterate rhythm. Afterwards, I bought her a drink, we kissed again and eventually she said goodnight and went home.

That evening and following into the early hours of the next morning, as you might imagine, I was on a massive high. This had been the first girl I had been even remotely intimate with since Loretta and it felt, well, pretty darn good. In fact, so good did it feel that it was almost like being sixteen all over again; the lust, the hormones, the first tiny droplets of male prowess. But, alas, the feeling of buoyancy, that sensation of being on top of the world, was not to last; *'Oh no what's this'* went the catchy yet woebegone lyric on cue as I became inexplicably ridden with guilt over my fleeting embrace with the rather youthful eighteen-year-old slip of a girl. And immediately, I began to question whether I had not been far too predatory in my approach, presenting the poor tiny creature before me with a rather uncomfortable ultimatum upon which she had no doubt felt obligated to cede; *Kiss me or else do not pass* being the rather indecorous proposition.

The shame that I was now some sort of sick and twisted *predator*, not to mention a step closer to being a fully fledged rapist, lingered like the piperitious whiff of cave aged *talleggio* for days, weeks.

"*You despicable little pervert,*" the gleeful gremlins celebrated. "*What* will *you stoop to next?*"

Of course, the alcohol did not help. It rarely ever does. I found that the voices, although often much quieter when subdued by the effects of wine and spirits would, over a period of usually around twelve or so hours, start to get louder, slowly but surely crystallising into a belated and rather blusterous paranoia which was always more powerful, more vengeful, more confusing than anything that my brain could conjure merely by itself and without such a toxic mix. Whatever the benefits of alcohol in the short term, it is never a surrogate for lasting consolation. Often it only sought to make things far worse and my perspective far more skewed.

Nevertheless I found often I could not resist. "Alcohol settles my nerves like nothing else," a friend of mine at Group later told me. "Sometimes I think it is the only thing that can calm me down."

And so it was, a few weeks later, I went out clubbing again. This time however, for a reason that I fail now to recall, I was markedly more tense; my mind skittish and mercurial. I felt so dangerous that at times it was like, at any moment, a police car might pull up beside me, lock me up in hand-cuffs and drag me away like something out of a well-known Kafka novel. My answer - to get as pissed as a newt; to utilise spirits and wine in a way that might stop me from feeling so irrecoverably on edge. And at first, the plan had worked nicely. Almost immediately having downed three shots of sambuca, my wavering anxiety started to steady and abate and, back in the game, I happened to clock a group of girls dancing to *Shake Your Ass* by Mystikal on the night club floor. Drunk and feeling brave, I decided to approach them by shuffling up uncomfortably behind their gyrating derrières; either they would oblige me, I thought to myself licentiously, by grinding against me (in the frivolous way some girls seem to do) or walk away in mild but harmless disgust. But whichever way it went, I considered, at least they would be given a *choice*. Which of course was the main thing.

Or so I had convinced myself.

Predictably, though perhaps more my by luck than through any sort of skilful execution on my part, the plan had worked perfectly well. A minute or so following my rather unseemly appropinquation, one of the girls, the slightly taller of the two, wearing denim hot pants and a low cut top, came up in front of me and started to grind berserkly against my trouser front, instantly causing my member to become mildly aroused. A few minutes later, after the track was up (the next song some emotional canticle about *separation* by Mariah Carey), the girl turned around to face me, kissed me saucily on the lips goodnight before caroming off with her equally underdressed compeer.

Another successful night out –or so it might have seemed at the time -but alas it did not stop my drunk and obsessional mind from once again twisting my fortunes into some sort of sinful or depraved indulgence. As soon as I was sober the next morning, I started to question intensely whether I had perhaps danced far too close to the *hotpants girl*; that maybe my groin had come into contact with her posterior before she had given me any sort of indication that she might be *interested*? Had I walked into *her* or had she backed up into *me*? The question of consent whirled around in my head like a police siren; could it be that, in a moment of mental abandon or selfishness, I had simply rubbed myself on her body, recklessly, without even so much as a second thought to what *she* might have wanted or to the numerous moral implications?

The term for this non-consensual paraphilia is actually known as 'frotteurism' and, according to Wikipedia, involves a man rubbing his erect penis against a non-consenting person for sexual gratification. And somehow I became filled with dread that this new label - this criminal charge - might somehow now apply to me. 'Fro...*tteur*' I scribbled down in my diary, simply adding this shiny new epithet to the rapidly growing litany of damming insignias. "I am a *frotteur*". The prospects were almost too much to handle.

Two innocent nights out (involving girls and alcohol); two dire spells of guilt. Eventually, I decided to knock the drinking on the head. It helped but it was not the complete answer. The guilt and paranoia continued to play havoc with my mind. Or was it my mind playing havoc with my senses? By the time the Easter holiday was over, I was convinced multiple times over that I was a man undeserving of a second chance. That I was, without question or pardon, a sexual deviant, the kind one must necessarily lock up and throw away the key for the greater good of all mankind.

When the holidays eventually came gloomily to a close, I knew things had finally reached an all time low. Mentally, I was a wreck. Yet still, I dreaded going back to university. As bad as things were back in Norwich, I knew things would be even worse *up there*. Up there, I had no one to reassure me. Up there, I felt almost totally alone. There was no palliative compassion, no one (with perhaps the exception of Gemma) who really *understood* me. I couldn't help but wonder whether one final trip to Lancaster, one final term away from home might just be the final straw.

I worried all the way on the train up.

* * *

According to William M. Gordon in his article *'Sexual Obsessions and OCD'*, the vast majority of people with OCD, particularly those with sexual obsessions, have what is termed 'variable insight.' That is they will suffer the profound effects of OCD without the ability to always discern their *symptoms* from reality.

"Often," Gordon goes on to say, "they know the obsession is false but occasionally it feels partly or fully valid. They are puzzled and frustrated over their inability to dismiss the obsession completely. Their insight is usually best when discussing the obsession with a therapist and worst when getting caught off guard by a sexual cue that elicits the obsession."

By the time university had started up again for the final term, it seemed like absolutely everything elicited such heart-stopping trepidation. Every girl I walked passed in the street, every female I spoke to on my course, every woman I served groceries to on my Morrison's check-out would make me flinch and then tremble with shame. As if I had just committed the worst crime imaginable or stepped out of the North Sea on a freezing cold winter's day.

During the times where my insight was at its lowest, I would feel unable to depart from my bedroom at all. Alone and trembling, I did not want to be out in public, to put myself and others at risk. Of course, staying in so much did me little good either. The time to ruminate further helped only in converting molehills into soaring great mountains; the fibres of my mind looping together, twisting and then reverse wrapping until finally creating a rope long enough and sturdy enough with which to ultimately hang myself.

I started to watch pornography. This wasn't intentional but an inevitability of being alone all the time and owning a laptop with internet connection. Unlike most lads my age (who I am in no doubt navigated porn sites as adeptly as bees collecting honey), internet porn was not something I had sought out before. The most risqué viewing had consisted of videos of Holly Valance on MTV (which I would watch on the family telly at home whenever I was on a sick day and both my parents were out at work) and a strange 2005 Italian film on satellite called *Natale a Miami* with the rather delicious Vanessa Hessler. I had not before delved into the depraved world of hardcore porn. Yet, after only a few moments of having typed 'sex' into the search engine, this new phenomena had engulfed my attention fully; a short, bitter-sweet flourish of excitement which followed each intoxicating new video or image.

And then one evening, alone in the house, I got to some sites offering what was rather sleazily plugged: '*nubiles*'. I looked on in horror but also with more than just a hint of excitement as pictures of girls that looked no older than seventeen filled my entire nineteen inch LCD display monitor. Certainly I had not set out to search for such profane imagery. Nor had I typed in anything untoward into the search engine (in my relative naivety I would only ever type in the words 'sex' or 'breasts'). Yet nonetheless, these images of young girls somehow left me curiously (and, yes, excitedly) wanting more. The sub-categories covered everything from girls in school uniforms having sex with their teachers to thin, emaciated looking girls, supposedly, having sex for the very first time (in some cases, losing their virginity) in front of a camera crew of leering middle aged fat men. And despite being somewhat disgusted by these rather obscene phantasmagorias (as well as feeling somewhat morally contemptuous for having allowed myself to continue viewing), I couldn't help but to respond with a somewhat boorish palpation.

Guiltily, I watched every last free video sample I could access. Some I even watched more than once. All the while, I couldn't help but wonder what it meant about me as a person. About the sort of things I might be *into*? As the weeks went by, and as the realisation of what I had done began to slowly but sharply sink in, I found myself wondering just how deep the depravity in me went; just how far the rot had seeped.

Of course, I did not at the time understand how porn sites were rigorously regulated. Nor had I considered how special cleanfeed filters were utilised by ISPs across the board so that, in reality, the girls I viewed online were only ever fully mature *women* in their very late teens or early twenties and certainly not the fifteen year old virginal school girls they so poorly imitated. Nevertheless, the fact that I had 'gotten off' on young looking girls, regardless of the authenticity of the websites in which they featured, was enough for me to question both my morality as well as my sexual inclinations.

"I thought I only liked girls with full, developed bodies," I panicked to Jake one evening on the phone. "But now I am not so sure. What happens if I am a...a... *paedophile*."

The prospects were almost more than I could bear.

In fact, so awful was the idea that I might be a nascent child molester that for days, weeks I remained beside myself with grief. A few weeks following my introduction into pornography, I wondered how I knew for sure I didn't fancy young children? How could I prove it to myself? How could any of us ever know for sure what we were truly, deeply turned on by? And the more I questioned, the more the uncertainty in me grew. Did I fancy women? Did I enjoy looking at adult female anatomy? Did I like big breasts? Had I ever really even been all that attracted to Loretta?

All of a sudden, it seemed, I had became tortuously unsure.

Of course, in many ways, it was almost funny to see how my mind had sort of taken me full circle - from deeming myself totally unsafe around women (due primarily to being an unflinching and paraphilic sexual predator) to holding an almost agamous disinterest in anything about them. If I hadn't been so terribly depressed, so totally and utterly taken in by such unadulterated nonsense, I might just have laughed the whole thing off. Though, at the time, there seemed little funny about the prospect of being a fully fledged paedophile.

Now of course, I find it one of the very *funniest* parts of my illness.

In the middle of July 2006, after three very tough years of study, my final year at university eventually came to a rather mercurial end. Somehow, I am not sure how, I managed to revise relatively effectively in between the cracks of near-suicidal neuroses and, to my surprise, passed every single one of my modules with an overall 2:1 with honours.

As soon as all the exams were finished, however, I went back home to Norwich. The term still went on without me but I did not want to stay. There were end-of-third-year celebrations and graduation balls. Not to mention the infamous Extrav Party, a three day partying event starting with Cartmel's evening of *'Superhoes and Villains'* and ending with Grizedale's notorious *beach party*. I willingly missed all of them. For me, there seemed little to celebrate. I needed to be back home. I needed to be back with my family.

And in many ways, I was right to crave familiarity. Following the end of university, as I had predicted, I started to feel substantially better. Unlike my housemates, whom I considered selfish and on the whole unfeeling, my parents cared greatly about my condition and I felt safe in their presence. Nevertheless, the obsessions continued to cause disruption. They came and went; I would ask my mum for reassurance, the symptoms would subside for a bit only to return again, more powerfully each time the cycle was repeated.

Still no one knew that my condition was actually OCD.

I never saw Loretta again after my return from university. I didn't bump into her in the street or see her at any reunion parties. Sometimes, I tried hard to bump into her. I would take long and pointless walks in and around the city with my best shirt on in the hope that I would see her and that she would see me and, at once, realise what she was missing and come back to me. Though this never happened. In time, I simply stopped caring. Or rather, I buried the emotions deep enough to enable me to move on. Eventually, the walks stopped and so too did any expectation that Loretta and I might someday reunite. I knew it was finally over. As the famous Smith's line goes: "I know it's over, and it never really began."

The feeling that I was a bad person, however, was far harder to shake off. As time went on and with increasing desperation, I craved the certainty that I hadn't done or wouldn't do something so horrific that I would not be able to forgive myself.

When the reassurance did not come, or come quickly, I found it almost impossible to cope.

I didn't realise it at the time but, through all the unending ambiguity and guilt, what I actually really wanted or rather, *needed*, was a quieter mind. To retrain my brain from scratch and simply to block out all that unhelpful noise. Though seeing and accepting this was not always easy. I knew that I would perhaps not be able to do this alone; to face these oversized *gremlins* by myself.

Luckily for me and after so many months and even years of suffering, I now finally didn't have to...

Chapter 9
COMING OUT

"Face the facts of being what you are, for that is what changes what you are."

- Soren Kierkegaard

"So there you have it," I turn to James in our usual treatment room. "*That* is my story."

James lets out this rather long exhalation. I have literally just given him chapter and verse on absolutely everything there is to know about me, about all of my *triggers*. If the secrets to my illness had not been fully promulgated prior to today's session, then certainly they had been now. In phosphorescent, Technicolor detail.

"The question now," James says rhetorically and in the sort of maieutic manner to which I have become accustomed, "is how we get rid of it." I look ahead, awkwardly.

"Yes," I say, looking thoughtful. "How *do* we get rid of it?"

The thought stays with me for a few seconds before, rather suddenly, it dawns on me how *loaded* a question this really is; like there could be just one simple answer. If only life were that easy. If only we can just wave a magic wand and all our problems disappear from sight; like grains of sand in an almighty hurricane.

"Well the way we get rid of it", says James, gleefully, interrupting me before I have time to think on it further, "is simply by realising that none of it is necessary."

"I beg your pardon?"

"That's how we get rid of it...the OCD...accepting that it just isn't *necessary.*"

I look at James querulously. Immediately I want to get up and argue with him. Tell him that he is wrong. That if it were really that straightforward, that one-dimensional, then surely I would bloody well have done it by now. Surely I would not have put myself, my family, through such full-on suffering if, with just one blink of an eye, it might all have been so easily avoided.

Except, well... I pause for a moment... I had never considered, until now, the reasons *why* I engaged in these pointless rituals. Often I just did what my OCD told me; perfunctorily, without question. Now, having raked through my past so meticulously, I have every reason to doubt my pathology.

Was it really *necessary*? Did I really *need* it in my life? Loretta, university, moving away from home – these had all been the triggers for my profound unease. The OCD had merely been there to provide some sort of structure around the chaos, to give me back a sense of *control*. Three years later and the fulfilment of such rituals seemed hardly to be in context.

"But if I don't do these things," I tell James, honestly, "then I run the risk of being a bad person. If I don't work out whether something is good or bad – or indeed whether or not I am capable of doing something bad – then I am surely acting recklessly, posing a threat to everyone around me. I cannot live with that."

James looks at me with a somewhat puzzled expression on his face, exaggerated because he wants me to consider my negative hypothesis a bit more carefully. "Maybe," he tells me, "you should try remembering a time before university, before meeting Loretta, *before* your OCD"

I squint my eyes slightly as I try to remember.

"Up until that point, you had seemingly made all the right choices. You've mentioned nothing to me about ever having done anything bad in your life; nothing before the age of nineteen that you *regret*?"

I nod in the affirmative.

"Then perhaps, far from you sticking to your OCD – which, let's face it, hasn't really been working great guns for you – you should go back to a time when you relied more heavily on your gut."

"My *gut*?"

"Yes, your gut instincts."

I pass James another querulous look. "You were fine trusting yourself before your OCD and nothing bad happened. Maybe it's time you re-introduce that trust."

I smile. I finally think I know what James is trying to say: getting rid of OCD is not just about stopping the rituals, it's about remembering who I am. It's about replacing negative beliefs with positive ones. It's about relinquishing my reliance on imaginary support structures. It's about *trust*.

I leave the treatment room that afternoon feeling buoyant, fresh and focused. I decide, there and then, to make a brand new resolution:

Over the coming months and weeks I will make every effort to try new things, to push the boundaries of my illness, to test out my true gut feelings in every which way I can.

I will endeavour, as they say, to *find* myself.

Who am I? Who *am* I? Who am *I*?

It's incredible how easy it is to lose yourself; to become nothing more than a living shadow, loathsome and empty; "The silence depressed me," remarks Esther in Sylvia Plath's *The Bell Jar*. "It wasn't the silence of silence. It was my own silence".

Without doubt, my three years through university and all the way up to my eventual diagnosis with OCD in 2007 had been perhaps some of the worst and toughest of my life. They had also come to represent a period in which my sense of selfhood and seity would be almost at its most exiguous and vapid. Over this relatively small yet substantial measure of time, it was as if I had allowed all or, at any rate, a significant part of my brain to deteriorate into this overgrown garden, untended, uncared for; a rough entanglement of fast enveloping bramble thorns, their long, sharp pedicles keeping me constantly caught up within myself and away from the much more sustaining, energy-giving rays of sunlight.

Following, in particular, my latter sessions with James, I decided that what I needed more than anything was to come back into the light. To plunge myself into all sorts of various different activities that would involve me once more engaging with the world around me. It was, as James had put it to me quite early on, "An experiment in living; a chance to find the hidden *you* which, up until now, has been locked away, rendered redundant by the onset of OCD." I knew I would need to engage in things previously off limits. I also knew I would need to step outside my comfort zone considerably; upsetting my OCD and possibly all my other internal cost-benefit subroutines in the process.

But I was sure – or at least as sure as I could be - that it would all be worth it... *in the end.*

And so, over a period of a few months, I threw myself into every new and exciting activity I could think of: I started salsa for example (which, admittedly, had lasted only two sessions and ended, quite abruptly, after I began to panic that I was dancing *too close* with some of the girls; *What happens if I get an erection and it rubs against them?*); I went to more parties (thus immersing myself with girls and alcohol; a most precarious mix even aside from the OCD); I even tried my hand, for a few weeks, at kung-fu (until I worried that my new skills would make me far too powerful and, therefore, *dangerous*).

Though perhaps most daring of all was a date with a rather dilettantish young barmaid called Candi, only nineteen years old, who had served drinks to Jake and I one warm summer's evening during a fairly random drive up to a convivial pub in North Norfolk. (Jake and I had often taken long drives out together during this period. We did it to clear our heads, to gain some distance from our so called 'problems'. In fact, right up until recently, we would routinely whirl around Norwich and beyond, talking, philosophising, putting the world to rights.)

That evening, in true spirit of pushing my boundaries, I had decided, much to Jake's disapprobation, to ask out this rather attentive and friendly barmaid (whom, for a reason unknown to either of us, had taken it upon herself to provide proper *table* service), and was most surprised when she simply responded with a smile and by scribbling down her name and number with a crayon on a used, scrunched-up serviette.

"You jammy git," said Jake as the two of us left for home that beautiful summer's evening. "Don't know how you pulled that one off so effortlessly."

Well if I didn't know then, I would certainly know soon enough.

That following week Candi and I met for dinner at an old Edwardian style seafood restaurant on Cromer seafront. It was, so she had told me, one of her favourite places to eat and I remember thinking at the time that this had probably meant she was a 'pretty classy bird'. A short while later, having found a quiet table close to the window, the food arrived and I sat back and watched as Candi tucked heartily into her meal. In the soft early evening sunshine, I couldn't help but observe a series of stil wooden bangles emanating up her left arm, going, quite unusually I couldn't help but think, all the way up to her elbow.

"Nice bangles," I said, with a mouthful of prawns and trying half-heartedly to generate some form of light conversation. It had actually been something I had noticed back at the pub, during our first encounter, but I had been too self-conscious to mention it then. Now, in the relaxed atmosphere of this top-rate seafood diner, I felt no such compunction. Alas, it would be the biggest mistake of the evening...

Candi immediately stopped eating and looked at me square on. There was a long, inexplicable pause before finally, rather candidly, the full extent of the truth of these rather prominent and meretricious charms was revealed: that in fact this gaudy miscellany of bracelets were nothing more than a token representation of each and every one of Candi's numerous sexual conquests; *"one for every man I've fucked,"* she said, with unflinching honesty.

Immediately, I began choking on my prawns: "I see," I said, in a complete coughing fit and, if truth be told, feeling pretty darned shocked to the core.

As you can imagine, following this rather brutish revelation, I had very little intention of sticking around. The two of us ate up quickly, I paid for the meal, we went for small drive in her car before, finally, I made my excuses to leave early. "Well it's a long way back to Norwich," I said politely, awkwardly backing out of the invitation for coffee at hers, "and, you know, I have work first thing."

Needless to say, my first date with Candi would undoubtedly be my last. In many ways, my gut feelings, which I had been aggressively instructed to trust, had clearly betrayed me. I had allowed myself to ask out what turned out to be a total sex maniac without ever once twigging that something might in fact be seriously wrong. That *she* might be seriously strange.

As the days went by, I found Candi's lack of communication to be somewhat of a blessing. Either she had taken the hint gracefully, respecting cordially my tacit derogation, or else had found me to be every bit as rank and off-putting as I had no doubt found her. Nevertheless, I couldn't help but worry *what if*. What if I had decided to sleep with her? What if I had then contracted an STI or lead her on in some way? As a red blooded male, desperate and alone, the thought of sleeping with her had certainly crossed my mind on more than one occasion throughout the date (despite not finding her attractive) and I couldn't help but worry about what that meant about me as a person.

"*But you didn't,"* said James, looking at me with mock perplexity during our session almost a week later. "You didn't sleep with her."

"But wha…."

"*What if*. Why worry about *what if*? *What if* never happened. You made the right decision. This is a perfect example of where trusting your gut worked for you. This does not need to be an exercise in beating yourself up."

I looked at him with soft, shimmering eyes; like something from a Japanese manga. I felt like I wanted to cry. "You're right," I conceded, making the slow yet revelatory transition from my rather darkened servility.

"You really cannot go on questioning yourself like this," said James finally. "You need to start believing in yourself."

I walked home that evening, reassured once more. Though I couldn't help but wonder how long the reassurance would or could last. How long it might be before the next hiccup, the next bump in the road. "I must start trusting myself," I said to myself over and over. "I *will* learn to trust in myself. I will learn it, even if it bloody kills me."

I got home that evening and went straight upstairs to look in the bathroom mirror. "Who am I!?" I shouted at myself in the mirror.

"I am a good person," I said to myself out aloud. "A GOOD PERSON."

At least, I *think* I am.

In the Autumn, I decided to join an OCD group. It had been the second thing on the link worker's list and, in the spirit of trying new things and expanding my horizons, I thought that this would be the perfect way of blending my own relatively *avant-garde* pursuit with something more conventionally therapeutic. I was right. I am proud to say that, after five years, I still attend the same group to this day. Though back then, I could not have known the myriad benefits or indeed the overall positive effect the group would have on my life.

"Do you think it's a good idea?" I asked James during one of our last ever sessions together, "I mean, now I'm feeling a little bit better, do you think it's *necessary*?"

"It certainly won't hurt," James replied, looking at me, almost quite proud of my progress. "If anything, you might be able to use what you've learned here to help other people."

"Yes," I nodded reflectively, "you might just be right."

And so, a week or so later, I attended my first ever group at the local forum. It was a cold and starry night in November and, as I arrived at the advertised rendezvous, I felt markedly tense. I did not know what to expect. I did not know what might be expected of me. As I walked in through the main entrance, I was greeted instantly by a rather elegant woman in her mid-to-late fifties with jet black hair and wearing a stylish leopard print pashmina shawl scarf. "Hello there," she said with a sort of swank gaiety. "Do come in. Come in. You must be Aron. My name is *Margo*."

I've mentioned Margo in this book a few times already. I am proud to say that I have actually known Margo now for almost six whole years. In that time, I have learned to trust Margo's opinions like I trust those of my own family and close friends. She understands OCD inside and out, understands the treatment as well as the pot-hole ridden road to recovery, and has thus dedicated her life to helping those suffering from such a wretched illness to get well again. She is a marvel, a gem, an inspiration.

Margo welcomed me into the group: "Isn't it wonderful to have such a lovely young *man* join us today," she told everyone as I shuffled nervously into the centre of the room. The group looked at each other awkwardly, a soft susurrus of salutation aimed imprecisely in my direction and I smiled demurely in return. Margo pointed over to a vacant seat in the far corner of the room (signaling the only free seat) and I followed her meandrous limb with razor precision. Sat to the right of me in a perfectly formed arc were all of the others. Well, I say *all of the others* but this is perhaps a somewhat generous use of the term. In fact, there were only three other members present that evening. I made up the fourth.

As the weeks went by, I learned that these three individuals were the group's regular attendees; the so-called '*core*'. "We're always very lucky to have a core," Margo would say each week with relish. "Others come and go but we would be absolutely nowhere without our core." In years to come, I would become the group's last and final core member, eventually taking a seat on the Board of Trustees and helping Margo on a weekly basis to establish the group as one of the first ever regional gatherings to offer both psycho-education and *'constructive empathy'*. Now I can proudly say, the attendance in each group session ranges from around ten (minimum) to as many as eighteen. The other week we actually had as many as thirty!

Yet back then, back at a time where my knowledge of my illness let alone the various treatment methods was scarce to say the least, the idea of *group* therapy had been a totally alien concept. I had not met a fellow OCD sufferer before that night. I certainly had not considered what it might be like to convalesce with them on a fortnightly basis.

"OK," said Margo, addressing the whole group with almost implausible beatitude as she brought the session to order, "let's introduce ourselves. I'll go first and then if we could all go round anti-clockwise, just saying a few words..."

The group nodded in unison as Margo drew breath only to start up again. This, as it happens, was the standard format of the group and still is. Often the introductions go on for so long, they even become part of the actual therapy.

"As you all know my name is Margo. I've been running the group now for over seven years. I am the group's founder and I have had OCD since a child. My OCD consists mainly of washing and a fear of contamination. It's been a long struggle and has included various stints in inpatient care. Now I can safely say, after many difficult years, that I am over the worst of it. I am almost 95 percent better."

And with that, the group all looked at each other, a mix of marvel and prostration in their eyes. They do this, incidentally, after every one of Margo's introductions; like they are always hearing the news for the very first time. I must admit, I do this too on occasion. Each session, Margo will regale the same promising statistic pertaining to her almost miraculous recovery and each time she does this, the group will not fail to *ooh* and *aah* in sheer astonishment. As OCD sufferers, we tend to cling on to hope. Or at least, this is what we do at group. Our attendance, of course, being the biggest indicator that we all still believe that recovery is more than possible.

One person, however, who had been a little more skeptical of Margo's miraculous recovery was 67 year-old Stanley, a retired deputy head teacher from Bungay. Stanley was very much subsumed by his OCD. He found it difficult to move on. Or so he told us that afternoon.

"OK Stanley," said Margo, turning slowly to face him, "would you like to say a few words now?"

"Yes," said Stanley, running his hands through a long white quiff of hair and smiling at the group. "Thank you. Hello everyone...yes...my name is Stanley. I have had OCD all my life. It was particularly virulent during my university years when I found I became obsessed with doing well; with competing with my peers. I found that my academic achievements were always under scrutiny from my masters and contemporaries; like I was always on the brink of some sort of grand failure. Then I became a teacher and the pressure and scrutiny continued even more. Of course, now I am retired I simply have so much time to think about it all; to reflect on my past dealings and the way I was treated. I worry quite a lot about what others have thought of me over the years, what they have said about me. What they have said *to* me. I cannot help but focus on all the times I have been criticized unfairly, been derided, albeit tacitly and undetectably, by other members of the faculty and said nothing. Why, *why* didn't I say something…"

Stanley shook for a moment in revulsion. He told us about one particular head teacher he had worked with back during the early nineties whom had been, allegedly, something of a bully: "He would rub us all up the wrong way on purpose. Why did I not stand up to him, say something back to him…"

The way Stanley went on to describe his OCD was both passionate and eloquent. Here was clearly an intelligent and well-read individual. Yet, somehow, I couldn't help but feel that poor old Stanley had missed the point somewhat. His tone suggested a belief in his own fixations as being bona fide and quite correct. Why *didn't* he stand up to his old headmaster; why on earth had he *allowed* himself to be so easily brow-beaten? Perhaps a more fitting question might simply have been, *'Why, after all these years, was he even still bothered?'*

It soon became clear from only two minutes listening to Stan, that there were perhaps plenty of sufferers out there who, quite contrary to the evidence, *believed* what their OCD told them. And this, I concluded, might very well have been one of the greatest obstacles they had to recovery. It has certainly been my own greatest obstacle.

Unfortunately, Ruth and Eileen have suffered similar such obstacles over the years. Though they might not have consciously recognized or appreciated it. They are the other two regular attendees at the group and, although I was sure they understood the rudimentary nature of OCD that much more than Stanley, they tended not to be able to apply it so well to their own set of depressing circumstances.

Ruth told us her story first. She told us of her terrible troubles leaving the house. How she had to perform certain rituals before she could even contemplate leaving each day for work. Sometimes these rituals would take literally hours on end as she meticulously set out to complete each abstruse routine, one after another, without interruption. She also told us of the therapy she was receiving from her CBT counselor. "He told me all about '*acceptance*'," she told the group, rather excitedly. "I have already started practicing it. I think it helps. I have tried relaxing more during the day. I even bake cupcakes on the weekends."

"And how about leaving the house?" Margo asked.

"How do you mean?" Ruth looked confused.

"Have you managed to reduce the time it takes to leave the house?"

"Oh…right…no." There was a pause. "But I certainly feel a lot better."

Margo re-constituted a smile and the rest of the group smiled along with her. To this day, Margo's reactions often dictate how the group will appraise another members' progress. After all, Margo is the *expert* amongst us. Not to mention, the only one of us to be fully recovered.

The next closest to recovery had, of course, been Eileen. Apparently when Eileen first attended the group she had been a quivering wreck. "I'm sure you won't mind me telling the group," Margo would say on her behalf, "that when you first arrived here Eileen, you couldn't even look the rest of us in the eye. You were so nervous, you refused even to speak."

Now, Eileen was so much more confident and comfortable with her illness. She told us how she was in fact almost *proud* of having OCD. "It's who I am," she told us. "I accept that now. I am fully comfortable with who and what I am."

Though a small part of me couldn't help but think (and in fact cannot help but still think) that maybe Eileen has been *too* comfortable over the years in accepting her OCD. Not to mention the limitations to recovery this evoked. Eileen finished telling the group every last detail of her OCD (as it turned out, she was quite the chatterbox) before attention fell finally onto the last attendee. Margo looked over sanguinely in my direction.

"Do you feel comfortable saying a few words?" she asked hesitantly, though with a cheerful optimism. "I know it's your first time so please do not feel obliged to say anything if you do not feel comfortable."

"No, that's fine," I replied, with assurance. "I am happy to say a few words." Which in many ways was true enough; I have never ordinarily been shy in coming forward. Despite the shame my OCD has thrust upon me, the guilt over the 'disgusting' nature of some of my obsessions, I have never been too ashamed to say what's on my mind. Or at least, I have learned to handle the inevitable shame and not let it affect me.

"My name is Aron," I said, "and I have sexual obsessions."

The group looked at each other, slight shock on their faces, and then turned finally to Margo for validation.

"Oh," said Margo, "I see."

Coming out with *sexual* OCD, in the beginning, had certainly not been easy. As I may already have mentioned earlier, this form of OCD in particular is a bit of a wheel within a wheel, a taboo upon a taboo. Subjects involving sexual depravity are often the very last thing we want to be discussing, particularly with those whom we love but also with those that we feel might be in a position to judge us unfavorably. However, following my initial disclosure, first with Gemma and then later with my family, I found it easier and easier to talk about my symptoms until eventually I started speaking about them quite routinely. Arguably, I talked about them *too* much.

Soon after I had divulged my inner-most fears with my mum (regarding primarily my having sexually assaulted Loretta), I found that the subject matter slowly but surely opened up to other, wider sex-related issues. My mum had provided me with so much comfort and relief -*"of course you're not a bad person"* - that I came to rely on her counsel simply as a matter of course.

The reliance on this rather gossamery support system would not always bode so well.

Unfortunately, as the reassurance persisted, so too did new worries spring to light, each one becoming more and more complex until ultimately they were beyond the mere common-place platitudes that I had no doubt counted on so fully only months beforehand. Instead they would need proper 'working out', sometimes with a pen, paper and a good few hours in solitary confinement. Here are a few good examples (although there were many, many more):

- *Is it bad if I roll over in bed with a girl, the two of us naked? What if I end up accidently or 'recklessly' penetrating her? Penetration, one must assume, takes a fair amount of* force. *I guess I would have to be rolling over fairly quickly (although, I am yet to unravel the true relationship between force and speed;* $\vec{F} = \mathrm{d}\vec{p}/\mathrm{d}t$*). Moreover, I'd definitely need to be at the correct angle and have the penis positioned right next to the vaginal opening. Without a good angle, penetration would be almost impossible. The wrong position would also potentially make things difficult. All things considered, I think it is perhaps pretty easy to determine that accidental or 'recklessly intended rape' (RIP) will include at least* two *of the following; force (speed in rolling over) + position + angle. The exception to this rule might be in circumstances where the person rolling holds a 'reasonable belief' that they will* not *penetrate in which case only one of the three criteria set out for RIP need be obviated.*

- *Is it bad to have sex with a girl under the influence of alcohol? How drunk is* too *drunk? Is the amount of alcohol the primary factor or is it the level of mental impairment that matters? 'Consent = Knowledge + Approval' or, as I like to refer to it, 'Consent =* "Approved knowledge".*' On that basis, a girl under the influence must not only say 'yes' but also have some deeper understanding and knowledge of the* consequences *of her actions before she can be said to have truly 'consented'. But how will I know if she understands? How will I know if she is not too impaired by alcohol? I guess there are a number of tests or questions one can tick off: Is she able to walk; is she able to speak coherently; can she identify the people she is speaking to; can she remember what has happened earlier in the evening and how she came to be in the position of now having sex? A girl must be able to demonstrate all of these things to a level of at least seven out of ten in order for them to be considered 'safe' to sleep with. N.B - this will not be based on an average but as a minimum score on each of the criteria in turn.*

As you can imagine, all these pretended scenarios, these catastrophically fashioned future-dilemmas, not to mention the complex 'working out' and strict regulations that would occur as a result, took up a lot of my time. They ate away at me and caused continued disruption to my day-to-day lifestyle. Nevertheless, I remained hopeful that I would eventually come through my OCD with my sanity intact. Luckily for me, James had warned me of the dangers of too much reassurance as well as the importance of *trust* and I had taken his guidance very seriously. "Remember to think with your *gut,*" he had told me. "Don't over-analyze or turn to others for certainty, trust in yourself." And each time I heard this message, my resolve would strengthen. Each day I trusted more I would be less inclined to carry out meaningless and abhorrent mental compulsions. It would be the start of a long and painful journey towards true mental wellbeing as well as the beginning of the end of the very worst of those two awful emotions: anxiety and guilt.

In fact it was a joint decision for my counselling with James to finally come to an end one rainy Tuesday in January. We had both concluded that, in spite of not being fully 'cured', enough progress had been made to, as it were, see me on my way. If I continued trusting my gut and kept on regularly leaving the house (and, of course, pushing myself whenever things got on top of me), I stood every chance of a full recovery. At least, that was the hope.

Though I knew it would not be easy. I knew it would take work, commitment and a fighting mentality. Getting well, as with any worthwhile endeavour, needs nurturing and tendering. It needs constant care, attention and dedication. As the eminent saying goes: "Many of the great achievements of the world were accomplished by tired and discouraged men who kept on working." Recovery is no different to this.

Following my last session of person-centred therapy, I continued attending group therapy regularly twice monthly. I found it to be both helpful and informative. I found that meeting other people suffering similar problems helped me to come to terms with my own illness. I felt less isolated and, by extension, less of a walking anomaly. It felt good to know that other people knew how I felt and could empathise, even if only partially, with the pain I went through seemingly on a daily basis.

Then during one group session that winter I got introduced to a guy called Ross. Ross, 35 years old, was my height, my build and, as it turned out, had most of my OCD symptoms. His OCD centred on sex and morality and was mainly *thought* based. It was like looking in the mirror. "Isn't it wonderful," said Margo one session to both Ross and myself. "You two have just *soooo* much in common."

Ross had actually been a long-standing member of the group for a good few years before my arrival but had never formed part of the *core*. He dipped in and out, often turning up only when he felt well enough (invariably this is the *worst* time to come. Or at the very least, is a time where one might least benefit from attending) and would disappear again for weeks, months. Though I always knew he would be back again; back, as it were, to fight another day.

Eventually, over the years, Ross and I became (and still are) very good friends; joined not only by our mutual suffering but through a cerebral cord, a thread of shared experience and intellectual understanding of our illness. Like me, Ross is a bit of a fighter. He resists his OCD when and where he can. Though, also like me, he has had to accept the limitations on treatment that exist not to mention the many pitfalls that one must inevitably associate with the journey towards recovery.

One evening when Ross was feeling a bit better, we went for a drink after group. Afterwards, we went for a drive to a patch just outside Norwich prison, located on the old site of the Britannia Barracks. We switched off the engine.

"Sometimes I like to come here to free up my mind," said Ross thoughtfully. "I find it so peaceful. I find I can really be in the *now*." Ross turned to me, looking overly serene. Ross had been struggling with his OCD for literally decades. He was the only other person I knew that went to GUM clinics regularly without having sex. Or worried about standing too close to women or children in supermarket queues. Now, finally, he seemed to have reached a point of calm.

"I can't profess to know the answers," he told me honestly. "Every time I think I've found the solution to my OCD, I find that it is all smoke and mirrors. All I can say is that this time, I feel confident I have found something that'll help. It might not work for you. I know it's not for everyone."

Ross handed me over a DVD. It was festooned in splashes of orange and green and was evocatively entitled, *'Eckart Tolle Awakening in the NOW'*. The back of the cover promised, quite magnanimously I couldn't help thinking, freedom for the *'thought possessed'*. Ross looked at me excitedly: "It's a spiritual DVD," he revealed. "Eckart Tolle is one of the greatest spiritualists I have come across. It has really helped me through some tough times. Like I said, it might not be your cup of tea."

Ross was right. It wasn't my cup of tea. A few days later, at home, I watched the DVD. I also read up on Eckart Tolle online and watched a few clips from his own live TV service, *'Eckart Tolle TV'* (which ordinarily, though perhaps unsurprisingly, required a *paid* subscription). I found his preaching to be, on the whole, rather too wishy-washy and thereby misleading: a litany of convenient and, in many ways, alluring truisms which, by virtue of their deceptively nebulous character and their widespread appeal, played on human credulity like an Italian accordion master plays the *Fisarmonica*. The brilliance of Eckart Tolle's works are, almost exclusively, the way in which they strike a chord in each and every one of us. We have all, at some time in our lives, suffered at the hands of our own thoughts and feelings. One does not have to have experienced OCD or depression or, indeed, any other form of mental illness, to have suffered, sometimes quite profoundly, at the hands of flawed or unhelpful thinking.

And it was over this small but inescapable truth, that I could not now help but question Tolle's seemingly *opportune* exhortation.

That said, I found I could not reject Eckart Tolle's mantra outright either. Not only because of the way it had seemingly benefited Ross but also because I agreed, at least in part, with the main tenets of what he was suggesting. The general message of Eckart's teachings pointed to an inner alignment with the present as being the key to tranquillity. That worrying about the future or dwelling on the past, of letting emotions and experiences cloud one's judgement, was anxiety-inducing and, ultimately, a waste of energy. I couldn't help but agree. OCD is, in essence, a propensity towards maladaptive habits. It is partial and inflexible and is a most unhelpful way of engaging with the world around. I knew I could no more accept my OCD as a viable way of living as swallow fully the proposed wisdom of one rather peremptory, self-designated messiah.

And so I started considering trying to live in the moment, of adopting a more non-judgemental stance to the past, to the future and to my own intrusive thoughts. I typed 'Being in the Now' into the internet. The search results went into their hundreds. The fifth result down talked about a new therapeutic application, a psychological faculty that had actually originated with Buddhist spiritual teachings and traditions from the East but that was now fast being adopted by the NHS as a way of combating stress, depression, substance abuse, and suicidal tendencies. It seemed intriguing and nothing that I had seen written before.

The technique was known quite simply as *mindful awareness*.

Chapter 10
A NEW AWARENESS

"The ultimate value of life depends upon awareness and the power of contemplation rather than upon mere survival."
- Aristotle

"Right then everybody," says Margo, addressing the whole group in unison, "I would like you all to close your eyes and focus on your breathing."

We do so. It is the first Wednesday of the month and we are all sat round in a neat semi-circle practicing mindful meditation – or *mindful awareness* as it is more commonly referred. Margo is standing at the far end of the room by the large sash window as she instructs us to *mindfully* bring our attention into the present.

"Now I would like all of you to concentrate on your chairs. Notice how the wooden spindles feel against your spine, notice how this new sensation gives you a *tingly* feeling that quickly travels upwards towards the small of your neck. Notice the hairs on the back of your neck stand on end. Now focus again on your breathing. Notice how you breathe in for the same length of time as you breathe out."

I try my best to focus on my breathing but cannot seem to concentrate or *stop* concentrating as is more aptly the case; the attempt at the former making things only much harder to achieve the latter. Instead, quite perversely, all I can think of, besides what's for tea, is well, how do I put this delicately, *sex*! And not just the clinical or scientific kind you might find in *Biology Today*. Oh no, not in *my* dirty little head. In the inner landscape of my own rather ill-regulated topography, countless corporal visages of bouncing female anatomy (jiggling bosoms and perfectly rounded derrieres) are grinding and copulating in almost every last corner of the terrain. In fact, it's almost like a scene from an X-rated MTV 'booty' video which, almost at once, sends me into a frenzy of hysterical guilt. According to an OCD rule I made up but a few weeks back, it is prohibited to think about sex in public because of the risk it poses of effectuating an erection which may then be seen by, amongst others, children but the quiet meditation allows my impish imagination to wreak havoc. *Tits and ass, tits and ass, tits and ass.*

Suddenly, though perhaps not surprisingly, there emerges a stirring in my groin and instantly I feel terrible, loathsome. I mean, what sort of dissolute human being allows, or worse still, *incites* such a turgid reaction and in the middle of a room full of innocent, and on the whole, middle-aged bystanders? What sort of person *gets hard* over no more than a few watery or muliebrous mental compositions? But then, just as I am about to beat myself up over this rather debauched *faux pas*, to try and work out how bad a person I must now be, I realise I am thinking again. I am thinking about thinking. I am *judging* myself. I probably need to stop. But how do I stop? *Shit, I'm still thinking.*

Eventually, after a few minutes or so of largely ineffectual meditation - in which I have probably done *more* thinking and not less (not to mention suffer plenty of anxious arousal) - Margo gently wakens us from our state of mindfulness and asks us to come back gradually into the room. The same room, incidentally, I am almost certain I never once left but in which I now sit with a most inopportune semi-*boner*.

"You may all now stop focussing on your breathing," Margo tells us calmly, "and open your eyes". We do so and are now all sitting peacefully with our eyes wide open, awaiting, with varying interest, the inevitable post-exercise dissection.

"So what did we all think?" says Margo, smiling rather fulsomely like a great, big, humanlike Cheshire Cat.

We all look at each other blankly and then back to Margo. There are five of us present today: Colin, Ruth (core), Brenda, Eileen (core) and Natalie. None of us are forthcoming. I look down at my crotch to check there is no erection and am relieved to discover that, as with the meditation itself, the effects of this rather *provoking* exercise have almost entirely vanished.

"Natalie, what did you think?"

Natalie is a bubbly and gregarious girl. She is also not afraid to give her true opinion. This is her second group session and already in that time she has been brave enough to tell us about her particular type of OCD (which is mainly centred around cleaning and contamination). "I didn't like it," she says, with unfaltering honesty. "I always find that focussing on my breathing makes me feel like I am choking. Like someone is strangling me to death."

There is a silence. I want to laugh but I hold in the urge to do so. Apparently, the feeling of choking is not all that uncommon with breathing exercises. It is an unintended consequence of this otherwise, (pseudo)-therapeutic endeavour. However, as I might instantly have suspected, Margo is not keen to discuss it further and so moves quickly on to...errr yes...*Colin.*

Colin is another newbie. He has been coming to the group for a little longer than Natalie, approximately the last six weeks, and is a rather bizarre chap. His OCD, like mine, is mainly thought-based though I haven't as yet managed to glean from him what type of thoughts he suffers with. Colin has his own views on where his OCD came from. His more recent theory is that it all resulted from years of breathing in asbestos during his time as a multi-tradesman for a social housing maintenance contractor. Now, Collin, who is in his mid-to-late forties, is currently unemployed and challenging, quite vehemently as it turns out, the government on their refusal to continue with his Employment and Support Allowance (otherwise known as ESA). He is adamant that his right to appeal on this matter constitutes an abuse of his Human Rights under Article 6.

"Well I actually didn't mind it," says Colin in his rather bombinating tone. "I always think it's quite good to meditate with others. I think it creates a really great energy. It reminds me of the energy I experienced not so long ago outside St Paul's Cathedral at the protest camp. I'm sure you've all read about it. I truly believe the whole thing is a democratic awakening. And it's not just London: this thing is going global. No more homelessness, no more tax revenues funding bonuses, no more fractional reserved banking."

At this, Margo looks, quite literally, dumbfound. Again, I feel the urge to laugh at this rather lucid segue off-topic. Though before I get the chance, Margo hastily looks over in my direction, her eyes gazing at me imploringly. I am her last hope. Her last chance of salvaging the evening's exercise. I decide I will not let her down.

"Yes," I say, before even being asked the question, "I think it was very good. Very good indeed."

Mindfulness, as I have already mentioned, is a practice that stems right the way back to the wisdom of Buddhist traditions over a millennia ago. Its original context is *religious* yet, interestingly, the health benefits are now starting to be realised more and more by the scientific community in the West with research pointing to associated improvements in both physical and emotional wellbeing. Most interestingly, growing research studies are pointing to mindfulness as being an incredibly useful way of helping sufferers of OCD in particular to redirect attention away from their bothersome intrusive thoughts as well as in getting them to challenge their own, often rather more deleterious belief structures.

The basic underlying principle of mindfulness is the idea that we should all pay much more attention to what is going on in the present moment without making too many unnecessary judgements; to view the world how it is and not how we fear it might be or what we have experienced it to be in the past. In other words, it asks us to take in everything that is going on around us as well as all the internal processes going on inside of us, our thoughts, feelings and physical sensations and then to simply refrain from labelling them. By resisting the snap judgements that we as humans make on a daily basis, the negative biases we learn through habit, we start to see things more and more clearly. Until eventually we stop automatically assuming the worst. We start being *neutral*.

All of this, of course, has some quite powerful implications for OCD in which automatic *negative* thinking is a key characteristic. Mindfulness teaches us to see each scenario afresh, to accept ourselves and the limitations over our environments as well as to tolerate invasive feelings of anxiety and dread. "We cannot control everything in our lives," Margo told the group one session. "And we should not attempt to do so. Overcoming OCD is not about increasing control. It is about acceptance. It is about neutrality."

Mindfulness in a nutshell teaches us to catch negative thoughts before they snowball out of control. According to Susan M. Orsillo and Lizabeth Roemer in their book, *'The Mindful Way through Anxiety'*:

"If people learn to allow even painful thoughts and feelings to come and go instead of ignoring them or trying to suppress them, their perspective can be completely altered."

Though despite the myriad benefits, I would be lying if I said I ever really tried practicing mindfulness to any great extent. I never sat cross legged on a giant soft cushion, spreading my weight evenly across each butt cheek, exhaling in and out with the rather distinctive insufflations of Darth Vader. Nor did I read books, listen to cassettes or even just simply attempt to relax more. Perhaps I should have. Perhaps it would have helped. Nevertheless, my interest in the *theory* behind mindfulness did set a powerful pretext for a particular treatment method in which I would, over time, become somewhat taken. The programme was known quite simply as *The Four Steps*.

The book *'Brain Lock'*, in which Dr Schwartz first presents his now quite infamous cognitive-biobehavioural self-treatment method (abbreviated to *The Four Steps*), had actually first been brought to my attention during one of our group sessions in the Spring of 2008 and bore more than just a simple likeness to mindfulness; it's simple structure not to mention its universality and user-friendliness being quite a powerful hook.

Step 1: Relabel
Step 2: Reattribute
Step 3: Refocus
Step 4: Revalue

For me, The Four Step Programme offered a new perspective, a fresh way of looking at this, otherwise, quite stale and menacing condition. It helped me to inject rationality back into my thinking. It allowed me to become, as Schwartz would have it, 'an impartial spectator', able to view my behaviour not to mention my emotional (over)reactions from a safe and objective distance.

Principally, Schwartz's cognitive-biobehavioural treatment (so labelled by the UCLA) draws together the idea that OCD has both a basis in *neuropsychology* (a proposition with which I have always been in firm support) with the idea that thoughts can be overcome simply by refocusing the mind (in a nutshell, *mindfulness*). The theory was neat, accessible and could be easily practiced alone and without a therapist. Quite crucially for me, it also recognised that OCD was invariably a separate and distinct formation; simply just a kink in my neurochemistry, a chink in my otherwise serviceable armour. For those interested in the *science* of neuroplasticity (which I very much was and still am), The Four Step Programme draws on the growing mounds of research pointing to the idea that by changing our thoughts and our behaviour we actually change the very neural pathways in the brain. It was and still is groundbreaking stuff.

"I think I have found a miracle treatment," I remember telling the group one session.

Though, like with everything, it was of course not without its flaws. There is still so much to do in the area of psychotherapy, particularly in relation to OCD. In many ways, some of the current treatments emanating from older Buddhist traditions, now being taken up by real *scientists* like Schwartz and the like, are merely just the tip of a very large iceberg. At present the iceberg is nearly almost entirely submerged. But as we all know when it comes to only partially observable icebergs, sometimes they have the ability to sink ships.

One thing with which researchers, psychologists and clinicians are all agreed; more work needs to be done in the area of brain mapping when it comes to gaining further insight into and providing suitable treatments for mental illness. Indeed, Dr Schwartz himself tells us:

"Understanding the relationship between what the brain does and a person's internal life is very important, both for medical reasons and because it is such a fascinating subject in its own right."

For me, Schwartz's emphasis on the brain - the medical labelling of OCD as nothing more than a biochemical imbalance - was incredibly liberating. It provided the first promising alternative theory to the one that so many of us, at least in the beginning, are forced to resign ourselves to: that the content of our intrusive thoughts actually hold some intrinsic and moral truth. That things really are as bad as we imagine.

"Our brains sometimes lie to us," Margo told us one group session. "It is important always to be as impartial as we can. To always be looking for the *evidence*."

And yet, the idea that the brain could be flawed or that *conscious* re-evaluation in particular might be the one true key to unlocking the troubles of the mind, in many ways, seemed to go against every piece of counselling I had ever received beforehand. For example, James, who had had the biggest impact on my illness to date, had always maintained that trust in our *gut feelings* was far superior to the sorts of cognisant and rational deliberation that was now being prescribed by neuroscientists and behavioural therapists.

And he was not the only one. According to Jonah Lehrer in his New York Times Best Seller, *'How We Decide'*:

"The process of thinking requires feeling, for feelings are what let us understand all the information that we can't directly comprehend. Reason without emotion is impotent."

Lehrer backs up his research with plenty of lovely, juicy brain science. Lehrer advocates that, buried deep in the brain, are dopamine neurons which connect all parts of the cortex and are responsible for many of our very best decisions. These neurons, as well as forming a part of the *subconscious* mind, also offer arguably the most versatile and failsafe decision-making processes available to us; their spindle cells constantly rewiring themselves to reflect new realities and new experiences.

It had certainly been a fascinating, if not groundbreaking proposition. Unfortunately it had also done very little to allay the sense of confusion I had now begun to feel.

Gut feeling or conscious deliberation? What to trust? Which to discard? Very soon I became obsessed by the brain, not only the implications that brain science had on treatment but also, as it would later turn out, the implications of all this groundbreaking discovery on my own moral OCD fixations with right and wrong. Could Leher's research actually point to an innate sense of morality in which *breaking bad* would be, like a man attempting to kick down a three inch steel-armoured door, almost inconceivable?

This idea of an *unconscious* moral faculty within the brain is echoed by Harvard University Professor and director of the Cognitive Lab, Marc D. Hauser in his book *'Moral Minds'*. He argues that, rather than morals being based wholly on society or on learned behaviour, there is instead a universal moral grammar underpinning almost all forms of moral behaviour. He draws an analogy with language: "The central idea of this book is simple: we evolved a moral instinct, a capacity that naturally grows within each child, designed to generate rapid judgements about what is morally right or wrong based in an unconscious grammar of action."

As you can imagine, over the weeks following my research into the brain, I drove myself literally balmy. Could I really now rely on research by the likes of Leher and Hauser to provide guarantees that I would always remain, for now and forever more, a 'good' person? Or was that simply just wishful thinking? Or even, dare I say it, *reassurance*. In the end, the endeavour to trust more and think less, quite ironically, had resulted in me actually trusting less and thinking more. It had resulted in me thinking about thinking. In thinking about every single decision, not merely the content of each and every moral dilemma but the way in which my mind processed, evaluated and, ultimately, adjudicated over each and every such obstacle and impasse, however small.

Eventually, the stress of it all made me ill. Regulating oneself needlessly is a thankless task. Not trusting one's own instincts, replacing them instead with the most galling and frustrating mental flagellation is a most exceptionable undertaking. Nevertheless, it felt like the only option available. The only way to ensure that I always made the best moral decisions.

The results would, in due course, prove disastrous.

Chapter 11
THE LOOKING DISORDER

"Curiosity is gluttony. To see is to devour."
- Victor Hugo, *Les Miserables*

In early 2009 I remember watching the 1999 film, *'The General's Daughter'*, directed by Simon West and starring John Travolta, and being gripped with fear. The film was not scary nor was it particularly bloodthirsty (I had watched all three *Omen* films as well as *The Hills Have Eyes* on numerous occasions without so much as a hint of vexation). Nor was it ever, at any stage, banned by film censorship organisations (*The Texas Chain Saw Massacre*, for example, banned in Norway, is actually one of my favourite horror films). But nonetheless, one particular scene had perhaps left a lasting negative impression on me. In fact, it had quite literally kept me up at night; a chill that shot down my spine like a ventrogluteal injection of Nalaxone.

The scene in question is the part in the film where Army CID Officer, Paul Brenner (Travolta), first stumbles upon the naked corpse of Captain Elisabeth Campbell, daughter of Lieutenant General Campbell, on the firing range at Fort MacCallum. As he is examining the unclothed and discarded carcass of the once very attractive female Captain (played by Leslie Stefanson), he seems to take a glance down at her bare breasts before declaring, rather vulgarly under his breath, *"What a waste."*

The look is very brief and the comment seemingly only a knee-jerk susurrus, but nevertheless the scene had somehow left me feeling incredibly uncomfortable. John Travolta, who clearly was meant to be the good guy, the *protagoniste*, had just eyed up a corpse; had ogled a naked dead body and taken his own sexual pleasure out of an otherwise heartrending *mise en scene*. Was this a truly morally virtuous thing to have done? The sort of behaviour becoming of a central character or mainstay? If this had been our very own loveable *British* Detective Inspector Jack Frost or Oxford-based Chief Inspector Morse, would we, as viewers, have been so forgiving over such a blatant indiscretion? Such an out-and-out show of impudence, disrespect and, let's face it, *necrophilia*.

My inability to accept that good people could sometimes do bad things or even that some things were bad only in certain contexts, was something I had always found difficult right from a young age. For me, there was always a right and a wrong; a 'good' and a 'bad'. The two were not usually apposite for crossover.

"Mum?" I would say as a three or four year old boy, rolling around on the carpet, playing with my figurines. "Who's right?" We would be watching perhaps an argument in *Neighbours* or a spat on Corrie.

"No one's *right,*" my mum would correct. "It's all a matter of opinion."

"Ok," I would say, "but which one is *more* right."

Such inflexibility regarding morality was, if you will, a sort of trademark characteristic of mine, particularly growing up. It is in fact a trademark feature of most young sufferers with early signs of OCD. Yet by 2008, this cute little intransigence, suddenly and out of the blue, worsened significantly, turning into an out-and-out OCD malfunction; an OCD *gremlin* if you will. My ability to trust my instincts, to accept that true morality sometimes rendered life in splashes of achromatic grey seemed now to be a conception somewhat lacking in my discernment. Following, in particular, the end of my sessions with James (which had, up until that point, helped me immensely), in a most bizarre and fervent gust, I began questioning almost every last morally ambiguous scintilla where some moral or ethical pronouncement could otherwise be drawn. I needed to know what was definitely 'good' and that which was unquestionably 'bad' so that I could be relatively sure I never inadvertently strayed into the latter (thus rendering my whole life invalid).

Looking, which was, I had concluded, exceptionally easy to do but which also seemed capable of being, almost in an instant, some form of heinous crime, literally scared the living bejesus out of me. *How,* I might hear you cry, would or could mere looking possibly make an otherwise good man 'bad'? Imagine if you will the following scenarios and you might, for just one moment, see where I am coming from: An old fart *perving* on a girl young enough to be his granddaughter (and by the way, when does merely looking turn into full blown *perving*?); a man glancing down the top of an unconscious drunk girl as she lies lifeless on the sidewalk; a guy watching (and maybe even enjoying) a fictional rape on TV (such as, *A Clockwork Orange*); a fella eyeing up 'on purpose' an attractive girl even for a microsecond while he is walking hand-in-hand with his bulimic or otherwise oversensitive fiancé *etc. etc*…I think you get the picture.

For me, the prospect of looking inappropriately at females (and thereby becoming a bad person) was far scarier than anything I had worried about before. Certainly far creepier than a group of psychotic mutants up a hillside in the Californian dessert. Glancing at a naked, dead girl lustfully, I had concluded, was one sure example of a totally immoral looking activity. Certainly it was enough to be filed unequivocally under 'bad'. Concordantly, it was this ridiculous conviction which had caused the 1999 box office hit to stir up such agitation. The paradox would be the start of a descent which would grip me for many months and even years to follow.

* * *

Conversation online with a good friend from work (Glen) actually as late as 2012. I am, at the time, watching an attempted rape scene in Rambo IV:

Me: Hey

Glen: Hey, you OK?

Me: Meh!

Glen: ???

Me: I am worried about perving on girls in films or TV that are a) dying or b) being sexually assaulted. The more I try not to look the more I want to. SO then I look. And if they're attractive I'll enjoy it.

Glen: On TV and film a lot is acting so not a problem, if it were actual life you can still enjoy a fitty but if they were being harmed you'd step in and help... stop over thinking and control the OCD.

Me: Yeah I know I'd help. But what if a girl is dying in real life of cancer and I take a sneaky peak at her breasts. It only takes one glance.

Glen: She can still be attractive so isn't a bad thing.

Me: Well what if I see a dead body in real life and glance?

Glen: And the chances of that are...

Me: Small. But it would be very bad.

Glen: I think if you saw a dead body in real life it would freak you and the breasts would be the last thing on your mind.

Me: I might still look for a second.

Glen: Yeah you would as it's human nature but I think you'd still be a bit more shocked and not thinking in a sexual way.

Me: This conversation is ridiculous isn't it?

Glen: A little but I know your brain whirs at a million miles an hour and sometimes the wiring gets a little fucked up...As you're mate, I may take the piss a lot and wind you up bit I think a lot of you and will listen to all the bollocks as you are a top lad and a bloody good friend.

Me: Thanks mate. I *think*.

The 'looking disorder', as I would later brand it, started actually just at the tail end of university, before then masked by the much more remorseless preoccupation that I was a rapist or a paedophile or some other form of perverse or sexual deviant. But a few months later, and following in particular my sessions with James, it would take on a much more central role in my moral fixation; powerful by virtue of its day by day significance, its subtlety, and its twisty, problematical character.

My moral dilemma was simply this: That looking at the female body (though, later, this would extend beyond just the body of adult women) could, in certain circumstances, constitute a crime of moral turpitude. That, in some extreme cases, not only could it transform me at once into some unforgiveable wretch but, worse still, might even be enough to cause genuine suffering. They say that the eyes are like the window to the soul; for me, my eyes had become an open fenestration through which it seemed wickedness could pour in and out without modulation.

The idea that mere looking could be dangerous had actually first been deposited in my mind during my final week at university, following a night out in Lancaster with Gemma. A guy in a night club had been eyeing her up because she was wearing a fairly short skirt and she had responded simply by whispering to me the following throw-away remark: "I think some men who stare at women should be locked up." Those words, which had meant nothing to me at the time, after a few days had haunted me greatly because, well, didn't *I* stare at women? Didn't I ogle girls in short skirts all the time? Did this mean I too should be locked away?

The fear of being a bad person by virtue of making women feel uncomfortable played on my mind for days, weeks. Like the post-war smog over the entire city of London in the early 1950's, my brain had become hooded, ensconced in the shadows of my own over-hanging introspection. Danger seemed to linger at every dark turn, with no guidance, no advice on how one might ultimately avoid the sharp, blackened-out corners and stay in the light. Eventually I decided I had no choice but to research the topic further, reading up on everything from Andrea Dworkin to Emmanuel Kant just to shed a bit of extra...*light*? However, just as with the fervent though ultimately futile searching online for information on STIs, what I found on the subject of *feminism* and female objectification more specifically had been deeply, deeply disturbing. According to radical feminist Catharine Alice Mackinnon, even looking at (pornographic) images of women posed grave moral issues. Mackinnon writes the following:

"A sex object is defined on the basis of its looks, in terms of its usability for sexual pleasure, such that both the looking - the quality of gaze, including its points of view - and the definition according to use become eroticised as part of the sex itself."

In other words, looking or *perving* (I really have never been able to define specifically what this rather pejorative term actually entails) on women causes them harm, stripping them entirely of their dignity and even their humanity. In much the same way as rape or other forms of violence against women, *perving,* I couldn't help but worry, seemed disconcertingly non-consensual.

Of course, the prospects of reducing women to no more than a helpless and devitalized immolation filled me with great levels of guilt. And not to mention uncertainty. For the first time in my life I questioned how I looked at women, when I looked at them, even the expression on my face as I smiled at them genially in the street. How could I be sure that the type of looking I partook in seemingly on a daily basis was not causing catastrophic anguish every time I so much as stepped foot outside my own front door? How could I be sure that, as a rather sex-starved and amatory young male, desperate and gagging for companionship, I might, at some point in my career of viewing women, have caused them to feel *objectified*.

"Mum?" I said in the kitchen one afternoon, my anxiety literally sky high. "Is it wrong to look at women *sexually*?"

My mum stopped still for a moment to consider: "I think the answer," she said matter-of-factly, not twigging that this question had in fact been incited by OCD, "is simply not to be too obvious."

Obvious, I thought to myself later. What in tarnation made looking *obvious*?

It would be perhaps only fair to say that, up until that point anyway, I did not nor had I ever suffered any compunction whatsoever when looking at girls I found attractive. I would simply look at what I fancied and enjoy it. I had certainly never considered whether or not I was ever being noticeable. Yet now, in light of my new revelation, I could not help but wonder whether this remorseless and rakish indulgence had been, to some extent, a rather dissolute undertaking. That, if some women, as I had now rather rigidly concluded, did indeed feel uneasy by being looked at by men in this way, then surely I had a duty to be discreet one hundred percent of the time, you know, *just in case*.

This, of course, raised the further question, and was a question I posed to myself on numerous occasions: What does it actually involve to look *discretely*? Maybe I was already being discreet, a natural instinct - or *daemon* - deep inside which would automatically trigger an alarm whenever I was looking too much or was about to get clocked (there is a brilliant article on *saccadic* eye movement and the role of the basal ganglia in modulating where our eyes go which I had read whilst compulsively researching the topic and which had given me a degree of comfort). Then again, maybe there was no such fail-safe mechanism at all and I genuinely ran the risk of being completely and utterly obvious every time I passed so much as a momentary glance. The doubts went round and around in my head; the answers seemed as distant to me as the Sombrero Galaxy.

And then one gloomy, destitute evening, alone and feeling pretty vulnerable, I decided to end the growing uncertainty once and for all. Or at least make a bloody good attempt at it. Rather sophistically, I decided to make up some *rules* in order to provide the ultimate set of answers to this rather nagging catch-22. That evening, I got out my notebook and pen (the same half-finished A4 paper bound notepad I had made my law notes in but a few months earlier) and began brainstorming.

What made looking 'obvious' was difficult to determine. I racked my brains like never before. Being so vague and all-consuming I knew I would have my work cut out coming up with some sort of workable formulation. Certainly it was a harder challenge than anything I had undertaken at university. Harder than property law and probate. Harder even than equities and trusts. Though after much contemplation, after hours and hours of over-thinking, I eventually settled on an answer I was happy with. I had concluded (perhaps rather fatuously I now accept) that being 'obvious' or 'noticeable' entailed any combination of the following behaviours (I wrote them down):

Looking for too long; looking at close proximity; looking at intimate body parts (like breasts and buttocks); *contorting* the body in order to look (for example, turning your head to catch a further glimpse of the girl who has just walked passed you); looking at someone who is conspicuously attractive (people are much more likely to think you're looking sexually if it's someone conventionally beautiful you have your eyes rested on); smiling while you look (indicating *pleasure* in what you are looking at) and looking in what I had deemed *'exposed public places'* (for example, a place without lots of people or landmarks around by which to obscure your perverted gaze - slightly more ambiguous than the others but worthy of codification nonetheless).

A combination of any *two* of the above, I wrote in my note book, would make the act of looking *'obvious'* (the act of being 'obvious' of course, being both proscribed and punishable by lengthy bouts of self-reproach). So, for example, I would be permitted under the rules to look at a girl's breasts, providing I didn't do it for ages and ages or that I turned around to catch a further glimpse. Similarly, I could look at a girl's ass whilst smiling but not in an empty public space and certainly not if she was conspicuously attractive, which would actually tick off as many as *three* from the checklist.

The rules, as you can imagine, were positively outlandish and yet for weeks, months, I lived by them. I *believed* in them. As one might expect, it didn't take long before these rather burdensome edicts had started making life needlessly complex; awkwardly and obstinately injecting the most pointless labelling into otherwise dismissible, day-to-day living. Censoring what I looked at became almost as ineffective and exhausting as one might imagine monitoring and reforming one's own blinking habits or even trying to control one's own intake of oxygen for each individual breath of fresh air.

Nonetheless, it did not stop me from trying...

Diary entry 1st September 2009:

Today during my shift, I am visited by a rather attractive Russian woman (I can tell she is Russian later by her accent). It has been a particularly boring shift, my mind drifting around, focusing on nothing in particular, when all of a sudden I look up to see this eye-catching young blond stood in front of me, smiling at me affectionately as she starts offloading some of her items onto my conveyer belt. She is wearing an elegant fox fur stroller, a low-cut fitted white top (no signs of a bra), a mini-skirt that would otherwise allow you to see what she had eaten for breakfast and a pair of designer sunglasses placed rather chicly upon her ornate *updo* hairstyle. Not surprisingly, I find I cannot take my eyes off her.

Later, as this attractive Russian finishes placing down the last of her items onto the belt, she arches forward over the table counter - in attempt, no doubt, to reach out for the separation bar - and, in so doing, inadvertently flaunts the whole front of her upper body; an unbroken corridor of air forming between her clothing and her torso, and going seemingly all the way down as far as the eye can see. And I can *see* literally everything.

At once, the situation causes me to go into a state of mild panic. In fear of having seen down her top, and thereby catching a glimpse of her full bosom, I turn my head away immediately, my OCD now flashing on full alert: *code red, code red.* Compulsively, I refer back to the rules I had made but a few weeks earlier. According to the checklist, looking at an 'intimate body part' at 'close proximity' is a prohibited combination. The fact that this rather striking *krasavitsa* might also be deemed 'conspicuously attractive' means that I have perhaps offended three of the criteria simultaneously. The guilt overtakes me like a thoroughbred racehorse at the Epsom Derby.

Enveloped in panic, I decide to look down and focus my attentions instead on opening plastic carrier bags, frantically pulling at them like a gopher on *Speed.* The sweat drips off me like rainwater. After I have finished bagging the last of her items - making sure the whole time to avert my eyes from her cleavage (as well as from the diamante thong she has purchased from the Home & Leisure Department) - I take her card and ask her if she needs any cash back.

"No zis is OK, ev-er-ything is very good," she replies in a low, monotone voice, each protracted syllable falling gracefully like snow-flakes from her raisin berry lips, before once again plunging her cleavage into my eye line as she reaches over to punch her PIN into the machine. Unbelievably my OCD is triggered for the second time. Though, this time, my self-control has been significantly perforated and seemingly I am unable to resist the urge to take that all essential look straight down her top.

At once I am a bad person.

A few milliseconds later, the luxuriant Russian looks up from her shopping basket and stares me straight in the eyes. It is unclear whether she has caught me in the act. Nothing is said. I can feel my tie clip stabbing sharply into my gullet as the shame and embarrassment cause me to become almost inconsolably grief-stricken. She eventually says thank you for her cash-back, gathers up her shopping bags and then walks off. I look at her once more as she moves – or *sashays* - away towards the revolving exit. She appears to be smirking to herself, though I cannot be sure.

As it happened, my looking disorder seemed to play up a lot at work. A supermarket is like one large consumer stadium, a bustling environment crammed with both customers and staff alike. There were often so many people to look at that, for my OCD, every shift was a field day.

Women, kids, the elderly - they were all subject to my OCD looking aversion. Each customer that travelled through my till would be like another looking dilemma just waiting to happen. Kids would climb up like monkeys onto my conveyer belt, old women would bend right over the checkouts in order to hand me their shrapnel and underage teenage girls, dressed as hookers, would try their luck purchasing cheap bottles of rosé and an assortment of different brightly coloured alcopops. Meanwhile, in the staff canteen, I would have to avoid looking at men's crotches as they sat indecorously on canteen benches or do my hardest to avoid glimpsing the often visible bra straps of some of my female colleagues whose inexpensive white shirts were often so translucent, they were almost entirely see-through.

One member of staff in particular who stirred up some rather definite bouts of 'looking' OCD was, perhaps unsurprisingly, ex-girlfriend Isabel. Isabel and I had, by this point, been broken up for a good few weeks but nonetheless my physical attraction towards her remained. So too did my view of her from the confines of my rather cramped little checkout. Sometimes, it was as much as I could do just to stay focused on the profusion of un-scannable broccoli or the constant sea of government subsidised powdered milk in front of me without succumbing to the urge just to peer into the cafe to watch her gliding around, as she so often did, like Mary Poppins, clearing up plates and taking food orders.

It would appear a particular hallmark of ex-lovers that they have this bizarre hyperawareness of everything the other is up to even after it has long ceased to be their concern. Perhaps it is the indelibility of intimacy (however paltry or fleeting) or the emotional upheaval of a messy breakup that keeps our attentions locked on our past relationships. Perhaps it is jealousy, habit or even just plain curiosity.

Whatever it was that made me want to keep on looking, I worried that my constant gawping might soon start to make Isabel feel violated. I feared that if she thought I was continuously staring at her that she might feel trapped, even frightened. And the more I tried not to look, the more I seemed to want to keep on doing it.

It is, it would seem, a curious impasse: of wanting not to look at a thing but feeling obliged to do so all at the very same time. The fact that Isabel would so frequently look back at me in return (possibly for all the same reasons), in many ways, did nothing at all to help assuage my ever-growing concerns. Instead, it seemed only to ever make me worry all the more; her looking at me, of course, meaning that there was always a much greater chance of my own viewing behaviour being clocked. And with each glance, with each momentary glimpse in her direction I could not help but wonder, *What if?* What if all my looking eventually drove her from her job? What would she do for money? Where would she go? Who would look after her?

'Proportion' is often the key word missing in the OCDers vocabulary. We affix ourselves to the drama, to this bizarre, almost incogitable mental embroidery. It was only *looking* that I could ever have been accused of in relation to Isabel and yet the consequence of this trifling and largely knee-jerk reflex could, at least to my own ailing mind, be responsible for seemingly the most unwelcomed and cataclysmic of outcomes. Unfortunately for me, it wasn't until much later on in my illness that I would come to learn of a whole series of heterodox and innovatory psychological labels peculiar to the language of OCD such as *catastrophising* and, of course, *magical thinking*.

Though back then, back when the neuroses surrounding this whole new looking dilemma - not to mention the rather warped conception of my own buirdly and atlantean efficacy - had all been quite new, I simply could not see the wood through the trees. For days, weeks, I worried about the effects my looking would have on Isabel. And not just the effects on Isabel but on me also. In particular, I worried profoundly about what all these new looking variables would do to the myriad rules I had made up only months beforehand. In this new world order, governed as it no doubt was by OCD, *rules* were everything. Now they had seemingly been undermined. Smashed to smithereens in fact. The stipulation that there needed to be at least *two* looking behaviours before any legitimate misgivings might be espoused on the part of the recipient did not cater for an oversensitive ex-girlfriend for whom it was clear only *one* looking activity was more than ample. The uncertainty was enough to make me sick to my stomach.

"The system is flawed," I wrote in my increasingly madcap diary. "This won't do. This won't do at all."

And so, in the absence of a functioning rule-based system, which, despite some obvious flaws, had served me well as a tried-and-tested code of practice, I found I now had to think fast on my feet; to devise, quickly, some new form of control strategies to stand in cogently in the short term. It did not take me long to come up with something lavishly self-harmful.

The first strategy that came almost axiomatically to mind had been *avoidance*; to simply hold off from looking at Isabel altogether; to expel fully her presence from my panoramic range of view. Not only, had I considered, might this be the most simple artifice for me to put into practice but would possibly also go some way in helping me to, as it were, 'get over' her emotionally; 'out of sight, out of mind' - *literally*! Unfortunately, this was always much easier said than done. The harder you try *not* to look, the greater the urge to do so. In much the same way as asking someone not to think about a pink elephant immediately conjures up that very simulacrum, the urge becomes consummated whether you like it or not.

And so onto the next steadfast stratagem which had been, admittedly, slightly more complex, involving the rather more cockeyed and nonsensical travail of 'testing'. OCD testing (*not* to be confused with ERP - more on that later) is a far less reported though nonetheless widespread OCD compulsion that is premised on the rather misguided conception that, in order to gain certainty over complex obsessions, one should first 'work out' parameters of safe behaviour by physically *testing* it. Sometimes, quite counter-intuitively, this can mean taking risks that our own OCD screams at us may, on some level at least, be unacceptable or even dangerous. But that, in the name of *certainty*, this might still be preferable - for example, eating the mouldy cereal you think you may have accidently given to the kids to make sure it doesn't poison you (and therefore poison the kids) or flicking through the images of *Gay Pages* to check it does not give you an erection (thereby categorically proving beyond all doubt that you are, unquestionably, one hundred percent *not* a homosexual). It should be noted here that, even when engaging in this form of *testing*, an OCDer is still never in danger of crossing the so-called moral threshold. As my latest therapist has often told me: "An OCDer will never cross their own bottom line."

Of course, this is no reassurance for the poor perturbed sufferer. Often blind to the truth and certainly unable to trust his or her own gut instincts, each so-called risk is like a dagger straight to the heart; an endless fall from grace; an all-too-familiar notification on *Zero Mission 2* flashing 'Game Over'. Nevertheless, it was with a terrible sense of unease and foreboding that I would purposefully look into the Morrison's cafe, each time firing my eyes at Isabel in short, determinable bursts; occasionally even fixating my gaze on her for whole seconds at a time. And every time I looked, I would hold my stare that bit longer. I was desperate to push the limits; to help determine what amount of looking felt acceptable or right.

Either by luck or simply courtesy of a far more sensitive inner *daemon* than I gave myself credit for possessing, Isabel never noticed any of these bizarre activities (or at least she never seemed to). Nor, as it turned out, did the testing do anything to calm or to quieten my burgeoning anxiety. Quite the opposite in fact: the more I tested, the more the uncertainty grew. Not to mention made me feel so guilty that at times I considered I might simply have no choice but to hand in my notice and be done with it. (Of course, I never did do this. For one, I knew that doing so might simply constitute *avoidance*, the first and arguably most extreme of the OCD stand-in strategies.)

In early 2010, after copious failed attempts at getting my looking at her 'right' (not to mention the fear that every shift I was *purposefully* running the risk of causing untold anguish), it was Isabel who finally left Morrisons to pastures new; first to become an occupational psychiatrist and then, later, a wife and full time mum. I remember vividly the day she left. "We said goodbye," I wrote in my diary, "she pecked me on the cheek at my checkout and I resisted one last time taking a glimpse of her hair, her legs, her long flowing Edwardian skirt as she travelled for the last time ever calmly and gracefully out of the revolving Morrison's doors."

A week or so later and Isabel's position in the cafe had been filled by an unattractive and outsized northern lass with greasy hair and a mouth full of fillings. By stark contrast to Isabel, this new replacement was a grubby looking piece with about as much grace and finesse as an Arctic musk ox. Not surprisingly, I had about as much urge to look at her as I had to read the full works of Eckhart Tolle or R D Laing.

"She's broken more crockery this week than the rest of the team combined," complained her cafe supervisor to me one afternoon in the canteen during break.

I smiled. It was, in so many ways, the best news I had heard in months.

Over the many years I have lived with OCD, it is undoubtedly the 'looking disorder' which had tied me up in the most knots; had left me so frequently feeling bewildered and frustrated as well as at a complete loss as to how to handle or prevent any of it from ruining entirely my quality of life. One of the main reasons for this, I have since concluded, is the rather intricate and contradictory way in which the various compulsions of this particular manifestation of my illness presented themselves. In many ways the urge to avoid and the urge to test are, despite both existing to alleviate anxiety and to ensure moral chastity, directives of a most contending nature.

Of course, this has had some serious bearing on treatment. In particular, it made it difficult to address each separate compulsion without accidentally engaging further in the rituals of the other. Below is an extract from my diary dated June 2009 which elucidates the quandary further:

If I look, I might be bad. If I don't look, I am denying myself the freedom to look as well as giving in to avoidance *compulsions. But then if I do look, I am testing myself (a compulsion). So maybe I shouldn't look. But if I don't look, I am denying myself the freedom to look...*

By resisting avoiding I was engaging in ritualizing. By resisting ritualizing, I was engaging in avoidance. There seemed to be no way out.

Unfortunately, once a life conundrum has been exposed, it is very difficult to come back to a point of half-knowledge; of amnesic concession. As a result of OCD, my looking at women remained unnatural for many months. It didn't *feel* right anymore; either I was looking too much or not allowing myself to look enough. Even the rules, which often I mistook for a solid compromise, a good and reliable guide for life, were synthetic and left grave room for doubt.

I would often go through all this with Jake in the car. I would nag him for answers; to indulge me in my restless appetence for solutions. Sometimes, he might be successful, momentarily, in quelling my unease but it would never last. We would be out drinking somewhere, usually a quiet pub up in North Norfolk, an attractive barmaid might be showing off a bit of cleavage and instantly the OCD cycle would begin all over. In these moments, the elementariness of looking would disappear faster than a rat up a drain pipe. Should I look? Shouldn't I look? Like forgetting how to tie your shoelaces or how to ride a bike, seemingly I had forgotten how to use my very own eyes.

As I hope you can imagine, losing touch with such a natural faculty, over time, became a most distressing and discomforting experience. It was exhausting and annoyingly ubiquitous. It was also incredibly unnerving. Often I wondered whether I might actually ever know true freedom again. Whether I might ever function 'normally'. Unfortunately for me, this compulsive dilemma would, over the weeks and months, not remain simply confined to attractive women. Or even just women. Indeed, by the end of it all, it stopped having anything to do with *sex* almost altogether as eventually, perhaps inevitably, my OCD woke up to its true potential.

Looking at women inappropriately was one thing but it hardly compared to other living objects such as old people, animals or even, dare I say it, *children*.

Once children were involved, I knew my illness would cripple me in ways not even I had dared to dread. The worst, as they say, was yet to come.

It is my experience of living with OCD that it always tries, where possible, to conjure the very worst case scenario; to generate as much possible anguish as it can and cause unspeakable mental devastation in its wake. For no one is this truer than for the OCDer with a heightened moral sensitivity. The worse the crime, the juicier the subject matter, the deeper the OCD will sink in its sharp, canine teeth.

Children in particular are, and have always been, an extremely sensitive and emotive subject matter; their need to be protected a fundamental and constitutive part of any upright, civilized society. Even as we speak, as I write this chapter, there are emotive headlines littering the news in the wake of a new report entitled *'Letting children be children'*. The report comes as a response to concern that children are being sexualised, in particular, by virtue of sexually explicit music videos, risqué pre-watershed TV and young girls acting as brand ambassadors in marketing campaigns aimed at children.

More recently, this topical debate has even found its way down to Norwich; featuring on the BBC television programme, *Question Time*, which took place in none other than Blackfriars Hall, located right here in the centre of the city not a million miles from where I still live with my parents. I did not attend, though watched it with my mum and dad in the lounge with both great interest and even greater dread.

My OCD regarding children affected me in much the same way as it had done with women (minus the sexual desire; that much at least I had managed to purge myself of during university). I feared looking inappropriately at a child as a result of the 'shall I look, shan't I look' monologue. What if I looked for too long? What if I briefly glanced at a child's crotch and someone saw? A man looking at a child, particularly in this day and age, is always under scrutiny. One false move may very well generate the wrong public impression: that such looking has been, in some way, *sexually* incited. After all, had we been talking about the fully mature anatomy of a grown female, the smallest of glimpses would most certainly have championed such uncomplimentary assumptions.

The thought that someone might think me a paedophile or, worse still, a child might *read into* my looking and suddenly become prematurely sexually aware scared me beyond all else. As with those less than scrupulous music videos and marketing campaigns now being bemoaned on *Question Time*, I feared that I too could be responsible for *sexualising* minors. Indeed, so scared was I of bringing such a colossal and deleterious outcome into being that, over time, I simply avoided children like the Black Death. I refused to walk passed primary or secondary schools and even stopped watching programmes like *2point4 Children* and *Malcolm in the Middle* (I'm not quite sure why I did this. After all, I knew only too well that there would be no chance of sexualising kids *over the TV*. At least, I *think* I knew that).

Though, in my heart of hearts, I knew this level of evasion would not remain a viable long term strategy. Blocking out great chunks of *life* never is.

"Expect the worst," Margo once told us in group. "Expect that, in all likelihood, you *will* encounter that which you most fear. For years, I had been afraid of everything from dogs' mess to wheelie bins. Trying to avoid these things, which were, of course, everywhere was only making matters worse; the unnecessary shock of encountering them each time only contributing to an already grievous state of anxiety."

A few months later, I would learn this lesson for myself. That, no matter how far we may try to run away, the OCD is always there, like Deputy Samuel Gerard from *The Fugitive* or even the ever relentless Javert in Victor Hugo's *Les Miserables*. It was an otherwise perfect summer's day and I was on the train to Southend (I was going to Southend to visit my nan who still lived down there) whereupon I found myself unexpectedly sat opposite a small boy playing with what appeared from my peripheral vision to be a bright red toy fire engine. "Look at my new toy," the little boy said to me, placing the engine onto his lap. "*Looook* at the red lights."

"Oh that's...err...that's very good," I replied, smiling diffidently, purposefully not looking at the toy positioned but a few millimetres from the boy's trouser front.

"You're not *looking,*" insisted the child, a look of annoyance knitted just above his eyebrows.

"I am...I...I..."

"Why aren't you looking? *Look*!" Immediately, my anxiety began to rise to almost ungovernable levels.

"Look, look, look, look, *look!*" the incessant chanting was now almost too much to bear until...

-"Come away now. Leave the nice man alone," eventually cried out the boy's mum in the seat behind, finally and in the same way dog owners will only ever bother to intervene the very moment their beloved flesh eating canines are about to tear off a huge lump of human skin with their long, mammalian cuspids.

"I'm not Mummy," insisted the snotty child, and putting down the fire engine on the seat next to him. "I'm *not* annoying the nice man!"

It was, in many senses, the *'nice man'* that had gotten to me the most, rankling duly through me like a very large and painful injection of potassium chloride. It was perhaps only by luck that on this occasion I had managed to escape the incident relatively unscathed, having avoided the urge to look and thus remaining, no less by the skin of my teeth, a 'good person'. Though I knew it would be perhaps only a matter of time before I did look inappropriately. That I transgressed my own rules. And the fear of doing this, of thereby becoming almost at once a loathsome human being, made me want to shut myself away, sleep like I had been cryogenically frozen and never wake again.

Of all of my OCD symptoms, my recovery from the 'looking disorder', particularly in relation to children, was perhaps the longest and hardest and was often met only with blank faces and brick walls by the professionals. There is very little published on this form of OCD and even less information available at doctors' surgeries and clinics. For those sufferers less familiar with some of the universal hallmarks of their disorders, I can imagine that this absence of information must serve only to add to what is already an extraordinarily isolating and baffling condition. From a clinical diagnostic point of view, it is perhaps all too easy for anomalous compulsions such as those mentioned above to lead to misunderstandings as to their meaning as well as even to out-and-out misdiagnosis.

According to Fred Penzel, Ph.D, founding member of the International Obsessive-Compulsive Disorder Foundation (IOCDF), OCD occurs "in a great variety of forms" and this can lead to an even greater number of sufferers not receiving "proper diagnosis of treatments". This he blames on the symptoms "not fitting the usual stereotypes associated with OCD" and the lack of information available on such symptoms. He cites in his article *'Here's Looking at You, Kid: People with OCD who notice things too much'* the example of a female patient, Marie, who cannot stop staring at the sexual body parts of her work colleagues. She somehow manages to convince herself that she is crazy or perverted or both because she cannot keep her focus away from the intimate areas of others.

When, eventually, she receives the help she so desperately needs, she is "surprised" to find out the problem is in fact OCD.

From this, Penzel contends that it is of vital importance that the proper information exists out there so that misunderstandings and misdiagnoses become far less frequent in the future:

"Although they [lesser well known forms of OCD] are not as well-known as some other forms of the disorder, they do affect numbers of people, and I think it is helpful for them to read about them, in order to see that they are not alone, and to help them to get some direction in finding treatment. My other hope is that clinicians learning to treat OCD will also become more aware that these problems really are OCD, or at least OCD related, and diagnose and treat them appropriately."

Often I had found it hard, almost impossible at times, to shake the feeling that my looking was not because I was a raging pervert; a bon vivant, a libertine, a *lecher*. Although my own understanding of OCD has always been fairly robust, in the absence of adequate information and professional advice (not to mention frequent and powerful twangs of self-reproach that crashed against me like waves against the seashore) I had found it difficult to convince myself of the rather more rational premise that my looking problems really were just symptoms of OCD.

In times of doubt, it is important to remember that OCD, despite having many different faces, is nearly always the same. "If it feels like OCD," warns Dr Schwartz, "then it probably is". As I have said before, the technical manifestations may differ but the fundamentals are, as it were, immutable. It is a lesson that I try not to forget.

It is a lesson that I hope you too will not forget either.

Chapter 12
"THE *RULE* OF LAW"

"Rules and responsibilities: these are the ties that bind us. We do what we do, because of who we are. If we did otherwise, we would not be ourselves. I will do what I have to do. And I will do what I must."
— Neil Gaiman, *The Sandman: Book of Dreams*

In June 2009, with more than a degree of gladness and after over five years of service as a complaining, ill-tempered check-out operator, I handed my notice in at Morrisons to pursue a career in law. It had come only days after an official letter of acceptance from Anglia Ruskin Law School and at first I had been over the moon.

"We're so very proud of you Aron," my parents had offered. "Our son, the *lawyer*."

And in many ways, admittedly, I had shared in their enthusiasm. Upon starting out promptly at this first-rate professional research facility in September, I liked the people on my course immensely and found the county town of Chelmsford to be much tamer and less hostile than the grittier and much more brutal city of Lancaster. Each day, I would journey to and from Chelmsford on the London Liverpool Street line to the Rivermead Campus on the banks of the River Chelmer which had both surprised me with its modern, colourful architecture and which had also quite effortlessly upstaged the comparatively bland, concrete jungle from whence I graduated two years earlier as a mere *Legum Baccalaureus*.

On top of the locale and the people (which, in case I hadn't mentioned earlier, was comprised *ninety percent* of women), I liked, on the whole, my lecturers as well as the canteen food (where they would serve dishes as extravagant as stroganoff and chicken curry just for lunch). I had even been quite impressed by the snazzy little Airblade hand dryers installed in pretty much all of the men's toilets which dried your hands in almost seconds and meant you didn't have to rely on the less hygienic cloth towel dispensers which I always feared simply wiped other people's germs straight back onto my hands (for those of you with contamination OCD it is possibly worth noting that research has proven that it is almost indisputably the other way around: that blow dryers, as opposed to hand towels, are the less hygienic due to the bacteria or fungi that tend to grow inside and which then gets blasted out).

Though one thing I did hate quite passionately was all the travelling. The long journeys to Essex and back on a daily basis were tiring and, worse still, seemed always to offer far too much time to think. In perhaps not too dissimilar a way as the trips to and from Lancaster only a few years earlier, time spent besieged in noisy, overcrowded train carriages (or cornered and trapped in the cramped inter-carriage if I was particularly unlucky) made me somewhat frightened and uneasy.

"The feeling of foreboding before a long trip on public transport," I wrote in my diary, "has never failed to elicit such profound symptoms of OCD. By the end of a journey I am nearly always a quivering wreck; never quite the person I was before I started." (It is perhaps little wonder that my two favourite songs at the time were *'Fear of Trains'* by the Indie *noisepop* band *The Magentic Fields* and '*National Express'* by the one and only *Divine Comedy*.)

Then there was the course itself. Although I had always loved the law - the principles, the social theories, the *history* - I found the Legal Practice Course (or LPC) - to be an experience quite disparate from the relatively abstract, carefree time studying as an undergraduate. By contrast to those rather casual and thought-provoking colloquia at university, law school was dry, meticulous and cumbersome. It forced us to look at bodies of regulations such as the Pre-Action Protocols, the Solicitor's Code of Conduct and, my own particular pet hate, the Civil Procedure Rules in lacklustre and painstaking detail. Some days, during the very driest of our lectures on the CPR or the various Practice Directives, it was enough just to stop myself running off to the bathroom to slit my own wrists with a particularly sharp, straight blade utility knife such was the level of sheer monotony.

Rules, in many ways - and on top of being deadly boring to learn about - are the antithesis of what it means to be free and even human. They appeal to our servility whilst, simultaneously, taking away our self-determinism so that we become nothing more than mere cellular shells, biotic automatons. And whilst some rules are no doubt essential for at least a partially functioning society, providing certainty and safeguarding rights and freedoms, others tend to fall down the all-too-easy trap of being either too draconian or, worse still, wholly prejudiced to suit a particular regime or agenda; *"Religions that are detrimental to Democratic Kampuchea and the people of Kampuchea are absolutely forbidden"* (Constitution of the Kyhmer Rouge); *"Marriages between Jews and of German or kindred blood are forbidden*" (Section 1 of the Nuremberg laws); *"Whoever, when the United States is at war, shall willfully...utter, print, write, or publish any disloyal, profane, scurrilous, or abusive language about the form of government of the United States...shall be punished by a fine of not more than*

$10,000 or imprisonment for not more than 20 years, or both" (The Sedition Act of 1918, United States of America).

"Any fool can make a rule," goes the popular expression by Henry David Thoreau, "and any fool will mind it."

It is a proverb with which I find myself now in almost one hundred percent agreement. Though it would be untrue of me to say that this had always been so. It would also be untrue to say that *all* of me recoiled from the relentless (and often dangerous) minutiae of rules so shrinkingly and so absolutely. In fact, to my own frustration and greater mistrust, my impish OCD seemingly loved the notion of *rules*. As the weeks at law school dragged by, the numerous legal precisions, the rigid codification and legal doctrine - aside from being duller than a grey sky in Morecambe - had seemingly provided an almost delicious pretext for my own neurotic mind-set; their structured arrangements and unequivocal lexicon capturing my imagination and helping to formulate my own set of OCD edicts and maxims. Based very similarly on the 'Looking Rules' I had made only a few months earlier, these rigorous laws would serve as a primary way of regulating my behaviour, ensuring I always conducted myself morally and appropriately at all times. One evening, in my ever misguided zeal, I wrote the below in my diary:

How does one truly avoid being bad? Is it even possible? I have been told, perhaps too many times now, I need simply to trust my gut instincts. That my intuition should be like my guiding beacon. And yet, it strikes me now that it would be truly ludicrous to trust such a flawed and antediluvian process so fully. How do I know, for example, that I am not naturally a psychopath? Could my natural urges be so readily complied with if that were truly the case? Moreover, how can I be sure that my own particular understanding of morality mirrors that of everyone else? How can I be sure that my moral compass may not, at one time or another, betray me or become overridden by emotion or temporarily broken? No, there must be something greater, something more concrete than mere flimsy intuition. Something which can both enjoin us to perform as well as provide us with a degree of certainty and, ultimately, safeguard us against harm.

How could I have missed it earlier; the answer is quite simple. The solution to all of this, undoubtedly, are rules.

And so, as the year at law school went on, I found myself drawn into this new preoccupation with rule-making like matter into a black hole, the life-blood being drawn out of me painfully and slowly as if undergoing a particularly savage medieval blood-letting. Very soon, rules had replaced almost everything else; instead of analysing *people* (a pursuit which often gave me great amounts of pleasure, particularly when aimed towards women I fancied) I analysed the rules; instead of writing in my diary about my day, I would cover the pages of my hyperbolic journal with endless practice directions and edicts. And not just in my journal. I wrote them on the train (on the back of lecture notes), I wrote them as draft text messages on my mobile phone; I even wrote them on the back of old shopping receipts. It was like having a brand new glistening pastime but without any of the attendant pleasure. And yet, to my illogical (or perhaps *overly* logical) mind, this was perhaps an almost indispensable way of ensuring my happiness: Rules='good'=*safe*='happy`.

Here are a few examples of some of the rules I made:

Rule 03

It is prohibited to think about sex in a public place (for the risk it poses of effectuating an erection) if any one of the following conditions are met;

i. *There is at least a 50/50 chance of children being present*

ii. *There is a at least a 50/50 chance of children becoming present at some imminent point in the future*

iii. *The environment remains static i.e. not simply 'walking through'*

iv. *The erection cannot be readily obscured*

v. *There is already a small physiological 'stirring' in the genital region*

Failure to comply with the above will render the perpetrator guilty of 'nascent paedophilia' and thus unforgiveable for a period no sooner than 5 years.

Rule 18

It is prohibited to lie to a girl before engaging in any form of sexual relations with her if two or more of the below are satisfied:

i. *A 'lasting' false impression is created*

ii. *That lasting false impression puts the liar in a favourable light*

iii. *The girl in question is engaging in said sexual relations in reliance on that false impression*

Failure to comply with the above constitutes an offence of 'non-consensual sex by deception', rendering the perpetrator unforgiveable for a period no sooner than 10 years.

Rules were, at least by design, a means by which I could remain feeling protected and in control. Paradoxically they were also, as I was later to discover much to my own regret, a pretty first-rate way of putting my whole future career into mild but palpable jeopardy. Unfortunately for me, by the time law school had ended, I had been so completely preoccupied with creating rules for everyday life, so utterly exhausted by the process of regulating every aspect of my existence that I had taken my eye off the ball almost completely when it came to my *real* law work. My final results were a fail in nearly every one of my core modules. That is with the exception of just one subject area.

Somehow, by the skin of my teeth, I had managed to scrape a pass in the one legal field that had perhaps always interested me the most (possibly because of how close it was to resembling a true rule-based morality): yes, you guessed it, *criminal law*. Being somewhat obsessed with standards of morality and social theory, I had always found myself fascinated by the way in which the Criminal Justice System seemed to both converge and diverge from morality in almost equal parts. Why were some morally contentious issues such as adultery, heresy and pornography permissible without limitation under the law yet other, arguably defensible acts, such as the medicinal use of cannabis and certain forms of prostitution, proscribed outright? What was the relationship between the Criminal Justice System and social morality? And why were some moral issues made into *rules* whilst others seemingly ignored or brushed aside?

With all these deeper questions floating around in my head, my OCD generating an almost unquenchable thirst for answers, it perhaps made a sort of sense that it be within this particular legal arena that I would invariably display the most natural aptitude.

A month or so after law school had ended, I eventually found myself a job. Somehow, I am not sure how, I had managed to put rule-making aside for long enough to concentrate on securing myself a place as a trainee solicitor in a small but highly successful provincial criminal law firm back down in Essex. The firm was called Kohlberg & Green LLP which, as it turned out, was but a stone's throw from where I had grown up in Southend-on-Sea in the fairly large and relatively new town of Basildon. The job would inevitably mean moving back down to Essex, away from Norwich; away from my friends and family. Arguably, it had been moving away from home up north which had been one of the biggest triggers of my OCD. Now, already ridden by painstaking rituals and obsessions, not to mention endless *rule-making*, I had decided, somewhat in two minds, to take the same, though technically reverse, course of action all over again.

"Are you sure you're ready for this?" my dad said one afternoon, concerned, particularly after my "funny period" up in Lancaster, that all this might just be too much for me.

"No," I said truthfully. "But what can I do? I can't let my OCD rule my life. I can't let it stop me realising my future."

"Between an uncontrolled escalation and passivity," warns Dominique de Villepin, French Minister of Foreign Affairs between 2002 and 2004, "there is a demanding road of responsibility that we must follow". It was unclear to me exactly whether a career as a solicitor of all things constituted *uncontrolled escalation* or the rather more desirable middle ground - "the road to responsibility" - but it was a risk I felt almost compelled to take. I owed it to myself. I owed it to my family and all the investment they had placed in my education and on my financial security to date. And so it was, that following September, having completed a whole year doing nothing but studying and wasting time with totally unnecessary mental rituals, I packed my bags, said goodbye once more to my parents, and decided, somewhat reticently, to make *rules* my new career. *If you can't beat them, join them,* goes the age-old maxim. It would be a choice I would come to both rejoice and lament in almost equal measure.

The very first rule I remember being met with in my new career as a criminal lawyer had been 'The Working Time regulations'. Being a solicitor, as I was soon to discover, was not a nine-to-five job. Nor was it a career that accommodated much in the way of a social life. Thus my very first sacrifice had been to sign a piece of paper stating that I would not object to working in excess of 48 hours a week for pretty much the rest of my working life. As it later transpired, it would not be unreasonable some weeks to expect to work in excess of seventy plus hours. One week, during the very beginning of my traineeship when everything still seemed like a rushed blur, it's possible I had worked ten hours straight every day for the best part of a fortnight.

Of course, nothing at school or university could have prepared me for such a striking intensification. Not even law school, with its emphasis on procedures and working practice, had offered any insight into the actual working day of a trainee solicitor. "If you think you have it hard now," said one hateful lecturer who we all disliked with similar acerbity, "then you just wait..." Somehow, I couldn't help but wish I had taken greater heed.

And so I worked. I worked and worked and worked, sometimes right until around ten or eleven at night. I would be writing up case notes or researching legal precedents or finishing off a particularly complex brief to counsel. A great chunk of the time I would be down the local cop shop shadowing the duty solicitor and learning how to advise drunken clients and handle awkward police officers who refused to give any preliminary disclosure (a frequent occurrence).

When I wasn't *in* work, I would find myself thinking or more aptly, *worrying*, about work. It did not help that all of the partners at the firm were especially strict and I found myself spending ever increasing periods outside of the office drawing up to-do lists and booking bail-back appointments with OICs just to avoid falling behind the next day and getting an almighty bollocking. As for the weekends, these supposedly restful bookends, these were invariably filled with catching up on useful reading or, on the odd occasion, standing in as duty solicitor (which of course meant the chance to go home and visit family and friends was greatly reduced, if not totally non-existent).

And yet, all that taken into account, it would be untrue to suggest that my life at Kohlberg & Green LLP was ever total hell. Far from it in fact. Despite some often very long hours and equally frightening bosses (not to mention a few all-nighters with fat Pauline, our designated supervisor, who made it quite clear from the start that she *hated* me with a passion comparable only to my own strong dislike for iceberg lettuces (which, irritatingly, had never once seemed to want to scan throughout my entire five years as an unhappy checkout operator)), the work itself was always remarkably interesting and, from the off, I was given every opportunity to throw myself right in.

Like, for example, the trial I was given to clerk at Basildon Crown Court after literally only a week or so in the job. Alan Stone, one of the senior partners, had instructed me to assist in the case of one of our most prolific clients - we'll call him Client X - up on a fourteen count indictment for sexual offences and I had literally jumped at the chance. It was a complicated, ghastly trial and had even been high profile enough to warrant drafting in one of chambers' very best advocates, the indomitable Maria Wainwright. The night before the trial began, I had sat up at the dining room table wading through the advanced disclosure, unused material and s.9 statements as well as read carefully all the witness statements from the four or so ill-fated victims, some of them as young as only fourteen years old. The accounts were harrowing, *tear-jerking* in parts. At other points, the content was almost wholly unreadable. And yet I simply loved the case from beginning to end.

It was a far cry from the lacklustre, often darn right pleonastic assignments we were forced to do at law school and for that I was everlastingly grateful.

People often ask me, now that I no longer work in criminal law, how I could possibly have managed to defend any man (or woman) as depraved and malevolent as Client X undoubtedly was. "It must have eaten you up inside," said one friend, actually quite recently, "especially with your OCD". And yet, perhaps surprisingly, I had never really viewed it like this. Instead I relished the chance to immerse myself in something so controversial, so delicious and *gritty*.

Ironically, I never once saw my efforts in criminal defence work as *immoral*. 'Equality before the law'. It was, if not totally essential, then certainly the cornerstone principle of a true and meaningful democracy.

There is this beautiful quote from the book and film *'A Man of All Seasons'* by Robert Bolt which I had read as a young man and which, to me, summed up the position perfectly. It takes the form of a debate between Thomas Moore, the protagonist, and the Witch Hunter William Roper:

William Roper: So, now you give the Devil the benefit of law!
Sir Thomas More: Yes! What would you do? Cut a great road through the law to get after the Devil?
William Roper: Yes, I'd cut down every law in England to do that!
Sir Thomas More: Oh? And when the last law was down, and the Devil turned 'round on you, where would you hide, Roper, the laws all being flat? This country is planted thick with laws, from coast to coast, Man's laws, not God's! And if you cut them down, and you're just the man to do it, do you really think you could stand upright in the winds that would blow then? Yes, I'd give the Devil benefit of law, for my own safety's sake!

That a set of moral codes, binding and justly administered, is desirable, in many ways, goes without saying. What is often less clear (and what became less and less clear to me not long after starting at Kohlberg & Green LLP) is whether the law - or at least, certain *substantive* elements of it - are always so morally sound. The law, as with the practice of it, has attracted varying degrees of criticism and condemnation over the centuries. And often for good reason. Despite the benefits of a rule-based system in providing a degree of certainty and impartiality, there are indubitably numerous difficulties, not to mention injustices, emanating from a one-size fits all system. Laws passed, rules promulgated are only ever as good or competent or, indeed, empathic as those enacting them. Aside from the more extreme laws proffered earlier on in this chapter, there are perhaps numerous examples even in our own legal system of the most incompetent and injudicious legislation.

Some of it still persists to this very day.

In my opinion, one of the biggest flaws of our current legal system is the way it in which it treats people who are not deemed as strictly 'rational' or who fall outside of the norm in terms of mental capacity. Despite having come on such a long way since the days of county asylums and the Lunacy Committee, the law is still, in many ways, dangerously unreflective when it comes to mental health. Where it does take note of the large minority of those living with some form or another of mental frailty or distress, it often goes far too far in applying harmful or, otherwise, unhelpful labels. There seems, at present, to be little in the way of a happy medium.

In his book, *'Law and Mental Health; A case-based approach'*, Robert G.Meyer describes it thus: "The legal profession cannot afford the luxury of conducting empirical research that would apply to each individual who comes through a courtroom."

In other words, the law is not able to accommodate *everyone*. It simply hasn't got the time or the resources. And this has had some massive ramifications, particularly on those with mental illness. From a *criminal* law perspective, the most controversial of these rather broad stroke approaches without doubt is the 'reasonable person' test. This so-called *objective* diagnostic used in establishing guilt or innocence in criminal trials, has long been criticised as representing a clear predisposition in favour of those fortunate enough to have the benefit of clear and accurate insight. It protects those who are deemed to function 'normally' whilst failing to cater for those with impairments, often outside of their own control. For more on this, there is a brilliant book by Mayo Moran, *'Rethinking the Reasonable Person: An Egalitarian Reconstruction of the Objective Standard'*.

Unfortunately, it is not just criminal law where such clear biases in the legal system occur. Under current UK employment law for example, people with certain mental conditions (including OCD) are actually precluded from such positions of responsibility as Company Director or even becoming members of parliament. Quite shockingly, The Juries Act 1974, still in effect at the time of writing, states that of those ineligible to sit on a jury, patients with mental health conditions are prohibited under Schedule I. This includes anyone who has a "psychopathic disorder, mental handicap or severe mental handicap, and on account of that condition either is resident in a hospital or other similar institution, or regularly attends for treatment by a medical practitioner".

Regrettably, *ashamedly*, OCD is still incorporated under this rather primitive characterisation of mental illness. When I heard the news actually only quite recently, I could not quite believe my ears. Not only do I find this an insult to the many highly intelligent, thoroughly discerning sufferers up and down the country, who I am in no doubt would serve so well as well-functioning Jurors, but it is also indicative of a flawed and half-cocked strategy on behalf of the Criminal Justice System to keep the process of deliberation a purely 'rational' one. So far as I am aware, no one is currently excluded from jury service under UK legislation for being a chauvinist, a homophobe, a closet racist, a militant feminist or even a religious fanatic; all these groups holding often to a whole plethora of strange, if not wholly inflexible prepossessions and viewpoints.

Recently, I got a chance at a national conference to speak with fellow OCD sufferer and MP for Broxbourne, Charles Walker, who, only a few months earlier, had rather bravely announced his condition in parliament, referring to himself jocosely as a 'practicing fruitcake'. I asked him about the Juries Act 1974 and how injudicious I felt it was. Being quite vocal and often abrupt in such political matters, I asked him what was being done about it. He advised that the law was hopefully set to change. "I cannot give you the finer details," he told me insistently, "but trust me when I say that it is most certainly in hand". He directed me to take a look at the notes from Hansard which were published online and so I did. The entry for November 2012, still available today, proposes some amendments to the Mental Health (Discrimination) (No.2) Bill and sets to lift, amongst other things, the bar on potential jurors receiving *voluntary* treatment. It seemed, at least in some small way, like a promising development.

In many other ways, however, the legal position, particularly in relation to the Criminal Justice System, had left a rather bitter taste in my mouth. Upon joining Kohlberg & Green LLP in 2009, ignorant to most of these legal prejudices and certainly not deeming myself to be 'irrational', I had not told anyone about my OCD. At the time, I did not consider it relevant. Now, in light of some of the wider and harsher judgements of the law itself, I couldn't help but question my aptitude more assiduously. Indeed, whether a career upholding a set of exclusionary principles and requiring, as it did, razor-sharp and detached legal *objectivity*, was something someone in my condition could truly ever master. The doubt generated over this rather desultory exigency, this new potential for failure, was, in many senses, a most unsettling knock to my confidence.

It would not, by any means, be the only knock during my very brief career as a criminal lawyer.

Ah yes, *failure*. The net result of our having lost all control, of no longer being in command of the outcomes or events in our lives. For an OCDer, the *prospect* of failure is nearly always a million times worse than the reality of it. Quite perversely, failure, when it comes - and it will come to all of us at some point - is often quite liberating. Or at least, it has been for me.

As the months working at Kohlberg & Green went on, so the pressures of real life mounted. The work was tough and the partners tougher still. They would howl when we didn't read 'All-staff' emails properly or understand how to use the air conditioning; they would rip up our work if it was too waffly or even fractionally inaccurate and woe betide me if I ever wore my single breasted Merino wool suit jacket to court with any of the buttons done up (as invariably I did to hide my bulging muffin top which I still felt unshakably self conscious of); "Undo your button *Gordon,*" Alan Stone would bellow. "It makes you look stuffy in front of the clients."

Of course, it did not help that I had not a practical bone in my body by the time I had rather naively left higher education and set upon this new career as a legal eagle. To put my lack of practical ability into some form of perspective, by the age of ten, I was still wearing Velcro shoes (unable to tackle laces until the summer before secondary school), couldn't make a cup of coffee until I was nineteen and my first kiss wasn't until I had left home for university. As I write this chapter, I cannot burp (in fact I have never burped; not even with the aid of fizzy drinks) and I am still unable to ride a bike (my friends at sixth form, upon hearing this news and being totally shocked by it, later tried to teach me on the spacious fields of Wacton Common. Needless to say, they had failed miserably).

How much of this inability to function practically is down to OCD, I cannot say. I certainly believe that a lifetime of intrusive thinking, of spending so much of my life stuck in the relative (un)safety of my own head, did not help. Certainly it had not fostered a more 'balanced' grounding. Now, all these years later, I found that it had affected quite palpably my ability to cope out in the *real* world; a world of courtrooms and judges, hard-bitten criminals, toughened police officers and, of course, case-hardened solicitors. Much of the time during my traineeship, I found myself to be nothing short of a fish out of water.

There are perhaps numerous examples of my practical failings during my time as a trainee solicitor but there is maybe one incident that stands out in particular to me now. It occurred on a Wednesday morning down at the magistrates' court and for the first time in my legal career, I questioned whether I was truly up to the challenges that my academic life, thus far, had led up to so perfunctorily and yet so apathetically.

Just to give you a bit of background, Wednesday mornings at Southend Magistrates' Court were always the very busiest. Offenders charged with an offence, unless they had been remanded in custody for a more serious crime, would nearly always be bailed to attend court midweek. During which time they would be introduced to our very own Alan Stone who would, in turn, take down their instructions, fill out a CDS 14 (legal aid form) and then represent them in front of the district judge or magistrates' bench.

That particular Wednesday morning, Alan Stone, busy with a rather pressing 'plea before venue' for one of our best and most frequent Kohlberg & Green clients - with no less than an impressive seventeen separate antecedent offences under his belt - had delegated the task of filling in the CDS 14 across to little old me. "It's for the lady over there on the bench," said Alan Stone, pointing rather haphazardly over to the drugged-up looking harridan slumped on the seat in front of the far courtroom. "Go away and fill out a Legal Aid form." Though never one for paperwork, and not having ever completed a form like this before, I literally blanched in fear. Slowly, painstakingly, I started to fill out the terrifying green form, doing my utmost not to make any mistakes - you weren't even allowed to go over the lines - when, no sooner had I rather cautiously and costively finished completing the last line of the client's address (and about to fill in section 29 on *Interests of Justice*), there was this loud, thundering clamour which shook me to the core; "What are you playing at?" howled a seething Alan Stone, his bellowing voice echoing magniloquently down the corridor.

At once, I looked up, like a rabbit caught in extra aggressive *HID* headlights and could not find the words to respond. Instead, I just stood there like a large, knobbly Amalfi lemon, smiling pathetically, gripped by anxiety.

"Have you not finished this yet! How can I trust you to represent clients if you can't even fill out a basic form!" Alan continued to yell, his eyes mad, his mouth frothing like an extra frothy mocha latte. "And why do you always look so *nervous*! Stop looking nervous!"

"Bu...bu...bu...bu"

I looked down at my feet, nervously not being able even to make eye contact. Indeed, if *stopping* me looking nervous had been Alan Stone's intention that very morning, he had perhaps only gone about achieving the very opposite; such a reprimand being nothing short of an ingenious method of both perpetuating my uneasy disposition as well as making permanent my pre-existing countenance.

"I'm really not sure you're cut out for this Aron," said Alan, finally, looking at my pallid skin and frightened eyes. "Perhaps this just isn't the job for you."

I looked down once more at my feet. I felt like giving up. I felt like crying my eyes out. Instead I decided to ring up Jake.

"I'm really not sure I can hack this," I said, miserably and scared over the phone that evening.

"You'll be fine," Jake responded firmly but sympathetically.

"But what if..." (*What if.* It had been a phrase I had made every conscious effort upon leaving home a second time to avoid. Now, in light of such brutal castigation, I felt almost justified in using it again.)

"You just have to give it a go Aron. You have nothing to lose."

And he, of course, was right. I did, in all fairness, have nothing to lose. Indeed, even Alan Stone himself had offered the following solace: "If you don't like it here, you can simply just leave. At the very least, regardless of whether we keep you on, you'll come away with a completed training contract under your belt." Consequently, over the next few weeks, like a snivelling kid having fallen off his bike and reattempting to get back on without stabilizers (oh how I know how that feels), I tried again. And despite remaining, at times, almost implausibly impractical, I hoped that the skills I did have would more than make up for this rather trifling shortfall. Academically, for example, I had always stood out: I had passed my Eleven plus (or selection exam as it is now known), gone to a grammar school, received a combination of 9 A's and A*'s at GCSE, 3 A's at A-level, The Humanities award for my school, a Norfolk County Scholarship for excellence in my field of study plus attained a pretty decent law degree from Lancaster University. Moreover, I was fairly good at public speaking, was pretty eloquent on paper and could grasp some of the more complicated facets of the law with little difficulty (my fellow students at law school had always been amazed by how easily I had grasped complex parts of land law such as prescriptive easements and adverse possession).

Surely, all that was enough? Surely all this highlighted my inherent worth, to borrow a familiar phrase, *beyond all reasonable doubt*? Unfortunately, as is so often the case when you are no more than a little fish swimming around in a massive great fuck-off pool, I would have to physically *prove* my capabilities. Or else fall flat on my face trying. The opportunity would come sooner than I anticipated.

A few weeks later, following the incident at the magistrates' court, I found myself stuck, once again, alone with the inimitable Alan Stone. I was in his office, getting him to check over my latest brief (which I had spent literally hours outside of the office preparing) when all of a sudden Alan turned to me, poised and with what seemed a particularly adventitious question to throw at me: "What do you know," he said teasingly, "about *the Criminal Procedure Rules?*" I paused for a moment in contemplation. It was certainly an odd subject to bring up and I was somewhat perplexed by his sudden and outwardly random inquisition.

Nevertheless, I could not at the same time help but feel ever so slightly smug. The *criminal* procedure, designed, in part, to mirror the *Civil* Procedure Rules was something I actually knew a fair bit about. Due primarily to my fervent OCD, I identified with these rules almost as intimately as some orthodox Christians are familiar with the canon of the New Testament. Though I knew that Alan would not expect me to know anything at all about them and so I decided to play this to my advantage.

"Well!" said Alan, impatiently, waiting for some sort of maundering, tongue-tied response from me. "What do you know about them then? Come on son. Speak up. Don't hold back."

And so, confidently and dare I say eloquently, I let rip: "The Criminal Procedure Rules," I said, repeating the words back for effect "if I am right in saying, which I believe I am, are a set of regulations, subdivided into 76 separate parts, which correspond to the various stages of a criminal case. They exist to ensure maximum fairness and efficiency throughout the entire legal process with the overriding objective being that all cases are dealt with justly."

And with that the room went dead. Literally, a pin-drop could be heard. Alan Stone eventually looked up at me dumbfounded, his jaw dropped so far down that for a moment he looked like something out of a Tex Avery cartoon. And then, for the first time since I had started at the firm over two month ago, he *smiled* at me. His smile was so warm and encouraging I felt almost like I could wrap myself up in it and float away. But in seconds the smile was over; his face dropped back, he pushed his glasses up from his rather large apex and resumed, rather too comfortably, his previously serious deportment.

"You're a fucking dichotomy Aron," he told me frazzled and somewhat effete, "a fucking dichotomy."

As the weeks went on, so the success stories racked up. Unfortunately so too did the mishaps. My lack of practical ability and common sense let me down on more occasions than I care to admit to. Constantly I forgot to shave or to undo my suit jacket. Persistently I lost my way at Crown Court or disremembered important clients' names. And whilst my memory in relation to case law, the Criminal Procedure Rules and PACE was second-to-none, when it came to booking bail-backs, collecting parcels from the Document Exchange and remembering to file travel expenses, I was positively awful.

Consequently, in late June, and after a few sleepless nights in deep but distressing ratiocination, I eventually came to the mewl and rather whimpering conclusion that a career in criminal law just wasn't for me. "Thank you for the opportunity," I said to Alan Stone, sincerely, as I handed him a handwritten letter detailing my reasons for leaving. (I did not tell him about my OCD. Instead, I simply made some excuse up about being homesick and missing my family and friends back in Norwich - which, actually, wasn't so much of a fib.)

"Well you know where we are if you ever change your mind," said Alan, quite genuinely, in response. It was perhaps the most positive thing he had ever said to me.

In so many ways, I cannot help but regret having turned my back entirely on a career in law. I do not feel I was driven out. Nor do I believe that it couldn't have worked. Just that my OCD, or perhaps even just my general character, had made life difficult. Sometimes nigh on impossible. I guess I'll never know just how far I might have been able to carry on had I resolved more determinedly to persevere or, even, whether or not I could have made the whole thing a glistening success.

Nevertheless, my ventures into criminal law were certainly not all for nothing. If anything, my time away had actually had a most positive impact on my OCD and, in particular, on the rather profligate rule-making. At long last and after so many months of unadulterated mental torture, I had started to see things in much greater perspective. I had worked with rapists, murderers, drug dealers and human traffickers. I had been involved with everything from child abuse cases to airport hijackings to multiple count conspiracies to commit armed robbery. All of which involved serious breaches of the law, major departures from the *rules*. And yet, even some of these so-called *low-lives* I had found to be fundamentally decent, their reasons for acting the way they had often a result of extraordinarily difficult circumstances and/or intolerably poor socialisation. Or even, in some unfortunate cases, full on coercion. For example, a girl I had helped represent, wailing with remorse, cried of a sexually abusive father and a callous and violent drug-dealing boyfriend (to whom she referred simply as 'the cunt'). Following two years of grooming and enslavement by the latter, she had gone from prostitution to, more recently, being forced into swallowing twenty cocaine capsules in an attempt to smuggle them discreetly into the country from Jamaica.

In so many ways, the great swathes of human fodder we so thoroughly represented were every bit as much a victim of circumstance as they were a cold or implacable perpetrator of crime. They were certainly, it struck me, not all beyond *forgiveness*. And on that basis, and for the those brilliantly pellucid moments of clarity, I knew, from a moral-visceral far deeper than my own rather more turbid OCD, that it was not merely an adherence to *rules* that made a person either worthwhile or wicked, virtuous or deficient, good or *bad*.

Following my rather terse period as a trainee solicitor in Essex, surrounded everywhere by fundamentally amoral rules and regulations, it did not take long to conclude that real life was not anywhere near as, well, *black and white* as my OCD had tried so doggedly to convince me. Certainly it was far less stark and uncompromising. "Never shall I make another rule again." Or so I promised myself with good intentions after my very last day in the legal profession, packing up my things and handing over my heavy workload of files and case notes to the poor sap whom would no doubt have to replace me. A few days later, my dad came to pick me up and drive me back home to Norwich and it was then that I made a sort of pact with myself. That I would not allow myself to ever become so enveloped by my illness again. That this would be, irrefutably, the first day of the rest of my OCD-free life. I was going to stay firmly, to quote directly the advice oft given to our clients, on the 'straight and narrow'.

* * *

September 2009. Afternoon. I turn to my mum in the kitchen. I have been back in Norwich precisely four weeks now. It is a beautiful summer's afternoon. Dad is out on a boat trip (he works part time as an auxiliary ranger for the Broads Authority) and mum is by the sink preparing dinner. "Mum..." I say, nervously.

"Yes," she says, half listening, half concentrating on boning the chicken for our pilaf. (Oh how I had missed that dish whilst I had been away in Essex masquerading as something out of a David Marnet screenplay; even now my mouth salivates at the smell of chopped onions and chicken stock from our kitchen.)

"You remember I told you about the case of Client X who had abused all three of his stepchildren?"

My mum turns to me slightly mystified. "Ye-*ess*," she says dubiously, going up slightly at the end to signify her mistrust. Clearly she senses trouble brewing.

"I smiled at him."

"How do you mean?"

"I mean...I *smiled* at him."

"I don't understand?" My mum squints, looking at me like she just knows the next line that comes out of my mouth is going to be total and utter garbage but that she will have to listen to it anyway.

"Well...the smile might not have been *pure*."

"*Pure*?" she says, confused.

"Yes pure."

Mum still looks confused and so I expand:

"It was during the second morning of the trial," I continue, "we were all in court and listening to the evidence of one of the key prosecution witnesses. The defence barrister had just tripped this particular witness up most spectacularly by posing the question, *'Either you were lying in your witness statement or you are lying now'* and she had literally fallen apart. But instead of feeling sorry for her, instead of hoping she would regain composure and continue giving evidence, I was, well, pleased. And that's when it happened. At least, I *think* it might have happened. I think I might, though I am not entirely sure, have turned to Client X in the dock and smiled. And now, after all these months, I am literally panicking like mad because I am not sure *why* I smiled. Was I pleased it was going so well for him? Was I pleased he might be let off? Did I *want* him to be let off? What happens if I was smiling as if to encourage him or to say *'Go on my son'*? How do I know that I don't actually quite like rapists? Or that I am not a secret rapist myself?"

My mum looks at me, slightly bemused and with what appears to be chapfallen eyes; "*Aron*," she turns to me, saddened and deflated because we have been here, quite literally, so many times before, "it really doesn't matter. You know it doesn't."

"But what if I smiled because I secretly like rape? Or maybe I just find rape funny? Or maybe..."

My mum interrupts, pulling her head closer: "You haven't *done* anything. You are a *good* person. You don't need to keep doing this to yourself."

"But what if..."

Mum and I go round a few more times, her offering reassurance and me rejecting it outright, until eventually we both just...*give up*. The problem - or so I repeatedly deceive myself – is that the answers my mum gives are never quite detailed enough. Never quite enough science or *reason*. Merely love and compassion, which I tend just to throw away like stale bread to the birds; as if they are the very last thing - and not the very first thing (which is possibly closer to the truth) - that may be able to help me through.

And so, as the days go on, I cannot help but think that what I really need to help me through this stomach-turning anxiety, to help me deal with all these new rather ugly-looking obsessions, is some more rules; a means of clarity and, indeed, *protection* from future misdeeds. Not surprisingly, like an addict going back to his or her substance of choice, I decide, once more, to put pen to paper, to make sure I never do anything like what I had done at Client X's trial again. Hurriedly, I write something down in a small spiral bound writing pad:

Rule 27

Smiling at anyone not associated with or being in any way related to the smile-bearer will be prohibited if any **one** *of the below conditions are satisfied:*

i) the 'receiver' has or has had a history of violent or sexual behaviour and there is no greater pretext for smiling or

ii) the 'receiver' has or has had a history of violent or sexual behaviour and there is a victim or witness in the same vicinity

Failure to comply with the above, I write down finally, *will make the perpetrator unforgiveable for an indeterminate period and a 'bad person' for a period no less than...*5 years.

Five Years. Ten Years. *Life.* It was all starting to feel pretty final. I get up nervously and walk to the bathroom. There, I gaze into the small circle of glass that is my dad's old retractable double-sided scissor shaving mirror and start to cry. I have let myself down. Let down my family. I have reneged on all of my promises and become drawn into my OCD yet again.

Worst of all, I know that it will not be long before I am forced to make the only pronouncement I ever can in times of such overwhelming anxiety: that I am, conclusively and quite unabashedly, a BAD PERSON.

Chapter 13
"SECRET WARS"

"In each family a story is playing itself out, and each family's story embodies its hope and despair".
- Auguste Napier

One thing that has remained steadfast and consistent throughout the various manifestations of my disorder has undoubtedly been the support I have received from both my parents. If my experiences with OCD have been erratic, unsettling and wearisome, the support I have had from my family has been everything but.

And yet, still living at home, I can only imagine that my suffering has not been easy on my poor old Ma and Pa. I can imagine that, at times, it must have left them quite literally at the end of their tether. '*Snap out of it!*' I can imagine they must have wanted to scream out. '*For goodness sake, why can you not just get a grip!*' Of course, it is rarely ever that easy. Nothing scary or habitual ever is.

With regards my own suffering, it has not always been easy to convey to my parents - or indeed anyone without OCD - the sheer complicity of what was going on inside my head. Ordinarily I am articulate and loquacious; I can put together the most fragmentary of thoughts seamlessly into well organized and beautifully constructed words and sentences. But when it comes to OCD, sometimes, it can feel almost impossible even to know where to begin. How does one successfully make clear to a loved one why they are washing their hands for the umpteenth time in spite of blistering, red raw hands; that, in their right mind, they know full well that their hands are probably already clean but that they are doing it anyway simply because they believe they must; one needless ablution after another. Not easy, right?

Well actually, it's possibly a lot easier than you might think.

I do not remember ever seeing my parents read any books on OCD. Nor did they ever go and get professional advice (bar seeing Dr Khanna when I was a young child). And yet, my parents, who were, in many ways, mental health novices, always seemed to have at least a basic comprehension of how my illness worked; how it managed so successfully to grip me in fear and influence my choices. Can human behaviour, however extreme, ever truly remain unfathomable to another human soul?

If OCD is anything like most other conditions (and I say this with considerable health warnings attached), perhaps all of us have an aspect of it, however small, in our lives. I am a great believer of wellness being on a spectrum. We are neither sane nor insane, mad or normal. That's not how it works. We are all only ever somewhere between two extremes. For example, often I will drink to get drunk or, even, get drunk to forget my problems (not that this is ever advisable - I certainly do not do it much these days). Though I am not an alcoholic. I do not crave alcohol nor do I rely on it to get by. I certainly wouldn't miss it too much if I had to go without. Yet I can empathize, even if only on a minute level, with an alcoholic who does need to constantly imbibe alcohol. I can extrapolate my own feelings and then magnify them by one hundred. At least, I feel that I can. I guess, in many ways, this capacity for congruity and *compassion* is what makes us truly human.

Of course, the connotations of all this are that I am perhaps not one of the few but one of the many; that my suffering is far less exclusive than I would otherwise like to have believed. Jon Richardson, Lancastrian comedian and regular fixture on *8 out of 10 cats*, has, for a long while, asserted quite publicly to having what he describes 'a strain of OCD', complaining in particular of being 'driven by a quest for perfection'. Yet, in a very recent OCD TV documentary entitled *'Jon Richardson: A little Bit OCD'* it was actually revealed that Jon, in fact, did not score high enough for a diagnosis of OCD, instead suffering only with what has since been described as a 'demanding perfectionism'. Does this mean that Jon now has no concept of OCD; that he is incapable of empathy? I do not for one moment believe it does.

How many people the world over check appliances, wash their hands once too often or ruminate over the significance of their thoughts? Most of us, at some point in our lives, question our decisions or even ourselves. I do not know many people who have *never* experienced these things...

And on that basis alone, I guess one has to ask themselves the following: Just to what extent is my OCD exclusively about *me*? How much of my OCD is a *family matter*; the causes as well as the experiences?

From the onset of having OCD up until, actually, quite recently, I thought, almost intractably, that my own OCD was the only incidence in the family. That my suffering arose from nowhere in particular and persisted in isolation from those close to me. Sure, there might have been blueprints in place for certain highly strung characteristics - in their own way, I think most of my family have a bent for worrying too much - but no one exhibited, or seemed to display, the typical hallmarks appertaining to a diagnosis of OCD. Looking back, I realise that, actually, they might very well have done. Sometimes when one suffers mentally, it can be all too easy to forget to notice the suffering of those around you; OCD, in particular, being a notably egoistical disease.

Of course, the above isn't just my own opinion but the viewpoint of medical science with more and more psychologists now coming to the fast conclusion that the link between OCD and genetics is by no means as insignificant as first it was thought. Research using twin studies, for example, have actually indicated that more than fifty percent of a person's risk of developing OCD is genetic. According to an article published by the University of Michigan Health System:

"Obsessive-compulsive disorder tends to run in families, causing members of several generations to experience severe anxiety and disturbing thoughts that they ease by repeating certain behaviors. In fact, close relatives of people with OCD are up to nine times more likely to develop OCD themselves."

No one is one hundred percent sure on how genes actually play a part in the disorder - most scientists are agreed that there is no one 'OCD gene' - nor to what extent genes over nurture (or gene-environment interaction) influence our brain chemistry. Research into the potential genetic etiology of OCD, which thus far has mainly consisted of family studies (including twin studies) as well as genome-wide linkage studies, is still very much in its infancy. Though that isn't to say that good progress has not been made. Regardless of the many blanks there are with contemporary gene theory, there is little doubt that new evidence is regularly coming to light, bridging the gap bit by bit, providing new and fascinating results with each new study that is undertaken.

For example, very recently, a study conducted by Dr Gerald Nestadt of the John Hopkins University School of Baltimore lead to the discovery of what has simply been described as 'genetic markers'. From such findings, explains Dr Nestadt, "We might ultimately be able to identify new drugs that could help people with this often disabling disorder." It is, in many ways, a most promising development and one which will no doubt pave the way for future research and RCTs.

At the very least, the evidence seemed almost conclusively to point to OCD being a 'family matter'. And on that basis, I started to wonder perhaps whether there could in fact be some signs of OCD running in other members of my own household. That perhaps I had thus far simply just ignored what was going on around me or, quite selfishly, failed to show the requisite interest. And so I take an opportunity now to explore the issue further; to work out once and for all where my OCD may have come from or even whether anyone else in my family is or has ever been a fellow sufferer.

My family mean the world to me. If my OCD over the years has made me self-centered, then I hope that, in writing this chapter, I can make it up to them all. I also hope it will serve as a useful reminder to all sufferers out there with OCD that we are never alone in our suffering. As with cancer or bereavement, OCD is in so many ways a *family* affair. It is an issue for the whole unit. And for that reason alone, the road to recovery should always be a journey shared.

In so many ways, my parents are not like many parents of today's generation. Nor can they even be comfortably aligned with a typical modern-day couple. That is by no means an insult to them. Together for over 36 years, my parents represent a happily married, middle-aged couple, contented, in the main, with their lot in life. Now they are both retired, they like, as my mum describes it, 'to potter'. And they have created a perfectly conducive environment in which do so. For anyone who has ever seen *'Another Year'* by the acclaimed write and director Mike Leigh, my parents resemble, in so many ways, the hard-working, down-to-earth yet unshakably devoted and loving cultivators played by Jim Broadbent and Ruth Sheen; sewing, tendering, furnishing, purveying and cropping until, gradually, producing a family home that would be perhaps the envy of even the richest of landowners. It's probably why I still live here at the ripe old age of 27. (That, and the fact that I, as with most OCD sufferers, am a great creature of comfort.)

The house we live in is detached, situated on an unmade road and positioned on top of a sloped lawn, the raised patio at the front of the house surrounded by an ornate concrete balustrade. At this time of the year, plants, shrubs and hanging-baskets propagate the area quite majestically: Begonias, Devon Wizards and a beautiful slowly maturing Magnolia Stallata. My dad has worked hard on the garden and loves to be outdoors, even in the deathly cold winter.

Now he is retired, my dad works as a volunteer on the Norfolk Broads as an auxiliary ranger where he patrols the waters, assists people with information on tidal conditions and safety procedures, gets involved with countryside maintenance and oil spills and even on one occasion had to help rescue a stranded seal on the shores of Hunstanton.

When we first moved here from our semi-detached Victorian House in Southend about eight years ago, we could not have dreamed of living in such a beautiful area of the country, against such a breath-taking back-drop. It had certainly been a far cry away from the run-down, black bin bag ridden streets from whence we came, where decent houses were increasingly being converted into flats and bedsits and crime and drugs seemed to be utterly rampageous. Nonetheless, this hasn't stopped my dad worrying, obsessing even, over whether moving to Norwich has been good for us. To this day, my dad worries about the effect moving has had on us all; whether a life in Southend would have provided us with more stability and opportunity. After all, weren't we closer to London? And what about all the family and friends we would be leaving behind? "Are you sure we did the right thing?" you will hear my dad frequently ask my mum, anxiety lacing his tone. "Yes!" my mum will yell back, clearly fed-up of answering this same question over and over ad infinitum. "You know we have."

I guess I never really appreciated that, for my dad, this recurring, intrusive and anxiety-provoking line of thought has been perhaps every bit as distressing as my own intrusive thoughts have been for me. The compulsive element in my dad's suffering appears to be absent - and perhaps that is because actually it *is* absent (after all, I am not advocating that my dad actually has OCD) - yet the periodic re-living of past events, of going over and over old ground, certainly suggests to me an element, if only the most infinitesimal fleck, of obsessive thinking. Who knows? It certainly does offer a small clue, a sneaky insight into perhaps where my own OCD may have unduly sprouted.

As with the outside, the inside of our house is, in many senses, just as impressive. Perhaps even more so. In our house the fridge is always full and the smell of cooking from the kitchen wafts savorously around the entire home; aromas of curry, casseroles and, my own personal favourite, chicken pilaf. My mum and dad are both great cooks, which is possibly just as well as my own culinary skills fall somewhat short of adequate (once I tried to make oven fish and chips: I ended up undercooking the fish and burning the chips).

As houses go, ours is kept in almost pristine condition; well decorated and always incredibly clean and tidy. My mum insists that every room of our four bedroom house should be dusted and hoovered thoroughly on a weekly basis. This, despite the disapprobation of my dad and I for whom, if it were down solely to us, there would no doubt be more dust motes floating about the place than Tutankhamun's tomb.

Though it would perhaps be unfair to say that my mum has ever been *obsessed* with the cleaning. She has never, for example, as truly obsessive cleaners might, applied soil retardants to the carpets or scrubbed the oven for hours at a time with industrial strength cleaning gel. She doesn't douse, buff, depurate or squelch. She also doesn't ever invade the privacy of my own room, allowing me to leave it junked up and un-hoovered for sometimes months on end; "It's up to you if you want to live in a sty," my mum will invariably jibe with mild chagrin (though never anything more determinative than that). No, my mum is not what one might describe an *obsessive* individual. Or, at least, she hadn't shown signs of being obsessive all through my childhood and teenage years. Unfortunately some things do not last forever. We are all, after all, a certain way until we're not.

In 2009, having lived in Norwich for over seven happy years my mum stumbled across hard times. The result was that she had become almost preternaturally fixated with her own and her family's safety. She would worry about everything from what went into our meals each day to the appearance of a new mole (indeed, the emergence of a new mole had always been a big thing in our household right since I was a small child. Everything from simple birth freckles to *intradermal nevi* would always have to be checked with painstaking care for having either changed shape or size).

By 2010, to everyone's surprise, my mum's internal conflicts, her constant worrying over her own and other people's health eventually saw her being referred to see a psychologist. It was a shock to all of us, not least because of how out of character her anxiety seemed to be but also by virtue of how late in life her symptoms had actually come to light. By that time, I had been to see more doctors, link workers and psychiatrists than I could shake a shitty stick at. I was *well versed,* so to speak, in my disorder. For my mum though, this had all been quite new.

It would be enough to unsettle our otherwise perky and contented family quite considerably.

"The job is unbearable," my mum confessed quite out of the blue one winter's evening at the dining table in front of both Dad and myself. "I'm not sure how much longer I can go on with it". And not being one for unnecessary histrionics, we had believed her at once. Mum was clearly suffering profoundly. Though the revelation, in many ways, had been something of a shock.

Upon moving to Norwich as long ago as ten years previously, my mum had willingly taken on the role of primary breadwinner, working, as she had done back in Southend, as a science technician in the local secondary school just down the road and for five years it had given her a great sense of independence not to mention providing a supplementary income for the family. She had loved it then: the science, the friendships, the camaraderie. Now, the very thought of it made her shudder from the inside out.

The main problem with the job, according to my mum as she explains it to me now (and notwithstanding any deterioration in her mental health - as I will go on to cover) had been the increasingly poor adherence of the school to general health and safety requirements. Students, with no training (or maturity for that matter), would be let loose with hazardous substances whilst teachers, who it seemed were getting younger and younger by the minute, had become increasingly more reckless, displaying as my mum describes it "a cavalier approach to safety".

My mum tells me the story of a sixth form class doing an experiment on bacterial conjugation. To complete the experiment, students had been instructed to place test tubes filled with a chemical solution known as Ecoli K12 inside a large, microprocessor-controlled water bath and then left simply to start multiplying. An ostensibly straightforward Year 12 task. Or so one might have assumed. However, not taking proper due care, this one particular spotty little sixth former had filled his test tubes right to the very brim before placing his solutions rather haphazardly inside the bath, causing them to spill out and contaminate the water.

Ecoli K12 is not, so my mum tells me, strictly speaking poisonous. However, that is not to say that it cannot become so. There is apparently always a risk that bacteria can mutate. And so, my mum, having already done a full day's work, was forced to autoclave the entire water bath, which took hours on end and which meant at least five loads in the pressure cooker.

Incidents like the one above were apparently frequent during this period which had slowly but surely dented my mum's confidence, generating ever increasing bouts of anxiety. Eventually, the safety of the students and teachers began to play so constantly on her mind, the thought of getting up in the morning and going to work, of being responsible for keeping everyone safe, physically turned her stomach. She worried continually about accidents and spillages. She lamented over the 'gun-hoe use', as she put it, of oxidizing agents and certain harmful acids in everyday experiments (which she would undoubtedly be tasked to manage and dispose of). In particular, she tormented herself endlessly over a particularly dangerous substance called copper sulphate, which she had told us all was notoriously difficult to clear up but which young, fresh-out-of-university teachers would insist on using almost as liberally as food colouring or baking soda.

"My nerves..." she told us all one evening, after a particularly awful day cleaning up this rather unpleasant chemical, "I'm not sure my nerves can take anymore."

And so it was, following my mum's revelation of the job becoming increasingly unbearable, that we had all decided that enough was finally enough. "Your mother has been through the mill for too long," said my dad, putting his foot down. And although he had always worried, often excessively, about money and security, he would not at the very same time have sat back and watched my mum struggle on. In 2009, my mum joined my dad permanently in early(ish) retirement. It could not have felt like more of a relief for all concerned.

Or at least it had done for a few months.

Unfortunately for my mum, as might have been predicted had we indeed been aware of what was *really* going on, the growing anxiety, the ever-present disquietude and unease would not end there. Underneath the surface, more sinister things burbled away assiduously, hanging, like the incorporeal scent of trouble, in the ever-thickening air.

In the Easter of that year, not long before her retirement, my mum had found a spot of blood on her nose. She and Dad had just come back from a holiday in Sorrento at the time and the sight of it had caused her some mild concern. "I don't like the look of this," she had told us all gingerly. And in many ways, she had been right to be ever so slightly troubled. It happens that spots of blood on the skin can, in certain circumstances, be indicative of the beginnings of a basal-cell carcinoma, a fairly non-metastasizing form of skin cancer which, although not life-threatening, may, if left untreated, lead to both cosmetic deformity as well as to the erosion of surrounding tissue. A gruesome if not mortiferous prospect. And on that basis, my mum, exercising perhaps only reasonable caution, had decided not to take any chances .

"It's probably just symptoms of menopause," said Dr Godbold at the local surgery quite dismissively a few weeks later, ruling out entirely the possibility that this might indeed be a form of skin cancer. "Thinning skin and psoriasis is incredibly common for a woman of your...*maturity*. I shouldn't worry in the slightest." Though something about his answer did not inspire much confidence.

And so, following her initial and unhelpful trip to the doctor's, my mum worried herself sick over all the possibilities, the endless uncertainty and, now, the lack of medical attention being shown. "You can't go on like this!" my dad eventually shouted at her one evening, more out of concern than genuine anger. "You're driving yourself doolally." Shortly after, at mine and my dad's insistence, my mum went back to the doctors, not once but twice more. On the first occasion, a rather rude young doctor, having kept her waiting for over twenty minutes and running totally over-schedule, had actually asked my poor mum to come back another time: "It's only skin," he had commented quite brusquely. The second time, however, noticing just how anxious my mum had become over her skin complaints, a different (female) doctor straightaway referred my mum to see a dermatology specialist as well as to a link worker for her burgeoning anxiety, which, by this time (and what with all the anxiety she had suffered at work) had gotten somewhat out of hand. "It might even be the case," said this new, rather more compassionate female doctor, "that the *anxiety* could be causing the nerve endings in your skin to become sensitive."

A few weeks later, much to everyone's surprise, my mum was diagnosed with the very basal-cell carcinoma she had all the while been dreading. And if ever there were a cause for her feeling anxious, for feeling out of control or of needing to check, double-check and triple-check her body for signs of frailty and malfunction, then it was this. For months following the diagnosis and long after the cancer had been removed (dealt with primarily by a microscopically controlled surgery known as *Mohs*) my mum worried excessively about her health and the health of her family; every lump, bump, tingle, itch, spot, blemish and discoloration was subject to rigorous scrutiny. Not to mention, at times, heart-stopping trepidation. Even cooking, something which she had always very much enjoyed, had started to become prohibitively toilsome. One evening my mum had made meringues for a family dinner party. For an unknown reason they had tasted slightly of lavender and for days my mum felt responsible for potentially poisoning us all. How could it have happened? Had she somehow managed to get washing-up liquid into the mixture? Maybe she had splashed fabric softener into the mix when she was doing the washing, the washing machine being only a few inches away from the oven? She was greatly relieved when she remembered the icing sugar had actually come from a friend, who, as we later found out, would spray lavender air-freshener into every room and cupboard as a matter of course.

Fortunately, as is so *infrequently* the case for so many, my mum's anxiety was dealt with rather quickly by the NHS. Unlike with the cancer, the doctors had been (surprisingly) quick to refer my mum for CBT and after only a few sessions she was almost entirely back to normal. Though nonetheless, the period of anxiety, the terrible unease which had visited upon my poor old mother, like the skin graft now permanently visible on her nose, would leave its mark. My mum, like the majority of sufferers, has what I like to term an OCD scar which means she is unlikely to forget the troubles and disquiet she had so unwillingly and so unexpectedly endured. Though, in many ways, I guess this isn't necessarily always such a bad thing. It serves, if nothing else, as a healthy reminder never to go down that awful road again, to deal with anxiety before it ever gets out of hand and to seek help the moment things aren't right.

For me, my OCD scar came a lot later. At first, it was more like a blister, susceptible to bursting. Prone to re-infection. Compared to my mum's, my own OCD was far more pervasive and, as had possibly already proven to be the case, far more long-term. It would, unfortunately for me, take more than just a few sessions of CBT to see me right again. Indeed, it would take almost every last fiber of my being.

Officially, I am the only one in my family with OCD. Unlike the others, I have a clinical diagnosis to my name as well as a miscellany of notes and doctors' records on the NHS National Network to back it all up. Though, as has been clearly demonstrated, I am not the only one to know how it feels to be anxious. Or to have experienced intrusive thoughts and compulsive inclinations.

In many ways, my mum, having gone through the more traditional symptoms of anxiety, helped us all to understand the types of thoughts I had spent so many years of my life trying with limited success to fend off. My mum's symptoms, as with the majority of those who first exhibit symptoms in later life, were very clearly *triggered*, the triggering event bearing much more than just a mild semblance to the presenting infirmity. My own OCD, by contrast, was far less easy to pinpoint and took a great deal of work in tracing back the triggering events. Yet the patterns were identical. Like I say, the mechanism of OCD is nearly always the same regardless of the manifestation (although it is now suggested that those with Pure O or a form of moral scrupulosity may in fact have a greater *cognitive* element; a greater tendency to catastrophically misinterpret the significance of everyday intrusive thoughts).

"I understand what you mean now about *testing,*" admitted my mum actually only quite recently. "Once when you and Dad asked if the Coke was alright to drink from the fridge and I said "yes" and then afterwards realised it was two days out of date, so awash with anxiety and guilt, I proceeded to drink a whole glass of it myself just to *test* whether or not it might be safe. I guess I didn't really consider the practical consequences if we *all* got sick."

In many ways, one of the biggest consequences of my mum's symptoms were that my own became far more difficult to conceal. Now my family *knew* what to look out for. The silences, the surliness, the constantly being, as it were, *spaced-out*. These were all obvious hallmarks of intrusive thoughts. Even now, close friends and family will often remark how they can almost *see* when I am thinking too much; as if a large white cartoon bubble has decocted up from my head, inside of which are sat two straight-cut gears, meshed together and circumvolving at literally hundreds of revs per minute.

It goes without saying that we invariably do more harm than good by our willingness to endure suffering alone. We are, none of us, an island, hatched in a pod and unique in our experiences. Our families notice and they care. Moreover, and as I hope this chapter has proven, they also have the capacity to *understand*.

Unfortunately, it would take me a long time to learn this lesson properly. Even after my mum's very similar problems with anxiety, for reasons unknown to me then, I still elected to suffer much of my OCD alone. I am not entirely sure why I did this. I like to think, looking back at it now, I did it to *protect* everyone around me, though I suspect my motives were slightly less gallant and far more self-centred than this. I did not like to constantly remind my family of my failure to get better is probably more like it. Keeping them worried indefinitely was one thing, displaying *weakness* was quite another. If my mum could get over it all so quickly then surely so could I. *Surely*. Couldn't I? *Couldn't I!?*

A few days after my mum's diagnosis, I went to write, as I did quite routinely, in my page-a-day diary and as I did so was hit with the biggest slab of anxiety I had endured to date. The thought that came over me almost as soon as I had put fingers to keyboard disgusted me in ways not even I felt possible. "At last, a *cancer* storyline," my little director's brain inwardly announced, immediately thinking of *Coronation Street* and *Eastenders* and how exciting their storylines often were by comparison to my own more feeble attempts. "*Finally*, something dramatic and interesting to write about."

But hang on a minute...this wasn't a storyline or a soap opera, this was real life. This was my *mother* we were talking about here! For heaven's sake, what sort of person derived pleasure or even satisfaction from thinking about their own ruddy familie's illness? From the tragedy that had befallen them? What sort of sick, *twisted*...

The guilt that ensued shot through me like a 500 Smith & Wesson, 50 caliber bullet.

Of course, the truth was that I did *not* enjoy my mum's tragedy. At least, I didn't enjoy the experience of it in real life. And certainly not the suffering it had caused us all afterwards. But on paper, separated from reality by syrupy black ink fused onto a single coating of calcium carbonate, a diaphanous, cellulose membrane separating almost hermetically the outer world from the inner, everything seemed different. In this world, *anything* went. And suddenly this unregulated macrocosm became, a bit like a dream about losing teeth or getting shot, a very scary place indeed. How had I allowed my imagination to remain so unregulated? How had I not questioned these utterly perverse thoughts earlier? Not surprisingly, my enthusiasm for invoking let alone chronicling this ill-regulated reality would eventually become all too much. "This will be my last entry..." I wrote with a heavy heart one evening, this before taking the rather more drastic action of tearing up all older entries in the months that followed. It had been the most painful sacrifice of my illness to date. It would be the start, unfortunately, of a most unpleasant second downward spiral and the most isolated few years of my life.

Chapter 14
HOME AND AWAY

"The voyage of discovery is not in seeking new landscapes but in having new eyes."
- Marcel Proust

Lying in bed, I awake suddenly.

The curtains in my room are slightly agape and the morning light is creeping in. I am unsure how this has happened because I am usually extremely careful to make sure both curtains are properly pulled to each night. I don't like any cracks peeping through the pleats and folds; I am frightened it will mean people will see in.

Maybe someone can see me now?

I get up and pull the heavy-pile faux suede curtains back together until there is not so much as a pin-prick of light and resume my lie-in. I nuzzle back under the warm duvet - that wondrous item of pliable quilt which, over the last few weeks in particular, has come to represent both safety and oblivion in equal measure - and lay my head back down onto my soft, welcoming pillow.

Only, I cannot relax. In fact, now I am awake, anxiety is already starting to rise luxuriantly. I wonder why the curtains had been left open in the first place. Had I done it on purpose? Had I wanted someone to see in, a child perhaps? Maybe I had secretly wanted them to catch sight of my semi-naked body or the erect penis-shaped dune in my duvet when I am lying flat on my back asleep? Perhaps I am secretly an *exhibitionist*?

I turn over in my bed and try to think about something else. To distract myself in whatever way I can. Though as darned luck would have it, the 'something else' I have unwittingly focused on is simply just more OCD. These days, it nearly always is. On this occasion, I am worried about something that occurred actually as long as a week or so ago and which has been playing on my mind almost non-stop for days. The incident in question (which perhaps isn't so much an 'incident' as an entirely passive or kinematic reaction on my part) is an inappropriate look I gave whilst watching an episode last Saturday night of *You've Been Framed.* An elderly woman at a wedding, whilst dancing on the slippery, laminate parquet dance floor, skids over ungracefully, baring her off-white bloomers (together with off-white wrinkly derriere) to a television audience of tens of millions and I had immediately taken the opportunity to glimpse up her skirt (if indeed looking *up* anything 2D is even possible; which I'm worried it might be). Why had I done it? Was it simply out of curiosity, a result of random saccadic eye movement or had I been actually *perving* on the unviable octogenarian? The thought that it may be the latter goes round and around like a bunch of Neopagan Germans around a floral centrepiece in my head. It is annoying, disquieting, *tormenting*. I feel so guilty that at times I wish I didn't even exist. Though this is not, I have since concluded, an option. There are only two *real* options: sleep or get up.

I choose to get up.

The alternative of course is to spend hour after hour in bed; sleep away my whole day until eventually I have mustered enough energy to attempt getting up tomorrow, or the next day or the day after.

This is not how I want to live. This is not how anyone is *meant* to live.

And so I get dressed and creep slowly downstairs. Mum and Dad have gone away to Somerset for the week, staying in a B&B in Shepton Mallet for their 35th wedding anniversary and I am home alone, unemployed and, if I'm perfectly honest, at a bit of a loose end. I should be looking for a job or, at the very least, getting myself down to the local job centre. Though instead, I am lounging around in my bedclothes, moping about an empty house and getting myself worked up over '*silly little problems*' as one therapist had indeed described them.

Only, as we all know, they are not all quite so silly. Some of them are pretty serious. At least, they are serious to me.

Half-heartedly, I walk into the kitchen and decide I am going to make myself some lunch - or perhaps that should be *brunch* - out of the fridge. It is only half past eleven but, now wide awake and actually pretty hungry, I can certainly use the distraction. Not to mention a small comestible analeptic. At the sink, I run the cold water to make myself a glass of orange squash and, as I do, I cannot help but notice a small black dot on the kitchen draining board. It is situated underneath one of the squares of our blue vinyl sink mat which, for some reason, isn't in its usual position in the sink. The black dot is too small to identify. It could be a speck of soil from the coriander plant we have on the kitchen window sill, a coffee granule or even a microscopic insect. There are a lot of tiny insects about the kitchen of late. Recently, we were bought a flamingo flower - or *Anthurium* - by some friends of my parents and the fleshy, pink spadix seems to be attracting fruit flies like no one's business.

The draining board is wet and the black dot is positioned but a few millimetres away from an otherwise lethal puddle.

Unsure whether the black dot is alive or dead or indeed inanimate (and not wanting to risk its near-certain drowning), I decide to lift the sink mat and blow gently against it in order to move it away from the wet draining board and thus from danger.

Under my moderately genteel puff, the dot travels wistfully away, gliding across the draining board like a skier across the smooth white Cortina d'Ampezzo and finishing up somewhere underneath the bottom of one of the kitchen units. In fact the dot is now half under the unit and half on the work surface. And this I don't feel at all comfortable with. I worry that the fly is now trapped and cannot move and that this is possibly just as cruel as letting it drown because this time it is *my* fault because I am the one who blew it there. So I use my finger - or more precisely my nail - to try and gently scrape the fly (or coffee granule or spec of soil or whatever the hell it is) out from the crack and back onto the surface. Only, my finger is too fat and I cannot get to it. I try again but to no avail.

Anxiety very quickly turns to frustration as I continue attempting to retrieve the black dot from the crack. Then, in a moment of malevolence or mental abandon or whatever else you want to call it, I press really hard against the black dot in order to pull it out. In fact, I press so hard that I know that I have squished whatever it is that I had, thus far, been making every effort to rescue and at once I feel a tremendous pang of remorse. The frustration has died down and now there is only anxiety. *What have I done?*

I've killed a fly in cold blood, that's what I have done. I am a *fly killer*. I go over to the fridge to make myself a sandwich. The guilt will linger for at least the next three hours.

The next morning, I am sitting at the family PC in the extension. I am surfing the internet, looking at nothing in particular when, all of a sudden, I come across a picture of a little girl on my home page. It is an advert for kids' clothing; a special twenty percent offer on a whole range of pink and purple cotton jerseys with button plackets (which incidentally is what the girl in the picture is dressed up in). And instantly there is this wring of self-reproach. At the very same time that the image of the little girl has popped up unsuspectingly on my computer screen, I have also crossed my legs, generating a mild sensation in my groin which immediately convinces me that I have, as it were, *done it on purpose*. That, on some level, I had wanted to attain some sort of accompanying physical gratification to the 'sexual' imagery on my computer display. The fact that I had merely crossed my legs to make them more comfortable or even to alleviate the anxiety (fidgeting being a well known response to elevated levels of stress) does not even cross my mind.

Nor does the idea that this feeling in my groin might merely be sensual; like yawning or stretching or scratching an itch. Instead, the fact that the feeling has emanated exclusively from my genitals is convincing me that the truth must be far less innocent. "You disgusting little paedophile," the gremlins attack, their words echoing around in the chambers of my mind. That children are about as attractive to me as an Ethiopian warthog or the leaf-nosed bat of Central America seems scarcely to factor.

Loathsome and ashamed, I eventually decide to log off of the computer and go back upstairs to bed. I draw the curtains until the room is pitch black. I cannot see anyone now.

Better luck job searching tomorrow.

Excessive individuation. The idea that a person may become unacceptably detached from his or her community. According to Durkheim writing in the mid-nineteenth century, this is one of the main universal causes of suicide. According to Margo it is also the cause (not to mention one of the profound effects) of mental illness. If there's one thing above all else that I have learned since being diagnosed with OCD: one cannot find true peace from avoiding life. It is not only a non sequitur but a complete and utter absurdity.

The other day I get a call out of the blue on my mobile from a good friend of mine called Freya. Freya and I used to work together at Morrisons - both on checkouts - and I literally haven't spoken to her in months. Now that I am unemployed and at a loss, I barely have contact with anyone.

"It's really great to hear from you," I say, honestly. "How have you been?"

She tells me, quite matter-of-factly, that she is actually not so good. That she has recently split up with her boyfriend of five years and is now thinking, very seriously, about quitting her job and *getting away for a bit.* "I want to go travelling," she tells me yearningly. "Just, you know, escape from it all. Life has become almost insufferable."

The news is impactful to say the least. I am not used to people telling me this sort of thing, especially now I barely speak to anybody. Freya in particular has always struck me as the real steady kind, composed, reliable. She is the last person I might have suspected would wish to throw down everything and set off dramatically into the sunset. *It only comes to show you,* I think to myself almost quite conceitedly. *Sometimes life can get on top of even the very best of us.*

That life can be hard, often unexpectedly so, is something I know perhaps only too well. Or at least it is something I have become familiar with in my latter years. Though it was not always this way. No sir-ee. Up until the age of eighteen I had been blessed with what I considered to be a rather care-free and easygoing existence. I worked hard and stayed focused on my studies and my career because I believed that life was ultimately good and that I would not have to worry about where the next dole of laughter or the next sprinkling of true happiness might come from. Now, happiness had to be squeezed out from half-empty tubes, extracted carefully from in between the cracks that formed sheets of ice over my whole entire life.

Perhaps now, after months of relatively poor mental health, I am finally ready to admit it, admit how I am really feeling; how shit everything has seemingly become: "I feel exactly the same Freya." The words fall out all too easily, like those small, pointless trinkets from a Christmas cracker. They are a surprise even to me, though mine is the tongue from whence they descend. Am I really feeling that low and subjugated? Is it really becoming all-too-much? Maybe I have finally, after such a protracted spell of suffering, just had enough?

There is a pause.

"Well then why don't you come with me?" Freya says, registering the melancholy in my tone and adapting quickly to my rather sudden adumbration. "Why don't you come with me to, I don't know...how about America? *New York*?" There is like this spontaneous upsurge of fervour in her inflection which, if I'm honest, takes me only further aback.

"I...I..."

"Oh *go* on," she says again, more insistently the second time around than even the first. "What have you got to lose?"

I ponder the question a moment: she's right of course, what *have* I got to lose? Let's review this very quickly shall we: no girlfriend, no job and wads of money in the bank (thank you WM Morrison!). Meanwhile, my OCD is so bad at the minute that sometimes it feels like I might simply just collapse under the weight of it all. Or else sit at home, alone, and rot in silence. Under these circumstances, there really does seem very little to think about.

"Bloody hell," I say, with a most unexpected gush of enthusiasm, "why the hell not!" And for the first time in months, it feels like finally there might really be something to look forward to; a small hairline fracture in those cold and exclusionary sheets of ice. It is the most hopeful I have felt for literary months on end. Unfortunately it is still a far cry from genuine excitement.

*

I have stopped leaving the house. Being unemployed has provided my OCD the perfect pretext it needs to keep me away from the outside world. Worse still, it would also appear that I have begun again to suffer slightly with what can only be described as an ancillary spell of 'looking disorder' (which, admittedly, is only getting worse as the days go on and the self-imposed curfews continue). I am afraid of what I might look at if I am exposed to large crowds of people. At home at least there is just me and my parents. TV can sometimes be an issue: close ups of people's crotches for example (the Pampers adverts are almost wholly unwatchable) and programmes containing scenes of a violent sexual nature. But on the whole, in the main, it's far safer indoors and I take refuge there.

Where I do go out, I make sure there are not too many people. Mainly, I go to visit Freya at her parents' home in Brundall to help plan our holiday to New York. Freya lives in a really lovely, three bedroom detached house just on the north bank of the River Yare and it is always a pleasure going round there. Her parents really like me. Or at least they seem to. Though we don't speak much. He is someone fairly high up in Norwich City Council. She is a teaching assistant at the local school. They trust me with their daughter. They think I am probably a good influence. I don't like to burst their bubble by telling them the truth.

And the truth is, well, that I am anything but *good*. Rather, I am a horrid, wretched, ignominious little creature. I am quite literally the worst person I know. It's just that no one seems ever to notice. Sometimes, I am utterly dumbfounded by how my malevolence and degeneracy have managed to go on for so long and run so deep without ever having been detected. I cannot help but worry that I am simply just living from one moment to the next on so-called borrowed time; simply waiting for the day I finally get caught out. I believe this is how most OCDers feel.

One evening round hers, Freya and I decide to go online in order to attempt completing the ESTA application form to get into the US. It is an obligatory form and one which must be answered one hundred percent accurately. We go through the questions carefully, one by one: 'Have you ever been or are now involved in espionage, sabotage, terrorist activities or genocide?' *Errr...not to my knowledge;* 'Have you ever asserted immunity from prosecution?' *Can't say I have;* 'Are you seeking entry to engage in criminal or immoral activities?' I pause in doubt. Suddenly, there is an imposition of unease. What do they mean exactly by *immoral*? If looking at someone inappropriately constitutes an immoral activity, then perhaps I am as guilty as sin. I wonder for a moment whether I shall put this on the form? Common sense dictates that I should not. Not if I want to stand any chance of ever getting into the US which, of course, I do. Desperately.

Hesitantly, nervously I select 'no'.

I hear from Ross. He isn't doing so good. "They altered my medication," he tells me by text message. "But it didn't help. So now I am on a much higher dose of clomipramine." Ross is still not working and by all accounts isn't going out much either. I haven't seen him in group for a good while now so I probably should have guessed that something wasn't quite right. "I know how you feel," I reply back to him, genuinely sympathetic. "I have been pretty low of late too." And so we decide to meet up for a few drinks one evening at our local pub (evenings are good. No kids around).

"So how have you been then?" I ask. "*Really* been I mean."

"Terrible." He looks at me imploringly.

"Ditto." I pick up my pint of pale ale and take a swig.

I tell him about my plans for America to get away for a while. I tell him that I need a bit of time just to clear my head. He tells me that he thinks a holiday is a great idea. "It'll do you good," he says with genuine consideration for my welfare.

We talk about his OCD over checking appliances (a new manifestation) and then onto my own moral OCD surrounding 'looking'. We go over some of the various different treatment methods, posing each other the same age-old questions: 'Have you thought of doing more meditation?'; 'Are you able to 'shelve' your worries?'; 'What about just accepting your negative thoughts and practicing *forgiveness*?' Sometimes it feels like we have exhausted almost every possible avenue and yet always we remain stuck, as it were, in first gear. I am sick of being wedged, fixed, *glued* to the same spot. Like I am in a constant state of treading water. A bit like in that psychological horror film *Open Water* about a couple stranded at sea, circled by sharks and jelly fish and battling extreme fatigue, hunger and mental exhaustion just to keep alive.

I wonder when living will start getting easier. When all of this circling turmoil might just...*fuck off*?

A few days later, Jake rings me up. He has some news. As part of his work at the university, he has been invited to speak at the highly prestigious International Conference on Acoustics, Speech, and Signal Processing being held later this month in Dallas, Texas. The conference is apparently the largest technical conference on signal processing in the world and Jake will be showcasing his latest research on visual-only lip reading identification technology. He has asked me if I want to come with him as his designated plus one.

"That sounds fantastic," I say enthusiastically, "I am packing my cases already." Which, actually, isn't so far from the truth. My trip to New York is but a few weeks away and following this I have already calculated that I will be able to take an inland flight straight to Dallas Fort-Worth with little inconvenience or expense.

And so it is, a few weeks later, I say goodbye to boring, stuffy old England and prepare myself for the trip of a lifetime to the grand old US of A. Quite by coincidence, the song *'Empire State of Mind'* has just been released in The Charts and is constantly being played on all the main radio stations. I find I am singing along to it constantly. I am hoping more than anything that an *empire state of mind* will be far worthier of my time than the current state of neuroses and despair I presently experience; the current, enervated trickle of serotonin that so helplessly and so futilely travels to and from the various lineaments of my mind.

"These streets will make you feel brand new," plays the music on my phone, now stored as my ringtone. I hope more than anything that they really might.

* * *

And so it is and here I am. It is a bitter cold February morning and I am sat at LaGuardia Airport awaiting my flight to Texas. My plane has just been delayed by approximately another three hours meaning my gate is jam-packed full of irked travellers and I am lucky to get a seat. One woman in a leaf green military jacket is looking at me as if I have just gone round her house and defecated in her lounge because I am sitting while she, with her giant canvas travel pack and matching wheeled duffel bag, is forced to stand. Though I do not feel guilty. I am far too busy fending off the myriad bad thoughts flying round and around in my head like luggage on a carousel to care much about my overall, generic unmannerliness.

I look down at my own, rather paltry brown vintage suitcase. For the last month or so, I have, quite literally, been living out of this very suitcase; travelling peripatetically from hostel to hostel, some of which with the worst amenities this side of the Atlantic Ocean. The last hostel in Chinatown had been the worst. Waking up each morning to the sound of a clinking radiator, a defiled bathroom, chicken gauge by way of a ceiling and the concern that roaming around in my hard, spring bed was a plethora of rancorous little bed bugs, had been dispiriting to say the least.

The reviews, which I am now looking at as a form of distraction, are even less inspiriting; "It's like a prison camp. I would not let my animals stay here," was but one of the critiques; "Last resort," said another angry commentator. "I created a trip advisor account for the sole reason of giving this place a terrible score."

Yet, New York itself, by stark contrast, had been utterly breath-taking; the cityscape awash with tall, majestic looking multi-storey buildings, grand fleets of golden yellow taxis and these rather heteroclite traffic lights which hung pendulously like the beautiful but narcotic South American *Angel Trumpet* next to billboards and sky scrapers. It had certainly made all the negative aspects of a life in hostels that much more bearable.

Nevertheless, and in spite of such amazing views and tantalizing scenery, my 'looking disorder' had played up for me something chronic. As gawking tourists travelled about with their heads permanently sloping upwards at the glowing lights, Art Deco spandrels and steel spires, I had, regrettably, spent my time looking, perhaps equally vertiginously, at girls of all shapes and sizes, *testing* myself, trying and failing to work out their various ages.

The unease had actually come about by the fear that perhaps American girls looked older than girls from Britain, creating, in my mind at least, an increased risk of accidently ogling someone who might in fact be *underage*. If ever you've watched one of those daytime American shows like *Sally Jessy Raphael* or *Jenny Jones*, you'll know where I'm coming from: 'corn fed' teen moms wobbling on stage with the anatomy of twenty year olds, announcing to the world how they were sexually active not long after they had learned to read and write. How did I know that the 'adult' girls I made eyes at on the streets of Times Square weren't in fact only teenagers in disguise? Or worse still, obese pre-teens who, by virtue of their preternatural sizes, were able to mask almost entirely their distinct lack of pubescence.

The worry had very nearly cost me my holiday.

Ironically, I had gone to America for a break from OCD. I had hoped that a new setting, a fresh, bustling environment, would break an otherwise stale and insidious cycle. I was wrong. Or at least, overly optimistic in my presumption. OCD is a thought-based disorder and as such resides *inside* of me. *It* goes where I go. And just as one cannot escape from heart disease or liver damage or even the emotional devastation of a bereavement nor can one ever truly run away from their own internal thought processes however far around the world they might travel in order to do so.

OCD is, in so many ways, the perfect travel companion: reliable, cautious and incredibly difficult to shake off.

And it is, I guess, for this very reason that, waiting here now at La Guardia Airport over three thousand miles away from Norwich, my OCD has risen to an all-time high. Who is safe to look at? Will anyone notice where my dissipated eyes are pointing? Will anyone wish to *report* me? It does not help that there are more people huddled around Central Terminal Building D this morning than there are visitors to the local Morrison's café on a Sunday afternoon (which, believe me, had been scary enough)!

Nevertheless, and in spite of this current spike in anxiety, I cannot deny that things have in fact over the last few days been gradually improving, particularly on the looking front. Slowly but surely, I have begun *acclimatizing* to American teen women and, as such, have managed to adjust my OCD rules accordingly. For the record and for those interested, the new and revised looking rules now state that I am permitted to look at any girl I want providing they are both over five-foot and look over 21 (which will mean I can be moderately certain that they are at least seventeen). And despite the fact that I know it will not be easy to age check every single youngish looking female before allowing my eyes to wander - not to mention from within a 750,000 square foot terminal covered floor to toe with passengers - I am glad I have established at least some degree, a minute element, of certitude over this otherwise quite indefinite and troublesome moral issue.

Other things have also helped bolster my mood over the last few days, the greatest of which is the prospect of seeing Jake. As it transpired, Freya and I had a fair few arguments during our time in New York (nothing too serious but enough to dampen the mood somewhat); whilst I had been keen to visit places like the Museum of Jewish Heritage and The Metropolitan Museum of Art, she had been far more interested in shopping at Bloomingdale's or Macy's or drinking expensive cocktails in Soho. It happens that Freya is far less cultural than me. Not to mention far more of a stubborn cow.

"I cannot believe you're dragging me all the way *there,*" Freya had complained as I tried to convince her to come with me to the Holocaust Museum in Manhattan's Battery Park one cold wintry morning. "As far as I'm concerned, what happened in the past should *stay* in the past!"

To the contrary, Jake, for all his faults, I know will be a much more amenable travel companion. Intelligent, well-read, *cultured.* He and I have been best friends now for almost a decade. And despite the odd bit of petty squabbling - usually over our various levels of indiscretion involving the other's latest love interest - we tend to see eye to eye on most things. So much so that he has stuck by me during the very worst and most frustrating of my OCD. He knows my anxiety is irrational and is separate from me. He also remembers what I used to be like *before*; before worry and guilt struck me like a right hook from Rocky Marciano in my late teens and early twenties.

I only wish that *I* had such a clear and remissive memory of my past.

Nevertheless, it is to the future now I look and, back in the present, the time is now almost 3 p.m., *local time*. It has been nearly an hour since the last flight announcement informing passengers of the long wait ahead and, as the crowds continue to fill the area like bilge water into a shipping vessel, I can feel my anxiety steadily start to rise again in almost sympathetic response. I seriously wonder how I will survive the next five minutes, let alone the next four hours. And, regrettably for me, things show little sign of getting any easier. A family, from seemingly out of nowhere, has just wandered over and stood right in front of me. They are so close to my face that I daren't so much as turn my head for fear of groping any one of them with my chin. I guess the rules of kinaesthetics or proxemics must necessarily be abandoned in times of great crowdedness. Inconveniently, the women of the family all have their backs to me and so I am unable to determine any of their ages or, more importantly, which of them are old enough to look at and the uncertainly causes immediate consternation. One of the female figures, perhaps the oldest looking of the clan, is wearing tight seamed jeans and has a rather nice derriere. Do I allow myself to look, potentially risking being a paedophile (as well as engaging in *testing*) or do I remain looking away, thus evading danger but also giving into the rather perfidious compulsive desire for *avoidance*? The uncertainty is crippling. I literally have no bloody clue where to place my sweeping, irresolute eyes.

And so I decide simply to close them. To take some deep breaths in and out and to start thinking - or *trying* to think - about the whole thing with much greater *perspective*; I mean, what does it really bloody matter where I look? Why do I think people might notice? Why do I think anyone will even care? It strikes me that there are so many things I could feasibly be looking at in an airport this size that someone would need literally to place two electrodes on the skin around my eyes and measure the change in the orientation of the dipole in order to truly pinpoint exactly where my eyes are pointing.

Nevertheless I am unable to curb the anxiety. Or to stop trying to *work out* once and for all the potential immorality of my actions. When the answers do not come or the reassurance that, in reality, it does not in fact matter a flying fuck where I look, I decide instead I must fix my attention elsewhere by gazing out of the large glass window in front of me and onto the concourse, *away* from other people. Outside, there are just a few men in fluorescent green jackets who all seem to be busy driving beltloaders and baggage carts or operating some of those state of the art refuelling pumpers. Some are even doing the unpleasant job of draining the onboard lavatories. There are no girls in sight.

In the background of my rather panoramic view, sits the ATC Tower, an aluminium construction with custom blue cladding which blends delicately into the skyline. The soffits and fin panels are a platinum grey which glisten majestically in the sunlight. Such a sumptuous sight, I cannot help but think. And for those few crystalline moments, so absorbed by the architecture and the activities of the ground control staff, I am almost totally oblivious to the hundreds of bustling people around me - or should that be, *on top of me* - and it feels good. Awesome in fact.

But alas, just as I start to lose myself completely, to become engulfed in this feeling of light serenity, there is a further flight announcement which brings me crashing back into the room with an almighty thud. A guy in a Southern accent and with an almost implausibly contralto tone, tells us that there will now be yet a further two hour delay on our already objectionably postponed flight and I am aghast. I look around, an expression of agony on my face. Instantly, I start becoming anxious all over again. What am I going to do with all this free time, I panic to myself? What will I focus on? How long can I realistically stay *looking away*? Maybe, I consider, I should go get something to eat. If nothing else it might kill a bit of time. Not to mention get me away from the hoards of delayed passengers, arranged like herds of buffalo, at my gate. Though it would seem that I am far from hungry. It was only a few hours ago that I was lunching at *Asian Chaio* at the terminal's main food court, stuffing myself full with bourbon chicken and fried wonton. In truth, I haven't been actually *hungry* since I arrived in the USA almost a month ago. Most of my intake has just been *comfort food*.

And so I end up settling instead on going to get a drink at Sam Adam's Bar. It seems an acceptable compromise and one which I take with relish. Once inside, I order myself a Boston Lager and hoist myself onto a retro-style Dinerware bar stool facing one of three 42-inch screens showing some obscure NCAA College Basketball match on ESPN. I don't understand the game in the slightest and make no attempt to try but nor am I bored either. In fact, I am actually, little by little, starting to simmer down a bit. It isn't so much the alcohol abating my nerves more than the realisation that I am in a bar- an *American* bar– and so will have very little chance of accidently clocking anybody under the age of majority, the legal limit over here being that much higher than at home. I am finally free to look wherever I like. Unsurprisingly, given such freedom, my eyes naturally stay glued to the dull though rather ostentatious charging and guarding of the Norfolk State Spartans, dunking and *layin* just a few inches from a row of liquor bottles above the bar.

Eventually, a few field goals and just as many pints later and it is time finally to return to the terminal gate to board the plane. I have now relaxed considerably and am not frightened to look at anyone anymore. Nor do I even have the *urge* to look at anyone. That is, all until I have gotten onto the plane and taken my seat. To the left of me there are a couple of sixteen year-old girls, giggling incurably over some magazine entitled '*Red Book*' (the American equivalent of *Woman's Own*), and I am set off at once. One of the girls has unexpectedly large breasts and I cannot help but notice how developed she appears in contrast to her respective maturity. Though, of course, I do not want to notice this. I would do anything *not* to notice. I look for only a micro-second at her cleavage but alas it is all too late to prevent...*whoosh* - another pang of guilt hits me like a sledgehammer.

Devastated, I rummage nervously through the on-flight bundle underneath my chair. There is a pair of earphones, a *'Plane & Pilot'* magazine and an on-board safety manual. Finally, I manage to pull out a complimentary sleeping mask which I am almost at once certain will do the job nicely. I place the mask over my head until my eyes are completely covered by the soft, poly cotton lining. At last. Blackness. I clench my eyes shut to make doubly, triply sure.

The time is 1 p.m., *local time*. Beautiful sunny skies are forecast across the state of New York.

An hour after my plane arrives at Dallas/Fort Worth International Airport, I greet Jake at the pick-up area just outside Terminal E. Quite inconveniently, it has taken three whole circuits of the airport grounds in a Green and Blue Terminal Link Van to get here; the driver had misheard me twice and taken me to the wrong terminal on each occasion.

"Terminal E," I had told him.

"*A?*" he had repeated back in his downtown accent and looking rather confused.

"Err...no...E"

"*A?*"

"E...for elephant!"

Jake laughs as I tell him this. And I laugh along too. It is a relief to see him. It is also a relief to finally be in Texas. It is warm here and already there seems to be an altogether friendlier vibe. Jake and I hail down a large green Chevy Uplander which takes us from the airport to our hotel in Downtown Dallas and, at last, it feels like I might just be able to sit back and...*relax*. As we approach the glittering, late-modernist, aluminium skyline of the so-called *Big D*, I get for the first time in weeks, a positive surge of emotion. Perhaps in a way that not even New York had been able to stir up genuine wonderment (mainly due to how equally oppressive and alienating it had all seemed), Dallas seems almost diaphanous by comparison (certainly it feels a hell of a lot more spacious) and, almost instantly, I have fallen in love with the place.

We pull up outside our hotel and make our way to reception. This four star hotel and conference centre will be our home for the next five days, as well as serving as a venue for Jake's International Conference on Accoustic, Speech and Signal Processing (ICASSP), and I am literally bowled over by its grandeur. The room we have been allocated is large and airy; the beds are custom-designed with mattress topper (*mattress toper!*) and there is a rather swish looking 42-inch LED backlit TV with Freeview and demand TV mounted onto the back wall. It is a far cry from chicken gauge and bed bugs and clinking radiators. Indeed, I am so glad not to be in yet another dire hostel in New York's cruddy China Town or crime-ridden Upper West side (110th street and above) that a hotel even half the quality and size would have more than adequately sufficed.

That evening, Jake and I decide, before bedtime, to go prosperously down to the hotel bar for a few celebratory drinks.

"This place is great," Jake says, as he pays for our beers with some freshly exchanged dollar bills.

"Here's to the rest of our holiday," I reply, clinking my glass of Bud Light with his and lying back into my soft, large leather sofa-chair.

Cheers. Or as they say over here in Dallas Texas, 'Cheers *y'all*'.

Whilst Jake is at his conference giving day-time presentations, I am off, like Christopher Columbus, doing some exploring on my own. One morning I decide to take an extra long exploratory walk right out across the Woodall Rodgers Freeway until, quite by accident, I stumble across what can only be described as mini-utopia: an avenue of Irish bars, sidewalk cafes and the best looking girls I have ever seen. This, I am later told by a random Latino babe, is Mckinney Avenue and today, as luck would have it, is St Patrick's Day meaning the whole place is brimming with bronze-pelted honeys in Shamrock green wishing everyone who passes a really *'happy St Paddy's Day'*.

Excitedly, I ring up Jake to let him know what I have discovered. “It's unbelievable,” I tell him with genuine amazement (the kind I can only imagine Columbus must have felt when he stumbled upon *San Salvador*). “You need to stop whatever you're doing and get here now!”

Ten minutes later and Jake pulls up in this bright yellow Dodge Grand Caravan with a grin from ear to ear. As it turns out, Jake is as much a fan of tanned American girls in skimpy green as I am.

That evening, having spent most of the afternoon getting lightly inebriated on pints of Guinness (after all, we were celebrating a *European* holiday), the two of us end up in a chic little bar called Sambuca Uptown speaking to a couple of hot girls propped up at the bar. Their names are Brittany and Kayla and they are seemingly drawn to our quintessentially English accents (they having approached us and not the other way around). Together, we down one *'Irish Car Bomb'* after another, this rather potent cocktail (comprising of Irish stout and whiskey) causing both Jake and I to feel ever so slightly sick, though for some unknown reason not conjuring the same effect on the girls whom appear as sober by the end of the night as they had done at the very beginning. Later on we find out that these so-called *girls* are actually both women in their mid-thirties - one of them actually a mother of two, the other a teacher in a local secondary school - and I, for one, am gobsmacked. Unlike the teenage moms on American talk shows or the older looking females on the streets of Time Square, the girls here clearly appear *younger* than they are in real life and, as a result, I am able to begin relaxing the interim pan-US 'looking' regulations which had so plagued me, particularly during my protracted stay at La Guardia's Delta Air Lines' boarding-gate. I am finally free to look where I want and it feels most liberating.

At the end of the evening, the two girls head off home (by car!) and Jake and I are literally left buzzing with elation; we have seemingly been speaking to some of the best looking girls in Dallas with almost next to no effort at all. “If any of this were to have happened at home, in the UK,” says Jake truthfully as we saunter slowly back to the heart of Downtown, to our hotel room, “we would instantly have assumed we were subject to some sort of cruel practical joke.”

As it is, both Jake and I will be pinching ourselves all the way back to Heathrow.

*

Almost as good as the women here is of course the food. Jake and I get the opportunity to frequent a variety of exquisite restaurants during our stay in Downtown serving a range of autochthonous Texan cuisine: barbeque ribs marinated in homemade barbeque sauce (Sonny Brian's), hand-picked prime beef steak (Dakota's), Texas Strip Dumplings and, of course, chicken fried steak in oceans of creamy white gravy.

The night before we are due to leave, Jake suggests going somewhere slightly different for our final meal. "How about *Hooters*?" he says with a degree of gusto. The idea instantly both excites and scares me in equal parts. As I think I may perhaps have mentioned earlier on, sex and OCD, a bit like the infamous Irish car bomb, is often something of an inadvisable mix. Sometimes, it can be a complete and utter recipe for disaster. Nevertheless, I cannot resist the urge to indulge in this once in a lifetime opportunity and I tell Jake that I agree it is probably a good idea.

"Oh go on then," I say, finally. "I think we're going to have to."

For those of you unfamiliar with the set-up, Hooters is a restaurant chain whose waiting staff are comprised solely of attractive young girls with toned, curvilinear bodies. The enterprise started out in Clearwater Florida and has since grown to be an empire of over four hundred odd restaurants, the title 'Hooters' a double-entendre referring both to the noise an owl makes (the Hooter's logo being an image of a barred owl) and the common American slang term for female bosoms.

However, as Jake and I arrive at this rather strange, sexed-up dining experience, we are surprised to discover how, well, *family* oriented it seems to be here. The place is positively littered with dough eyed couples, respectable, middle-American families and kids...loads and loads of *kids*.

Where are all the seedy, old anoraks, I think to myself? Where are all the leering, sex-deprived young adolescent males? Are Jake and I really the only two *debauchees* in the whole diner? The only two individuals here just to check out and leer at an array of scantily clad *broads*. Instantly, I feel inconsolably ashamed. Worse, I feel like a pervert...

A brunette with a tight white T-shirt and large, double D breasts eventually comes up to our table to take our order: Naked Wings for me, Chicken Strip Cheese for Jake. When she goes, I look at her peach-shaped bottom and then, as she sashays over to serve another table, I gawp again at her pert breasts. No one else seems even to have noticed her, let alone clocked her most spectacular physiology. Am I bad person for noticing? Am I bad person for being such an outrageous lecher? For potentially turning this unassuming young waitress, eager just to earn an honest crust, into nothing more than an object of male rapaciousness.

After our meal, Jake and I make our way back to the hotel for our last ever night in Texas and I cannot help but worry all the way back. In fact I am still fretting by the time I am ready to board the plane hours later the next day. I can only assume that it is the rather desultory prospect of returning back to the UK that is to blame here; for triggering this new wave of anxiety which I have dealt with in my usual unhelpful and counter-intuitive way. Though I know that, in reality, this is just one of a large number of things that could have set me off. It really doesn't take much.

The holiday is over and I am actually finding it difficult to come to terms with. Unfortunately, the OCD lives on. As we fly over Nova Scotia, The North Atlantic Ocean, Tralee and finally Heathrow, I wonder when it will all come to an end. I wonder when my break from OCD (and thus my chance to live a full and happy life) will truly begin. I finally conclude that running away or hiding at home is no longer the answer. That if I am to stand any chance of being well again I am going to have to face up to my problems, once more, head on.

I am going to need to seek help. And this time, I am not going to give up until I am healthy and well.

Chapter 15
"STILL ILL"

"The most fatal illusion is the settled point of view. Since life is growth and motion,
a fixed point of view kills anybody who has one."
-Brooks Atkinson

And so in the winter of 2011 I finally decide to go back to the doctors. Since returning home from the States my OCD has progressively worsened; each day becoming more frustrating, more unbearable, more distressing than the last. All the various techniques that were so keenly catechized over the course of various counselling sessions and treatment programs, have become lost or, more aptly, twisted and contorted by my own over-analytical mind. *'Analytical Aron'* is actually how I'm known at OCD group. I cannot fault the veracity of this alliterative assignation. Just as I cannot deny the grief my analytical tendencies have caused me over the years.

The morning of my appointment, in the comfort of Dr Goldstein's sea green office (yet *another* doctor at the same surgery), I convey my predicament with surety and conviction; the sort of expertness that one comes to expect from a seasoned surgery goer. As I had anticipated, Dr Goldstein looks back at me blankly, bewildered. OCD is simply just not that well understood by general practitioners. Luckily, I had prepared for such vacuity and as I begin to offload, Dr Goldstein instinctively looks down at the black computer keyboard in front of her.

I talk; she takes notes:

D. Goldstein:
24-Feb-2011
ASSESSMENT
HISTORY:
OCD since university (5 or 6 years) Perhaps had some signs of it when a child

PROBLEMS:
Intrusive thoughts about morals; trying to work out whether he is a bad person, how to avoid getting himself in situations where his morals are questioned, trying to work out if his actions are bad or not bad.
Is too analytical

Can't trust himself.
Some thoughts about what he looks like (mild BDD?) resulting in compulsive face checking in any reflective surface.

EXAMPLE OF THOUGHTS: 'how do I know I haven't been a bad person? If I don't think about it I might do something bad.
Emotion; anxiety
Behaviour; dwelling on thoughts until I can work it out. Makes rules for future behaviour, excessive avoidance (not looking at people, avoiding places etc) Seek reassurance

DRUG/ALCHOLOL; only social alcohol. No drug

RISK; none

PAST HELP; CBT group support, mindfulness, counselling

OUTCOME;
Accepted for CBT.

It is a few months later when I finally hear back from the NHS. It comes in the form of a letter: "We are pleased to inform you," reads the belated dispatch, "that we have booked you a series of appointments to see one of our trainee therapists starting in April and continuing for up to a maximum of twenty sessions. Please call the below number to confirm your appointment if you wish to proceed."

I look at my mum (whom happens to be in the room with me as I open and then read through the letter) in utter horror; "A *trainee,*" I let out in an appalled tone. "All these years a sufferer, and the only thing they can offer me is a bleedin' *trainee*."

My mum looks back at me sympathetically though slightly more unaffectedly than I might have otherwise preferred; "Just give it a go," she replies calmly, diplomatically. "You have absolutely nothing to lose."

She, of course, is right.

And so that afternoon, begrudgingly to say the least, I phone up my local NHS mental health service to confirm my first appointment.

"Right then," says the rather officious woman on the other end of the phone, coldly summarising the call, "that'll be 5 p.m. Thursday March 30th to see Joseph Carpenter at the West Pottergate Health Centre on Earlham Road. Please do not be late."

"Fine, thank you," I say, putting down the phone without even so much as an affirmatory goodbye. Though in truth I am about as far from fine as I have ever been. As I later put it in a text message to a friend: *"I am about as far from fine as a waterbuck in a lion's den."*

A few weeks later, after what feels like literally a lifetime on the waiting list, my appointment for CBT eventually comes around. By this time, my OCD has become so bad I am scarcely able to go five minutes without a great rush of anxiety. Triggers, it seems, are absolutely everywhere: an advert for nappies on the TV, an awkward glimpse up the skirt of a manikin, a vignette of a nude child in my own mind's eye. And now, as I arrive over fifteen minutes late to my first ever session of CBT with trainee Joseph, I cannot help but feel foolish for falling, yet again, down the same forsaken trap.

Why am I late? The answer, as always, comes back to good old reliable - or should that be *unreliable* - OCD.

I had, as it happens, been relatively hopeful as I strolled calmly and on time along the main road headed for the West Pottergate Health Centre this rather mild and temperate winter's evening. I had been trying carefully to compose myself, to think constructively about what I might say, about how I might accurately convey my symptoms, when, almost out of nowhere at all, anxiety had struck like a blow to the back of the head. Unwittingly, I had stumbled upon a beautiful white and marble butterfly which had somehow become stuck to a piece of chewing gum right smack bang in the middle of the pavement which had caused me a considerable degree of distress and anguish. *Should I help it?* I panicked to myself, anxiety now rising fast and pressing uncomfortably against my rib cage. *Or should I leave it well alone? If I try to pull it away, I may accidently pull its wings off. If I leave it, I will undoubtedly be responsible for bringing about its continual suffering.*

The dilemma, like so many of the other thousand or so predicaments that invade me on a daily basis, went round and around in my head like a 1300 watt cyclone vacuum cleaner. During these 'moments of madness' as I now like to refer to them, it is nearly almost always impossible to make a good or rational pronouncement. When anxiety is involved, even something as simple as whether or not to eat lunch or use the lavatory can feel like a real *Sophie's Choice*. Though, conscious of my impending appointment and the consequential strain on the NHS should I arrive late, I knew I would need to make a decision and make it quickly. And so I brushed my hands together, *manually* shifted gears, and continued on 'bravely' about my journey. Only, as I did so, to my utter disbelief, anxiety somehow managed to strike me for a second time, this time upon joining onto the main section of Earlham Road. In my haste to get to the health centre - not least because I was now actually physically eating into NHS time - I had begun, quite unintentionally, to swing my arms, violently, recklessly, oblivious to anyone walking behind and was devastated to discover, upon turning my head behind my left shoulder blade, a woman in a cheap Down Moncler jacket, pushing a pram a mere two or so metres from my vacillating carcass. Immediately, I panicked about just how near my swinging hands had come to touching her body; had I secretly done it on purpose, to touch her leg, to touch her vagina...to touch *the baby??*

For the remainder of the journey, petrified that this final act had now somehow transformed me immediately into a rapist or, worse still, a paedophile, I walked so slow I might just as well have been on all fours crawling. All the while, my arms remained fixed firmly to my sides like a Russian doll or an Elizabethan Irish dancer. Until eventually, *finally*, I had arrived at my destination.

Which of course is where I am now. Late for my appointment and being rather unfairly chastised by the evil-looking receptionist manning the front desk; "You're *late,*" she says, judgementally, as I attempt to apologise, understandably looking both exhausted and dishevelled; sweat dripping from my forehead like goblets of rainwater down a nickel-chrome laminated car window. The old bat, snarling under her breath whilst still somehow remaining ostensibly 'professional', proceeds to usher me into the correct treatment room where, shortly after having made my entrance, I throw off my jacket and flop onto the only available plastic-backed chair in sight. Joseph, who no doubt has been sat here for a good twenty minutes or so, looks up at me and smiles. "You must be Aron," he says in a friendly though nervous tone, observing my ruffled deportment and kindly turning a blind eye to my tardiness. "My name is Joseph. How are you?"

I look down at my feet. *How do you think*, is what I feel like saying. "Not great," I say instead rather more tactfully. I slide back into an upright position, hooked forward like one of those large, carved stone gargoyles I saw so frequently perched precariously atop New York skyscrapers. I do not look up or around me and, consequently, have barely noticed the pale, pastel blue walls or the brown wooden desk upon which sits an old Windows Millennium edition PC. Perhaps most importantly, I have not really paid much attention to the grey, rather timid looking *trainee* sat nervously but patiently in front of me, about to work his very first case of Pure-O.

"Well if you just sit back. Relax. Get your breath back and maybe we can help sort things through," says Joseph, quite uneasily. I look up for the first time and attempt to recompose myself.

Joseph starts by asking me to explain why I am not feeling so great and the nature of my OCD more generally. I peer back at him importunately and, unable to contain my epic tales of woe for a moment longer, I let it all out, every last detail. It rolls off the tongue like a round of double Gloucester cheese down a particularly declivitous hillside. I tell him I am afraid of looking at people, of accidently (but perhaps also on purpose) touching women and children, of having inappropriate sexual thoughts and of being a raving *pervert*. I ask him if it was bad that I smiled at a sixteen year-old last week thinking she was eighteen? Or whether it was wrong that I glimpsed at a girl's crotch on the bus and then smirked involuntarily? Is it bad that I looked at the breasts and vagina of a septuagenarian on a park bench last Thursday?

The list of my concerns and potential malfeasants go on and on like an old 1996 advert promoting Italian washing machines. In response, Joseph simply looks at me with an almost vertiginous confusion and smiles quasi-moronically. "You're going to have to speak a lot slower," he tells me, again laughing nervously. "I'm finding it hard keeping up."

His perplexity instantly strikes me as quite bizarre. Not to mention curiously maddening. *What is he finding so difficult here,* I think rather hotly to myself. *Surely this is all pretty straightforward stuff?* Nevertheless, not wishing to appear ungenerous, I go through the list again, this time a bit slower and with a little more by way of elucidation.

It does not help.

"You seem to have so many different OCDs," Joseph responds still seemingly bewildered. "Perhaps we could just deal with one thing at a time."

"I haven't got lots of *different* OCDs," I respond back, the aggravation rising again in my tone. "It's all the same. It all follows the same *pattern.*"

"Does it?"

"Yes. Of course it does!"

"I guess," Joseph shrugs, picking his lip, still not fully committing himself to this line of thought. His apparent incomprehension is now more than I can stand and, as he continues to fumble unskilfully through the session, I sit back in my chair, slumped back and switched off. As far as I am now concerned, Joseph has blown it entirely and consequently I have lost trust in almost everything he has to say. Nevertheless, he proceeds to ask me a few background questions into my illness - how long I have been suffering, when I first noticed it, when I had first gone to see about it - and I answer each interrogative with little more than monosyllabic grunts. Eventually, after ten minutes or so of this benign probing into my condition, the questions stop abruptly. It is now 6 p.m. and seemingly my session has come to a rather sudden end. Indeed, so keen to draw the session to a close, Joseph actually manages to end mid-sentence, the fifteen minutes lost at the beginning scarcely to be recouped. (This has always been a massive gripe of mine, though not simply just confined to Joseph. One could literally be dangling on a life-changing precipice; on the very cusp of a breakthrough leading to undoubted recuperation and the session would still always have to end *on time*, at a pre-designated juncture.)

"We will discuss further the *content* of your obsessions next week," Joseph tells me cheerfully and with what appears to be a touch of relief as I throw on my coat and get ready to leave.

"If there is a next week," I mutter faintly under my breath.

When I arrive home that evening, as you might expect, my mum asks me with interest how my session had gone.

"Awful," I tell her frankly, not sparing anybody's feelings, least of all hers. "The man doesn't understand a bloody thing. I would be better off counselling myself."

My mum looks at me imploringly. "Well, maybe next time will be better eh?"

"Maybe," I say, dropping my voice down to an inaudible whisper. "And maybe I'll also have children with Kate Moss." And with that I slope off to my room to worry some more about kids, old ladies and...*butterflies*.

It has often been said that a bad thing poorly expressed is a lie. I don't quite agree with this statement but what I am sure of is that both clarity and insight are of vital importance when it comes to good therapy. Without it, the counsel is merely a regurgitation of what could otherwise be imbibed straight from a book or an article online.

Unfortunately - though perhaps not too unpredictably - as the sessions with Joseph went on, so the misunderstandings and fumbling persisted. We locked horns on so many issues that I found going there only ever seemed to make my OCD worse as opposed to better. Sometimes I couldn't help but liken seeing Joseph to a rescue attempt from choppy waters by a lifeguard with no arms and no legs.

Though, looking back, I can also see that my own attitude did not always help. My grossly analytical tendencies which so often served me well academically, invariably demanded, perhaps inappropriately, an equal, if not superior, intellectual understanding in those masquerading as so-called experts and therapists. I found it difficult to trust and even harder to accept advice that hadn't first been subject to rigorous authentication.

"You should give people a chance," my mum would say. "You can't be helped if you won't *let* yourself be helped."

Again, she was right. But perhaps not as entirely as I had first ceded...

Therapists, in many ways, as I have since reflected, are like clothes shops; some outlets can be niche and high-quality (Selfridges for example) whilst others can equally be cheap or tacky (I'm thinking the Bargain Bin at QD). What I'm trying to say here is that just because a shop sells clothes does not mean we should buy from them. Nor would we expect people to put up and shut up when it comes to wearing clothes they do not feel comfortable in. Not all clothes are equal. *Shop around*! You never know what you are missing until you explore the options further.

Certainly over the years I have had cause to question the aptitude of many of the therapists I had encountered, particularly the ones that were thrust upon me (as opposed to ones, later, that I chose for myself). At best, the majority seemed to have only a very cursory understanding of the handful of spectrum disorders to which they must apply a blanket CBT approach. At worst, many of them simply did not understand the disorders to which they were designated to treat at all.

Portentously for me, Joseph was perhaps a firm example of the latter. Had I known then what I know now, had the confidence then that I do now in sheer abundance, I would no doubt have insisted on seeing someone else; someone more experienced. I would certainly have insisted on *shopping around*. Alas, it would be a lesson I would have to learn the hard way and, regrettably, quite late on in my journey. For now at least, I was stuck with what I had. And what I had was far, far from ideal.

"Treating OCD is actually very simple," insisted Joseph during actually only the third of our sessions together. It was a cold miserable afternoon in February and immediately his optimism put me on edge. Not to mention invoked deep scepticism. What did he of little qualification and with certainly no personal experience know of OCD? Of the way it so mercilessly gripped its victims and didn't ever seem to want to let go, like a ferocious Siberian tiger seizing on human flesh? What did he know of the torment, the fear, the *shame*. No doubt his conviction was based nearly entirely on what he had read in some instruction manual or on some pithy crash course. Like many CBT therapists, Joseph knew the rudiments of OCD predominantly through a book.

Yet it was on this rather flimsy basis that Joseph, already detecting my censor but somehow remaining unable (or should that be *unwilling*) to change tact, came out with the following; "I am sure, as sure as I can be anyway, that the way to tackle your OCD is with behavioural experiments or, as it is often referred, *exposure and response prevention*."

And with that, the room fell into total silence. I sank so far in my seat I thought I might simply slide off the edge and down a never-ending hole in the ground. The thought that this facile and rather abecedarian method, above all else, might be utilised almost exclusively in my recovery made me shudder as if suddenly visited upon by the apparitions of all the local dead. That Joseph had even suggested such a course of action made me angry. Very angry. And not to mention anxious. Indeed, had I not been so afraid of expressing my true emotions in public, of being seen as an out-and-out *sissy*, I might simply have run out of the treatment room then and there.

Exposure and response prevention or ERP as it is often abbreviated was something that had invoked cynicism, if not total disparagement, in me right from the very moment I had first ever read about it. In fact, I often held ERP in much the same regard as many of the poor therapists that I had unwillingly endured during my various travels through therapy. I hated it. I hated the very idea of it.

Before I go into a whole diatribe on why I found ERP often so unhelpful it is perhaps only fair to first mention what it is and why it is used. ERP is certainly not without empirical justification. In fact, according to nearly every bit of scientific research out there, it is this form of therapy which is heralded the most effectual in treating the more general symptoms of OCD. The principle behind ERP is simple and the methodology can be split neatly, all too conveniently some might argue, into two crucial tenets: 1) Exposure to feared stimuli and 2) A discontinuation of an escape response. The best way to explain it is perhaps by reference to a common example:

Imagine if you will a patient who fears touching dirt. He avoids fields or places where there is any sort of mud or feculence. Under ERP, he might be asked to face his fears directly by repeatedly touching his most feared item (exposure) and then resisting the urge to wash afterwards (prevention). This is in turn causes what is known in the field as *habituation* whereby the previously feared stimuli - in this case mud or dirt - no longer induces in the subject or patient any apprehension at all. Over time it simply stops being a problem altogether and the patient slowly but surely begins to make a full recovery.

It is, in many ways, a simple and quite perfunctory process which no doubt is part of its main appeal. According to the NHS website on the effectiveness of ERP: "People with mild to moderate OCD usually need about ten hours of therapist treatment." No doubt such a package is exceptionally attractive for a budget-conscious NHS. For a Society concerned perhaps as much with getting people back into work as they are with mental health per say, I can imagine how such a quick turn-around might more than readily suit the overriding agenda.

Unfortunately what is convenient does not always equate to what is right. Or helpful. Or useful. And whilst ERP has been shown to work well with perhaps more conventional forms of OCD (i.e. for people with something quite *behavioural* like washing or checking), for those of us with a version of OCD such as moral scrupulosity or a more cognitive variation thereof, I think the results can, at best, be quite hit-and-miss. Though, unfortunately, the research remains woefully lacking in this area. According to a study conducted in 2005 by Elizabeth A. Nelson et al and published in the *Journal of Anxiety Disorders,* volume 2, issue 8: "Scrupulosity is often encountered among individuals with obsessive-compulsive disorder (OCD), yet relatively few studies have examined this particular symptom presentation."

The main problem I encountered with ERP was that my own type of OCD was often incredibly *hypothetical*, intuited by an array of cognitive biases and premised on often highly un-testable, moral dilemmas: *'Am I a bad person if I look at a girl's crotch?'* or *'Am I a sinner if I happen to touch my penis at the same time an image of a baby has come into my line of sight?* or even, *'Am I a pervert if I imagine myself quite randomly having sex with a rather provocative looking Labrador?'* The answer, I assure you, is not to stare, as ERP would have it, inappropriately at female labia, masturbate over minors or seek out canine pornography. (It is perhaps worth noting here that any therapist that asks you to do any of these things is either dangerously missing the point or a complete nut bag (most likely both) and needs urgently to be struck off.)

Moral scrupulosity, unlike other more mainstream manifestations of OCD, on the whole, tends to invoke more complex obsessions and self-dialogue. And unlike, for example, our understanding of germs and the rules pertaining to their proliferation (as in the case of contamination OCD), there are scarcely any singular, objective *moral* truths when it comes to religious or secular moral scrupulosity. And this leaves us with more than just a few unanswered questions when it comes to determining 'acceptable' exposure. To what extent can or should "reasonable risks" be carefully incorporated into the therapy? What even is a "reasonable risk" when it comes to *ethical* behavioural parameters? As Jonathan D Huppert and Jedidiah Siev point out in their article *'Treating Scrupulosity in religious Individuals Using Cognitive-Behavioral Therapy'*:

"In EX/RP we increase the level of risk without going to the point that the level of risk is forbidden by religious law... This approach is similar to standard EX/RP for other forms of OCD, for which the patient takes risks during which they are confronted with the uncertainty of the feared consequence without truly actualizing it. This is very clear in treatment of harm and sexual obsessions, where actual engagement in the feared act is typically immoral, unethical, and illegal, in which case in vivo exposures involved normal behaviour during which the patient is confronted with fears and uncertainty (e.g., a mother who fears stabbing her children dices vegetables with them in the room)."

For me personally, this whole notion of 'normal' exposure raises two rather pronounced problems which are as follows: 1) Effective ERP, unlike cognitive-biobehavioral self-treatment (such as Dr. Jeffrey Schwartz's *Four Steps*), cannot be practised alone or even with only a semi-competent therapist and 2) who determines the morally "acceptable risks"? In the study above, there are suggestions that "if the therapist is not sure about whether a planned exposure is in fact a true violation of a religious dictate then clergy should be consulted". But what about for a moral atheist? What about for a virtuous agnostic merely desperate at all costs not to be deemed a *bad* individual? Surely such an endeavour, although well-meaning enough, simply feeds the misguided conception that moral certainty on some level should still be sought. That moral objectivity is in fact even possible. By contrast, a treatment programme promoting trust in gut feelings, acceptance and a recognition of OCD symptoms as purely *egodystonic* might be much better placed.

Of course, now I can appreciate that the above appraisal may be ever so slightly inerudite. As a result of extremely helpful therapy I received much later on in my illness, I now know only too well that traditional ERP can indeed be applied effectively to moral OCD. *How*, I hear you ask? Well it's actually pretty simple when you consider it carefully: one must simply expose themselves not to the moral behaviour, as in the case of scrupulosity, but to the hot *thought,* 'I am a bad person'. The response prevention then comes in the outright refusal to engage with that particular thought - i.e. *not* 'working it out' or *not* making rules. In the case of Pure O, thoughts are often dealt with by the OCDer with *cerebral* compulsions. It therefore only stands to reason that ERP in this respect must be aimed at reducing the *thoughts* and not in testing the outcomes - which in some instances may actually serve only to incite further ritualization, further 'working out'.

As with perhaps the majority of OCDers with moral scrupulosity, my own OCD thoughts would often be framed more as an interrogative than as a statement of fact: *'Is* it bad if I do X?' or *'Am* I a bad person for doing Y?' rather than, "It *is* dangerous to do X" and "I *must* avoid Y". With regard the latter, traditional ERP, which involves actually *doing* X or trying out Y can, I imagine, actually be quite effective. With regard the former, it perhaps does no more than simply generate yet another OCD ritual: an endeavour to create certainty through *testing.*

"We must not allow OCD treatment to simply become part of the ritualising process," warns Margo. "Such an outcome would be most counter-productive."

And so there you have it: complicated thoughts and rituals requiring perhaps more than just a straightforward, one-size-fits-all treatment plan. It was, in so many ways, beyond the remit, or maybe even the expertise, of poor old Joseph.

Nevertheless, often during my sessions, I would give Joseph every opportunity to regroup, to consolidate his knowledge and think about the condition much more discerningly. I would often, for example, express my concerns over the intricacies of ERP in the vain hope that some of it might just register but, alas, the vast majority of it would go right over his head. Unsurprisingly, Joseph's inexperience meant that he was often unable to address much of my apprehension and was either too proud or confused (or both) to go out and source me the answers from elsewhere.

"I am worried about purposefully getting an erection in public," I told him, maybe too candidly one session (and back when my own understanding of ERP was pretty substandard). "I'm worried that if I think about sex deliberately whilst I am out in public it could give me an erection. If people then *see* my erection, I am automatically a bad person because I caused it to happen on purpose."

"I see," said Joseph, stroking his grey-brown goatee, looking cogitative. "In that case, maybe you should just try *not* thinking about sex." And at this, my jaw dropped, both my eyebrows catapulting skyward, forming a rather pronounced single stray crease in the middle of my forehead. I simply could not believe what I was hearing.

"But if I try to *avoid* thinking about sex," I responded, somewhat uneasily, "then surely I am engaging in a *compulsion*. I am engaging in *thought suppression*." Instead I told Joseph that surely the answer was to think about sex as much as I liked. To put my OCD beliefs to the test by simply just letting go and doing whatever came naturally. Surely, if nothing else, this was much more in line with traditional ERP...

"No!" Joseph cried out, an unintended plaint in his pitch, the force of which making me jump up in my seat. "Per...perhaps that would not be such a good idea." He gave me a final beseeching look; "W..we..we might have to look at this in more detail next week."

And with that I looked down despondently at my watch. It was 6 p.m. The session had officially concluded. There would be no more discussion on the topic for at least the next seven days.

As the Spring slowly approached, cherry trees abundant with clusters of Bavarian cream white, evergreen herbaceous plants in the throes of producing vibrant pinks, yellows and reds and bell-flowers displaying the most radiant and breathtaking flashes of blue and purple, my OCD had grown into a full blossom all of its own. Each day, whilst the sun shone brightly up in the fluttering Columbian blue sky, my mood remained dark, deep, impenetrable. It was like a black cloud that would not pass, a dark tunnel that I simply could not dig my way out of.

It seemed, perhaps now more than ever, like all hope of recovery was fast slipping away; further and further like fine sand through the lithesome fingers of a child. My sessions with Joseph were proving to be most unfruitful indeed; each futile session only making a lifetime of suffering seem that much more likely. And of course, that much more awful by virtue of its endlessness.

I felt low most days. Some mornings I would wake with a tinge of disaffection which would make it hard, very hard at times, to get out of bed. I didn't feel up to socialising and, instead, looked forward to hot baths (this, despite the warmer weather) and going to bed as early as I could get away with. I felt generally less motivated. I barely sent text messages and gave up on phone conversations almost altogether.

I had, in many ways, hit my *lowest* point.

Yet, nevertheless, it would be inaccurate of me to say now, in light of everything that I have subsequently read on the subject, that what I was experiencing back then was the emergence or first signs of clinical depression. Or even clinical dysphoria. In many ways, my growing anxiety, the full-on disquiet that intuited my thinking, although bringing me down at times, was perhaps the biggest indicator that my zest for life remained in fact quite steadfast; after all, only someone with such a heaped and vested interest in *living* could possibly care so much for the supposed consequence of each and every minor thought and action. Indeed, the infertile energy, the mental waste that one must somehow associate with anxiety, is at the very least, an indicator that we do indeed still care. That we have not given up on life. That we have not given up on ourselves.

Nevertheless, depression and OCD are far from divorced. According to OCD UK, one of the UK's leading national charities, roughly three out of every four people with OCD have concurrent co-morbid depression. That is to say, 75 percent of all sufferers will, at some stage in their illness, suffer some or all of the following symptoms (which again, are listed on the OCD UK website):

- Low mood.
- Lack of interest in and pleasure from usual activities and interests.
- Poor attention and concentration.
- Suicidal ideas and feelings.
- Loss of energy
- Loss of sexual desire
- Feelings of guilt or shame.
- Extensive pessimism
- Feelings of worthlessness or hopelessness.
- Disturbed appetite, usually associated with weight loss or weight gain.
- Disturbed sleep, often causing waking in the early hours of the morning and a feeling of being unrefreshed by sleep.

Looking at the list in all of its reductionist candour, I can certainly place a mental tick by a good third of them. The main one for me, however, has always been the guilt. As I hope has become abundantly clear by now, my OCD frequently inspirited feelings of colossal self-reproach and shame. Sometimes the guilt would weigh down on me so heavily I could scarcely have found the energy to bring myself to stand upright.

Fortunately for me, the other symptoms were far less frequent and, in many cases, were not even present at all. Scarcely did I feel worthless or hopeless. *Never* did I suffer suicidal thoughts and feelings (*suicidal ideation* is how it is often referred and involves an unusual mental occupation with ending one's own life).

My appetite, sleep patterns and sex drive also remained, on the whole, fully intact (sometimes a particularly unpleasant sexual obsession might temporarily put me off of eroticism and sex more generally. Though mostly my sexual OCD had no de facto link with my libido).

I guess, on that basis, I am one of the lucky ones. Although I suffered certain symptoms of depression, I certainly could not have been labelled a true depressive. Indeed, when not drowning in anxiety, I was actually pretty happy-go-lucky. Some mornings, where there was no OCD, no spikes of anxiety or guilt, I would wake with an almost solipsistic optimism, an ephemeral surge of exhilaration from nowhere in particular, as if a fidgety, galvanic infant on Christmas morning. Sometimes, I forgot to be grateful for those small blessings. Often I would overlook the worth of *intermittent* happiness as if somehow cancelled out by the surrounding misery.

"Sometimes, it really is unbearable," said one of my friends at group who suffered terribly with both depression and OCD (and eating disorders...and body dismorphia). "I can't leave the house. Sometimes I have days where I sleep for more than sixteen hours at a time."

A spiritualist friend of mine once told me that, as living creatures, we are all only ever given as much suffering as we can deal with. To me this is bullshit. For some people, their suffering can be like a bottomless pit. For others, their suffering is so bad they feel they have no choice but to end their lives. Some succeed.

It is generally estimated that between five to 25 percent of people with OCD will at some point attempt to end their lives. Whilst most OCDers will tend to go on fighting and simply struggle through their symptoms - hence *The Walking Worried* - we must not forget those that are so stricken by the torment of their illness, the agony and helplessness of it all, that they feel they can no longer go on. There is a wonderful though difficult book by Louis Chaber entitled *'The Thing Inside my Head'* which chronicles beautifully and eloquently the suffering and the agony of her daughter Sybil through OCD and Anorexia Nervosa as well as her and her family's distress at the loss of their daughter following her tragic suicide whilst still in hospital. It is, in no uncertain terms, a wake-up call to all those who may wish to trivialise the condition as well as to the professionals out there designated to provide and administer cohesive and effective treatment therapies.

For me, it was a beacon of hope; a reminder to count my blessings. Without a doubt, I am one of the lucky ones. I work, I socialise and, to a large extent, I enjoy my life. I try not to forget that whenever I am feeling too sorry for myself or start believing that I have it so much worse than everyone else. I hope most sincerely that I never have to find out first-hand how hard living with clinical depression or having to battle constantly with suicidal thoughts must be.

"Be kind," Plato warns us, "for everyone you meet is fighting a harder battle." Never has there been a truer aphorism.

After Spring, came slowly and gradually the summer. And with the sunshine and warmer weather came, finally, actually a bit of a breakthrough. After what had felt like months of banal and two-dimensional counselling from Joseph and censorious, polemic resistance from me in response, we finally stumbled on a course of action that we could both work on. *Together*.

One afternoon, during one of our final sessions, Joseph told me of there being this list of common cognitive distortions in OCD and my ears pricked with interest. Joseph, who had clearly done some of his own preparation, handed me a black-and-white photocopy of a page entitled *Types of OCD Beliefs* and on the page, clearly laid out, were a list of five or six or maybe even as many as ten different 'faulty beliefs' distinctive to OCD. Joseph began reading them aloud. There were, amongst others, 'over-importance of thoughts' (the idea that one places thoughts and actions as moral equivalents), 'inflation of responsibility' (discounting the parts that others may have played or the influence of circumstances outside one's own control), 'overestimation of danger' (the likelihood of something bad happening being unrealistically high), 'need for certainty' and 'intolerance of anxiety'.

Underneath the main 'faulty beliefs' there were a list of sub-beliefs or 'cognitive errors', described as inappropriate mental filters by which a person with OCD may come to see the world. These errors included, amongst many, 'polarized thinking', 'labelling', 'overgeneralization' and 'mind reading'.

"When you feel like giving in or even *buying in* to one of your intrusive thoughts," said Joseph quite informatively, "you can use these labels to help gain clarity and objectivity."

"Yes," I said, feeling a surge of excitement. "This is good. Very good."

And so, over the next few weeks, I started to use this new way of labelling my cognitive experiences to help me identify when and where I was having an OCD thought. I found it to be, on the whole, quite effective. I also found it to be an extremely useful expansion on what I already found most helpful about Dr Schwartz's Four Step Programme. Any therapy that attempted to separate *me* from my OCD, which enabled me to regain some form of *perspective* was a treatment method I was more than willing to embrace.

"I want you to really practice using this list whenever you feel like you are about to give in to a thought," said Joseph. "Pretend that you are in court weighing up the evidence. Look for the evidence to support your OCD thought, write it down if necessary, and then, with reference to the list, look for the evidence against. This should help you always to come to the right conclusion."

In actual fact, looking for the *evidence* was not a new concept to me. Notwithstanding my legal training, Margo had mentioned the importance of evidence on numerous occasions in group by reference to something called '*Theory A and Theory B'* which I had always found most helpful. The idea behind this simple but effective cognitive strategy, first proposed by Professor Paul Salvoskis in his groundbreaking work *'Breaking Free'*, is that the meaning we assign to our thoughts do not always equate to a true or factual representation. In other words, the OCD beliefs we hold close (and which lead invariably to the performance of unnecessary safety seeking behaviours), may in fact not always be the correct way of viewing the world at all. Salkovskis makes the distinction between true danger and mere *worry* about danger.

To put this into an OCD context and drawing from my own personal manifestation of the disorder, the negative hot thought '*I am a bad person who likes to make women feel violated just by looking at them'* (Theory A) might be turned immediately into Theory B, '*I am a conscientious, responsible person who is simply* worried *that normal looking* **may** *lead to women feeling violated.*'

It was a simple enough conversion. But how do we make the leap from one world view to the other? Salkovskis asks us simply just to look for the evidence. What is the *evidence* I like to cause women to suffer by looking at them? Have I ever enjoyed hurting them before? Have any women ever come forward to say that I have upset them or harmed them in any way? Is it not true that all men look at women during the course of their day-to-day business anyway?

The evidence, when applied in this way, nearly always provided support for...yep, you guessed it, *Theory B*. And, on that basis alone, I liked it immensely. It was reassurance but not in the traditional sense. It did not provide *answers*, merely helped one to rationalise their thoughts, to see things in a bit more perspective. *Ei, non qui negat*; "The burden of proof rests on who asserts, not on who denies."

Yet there is a big danger that evidence gathering of this nature can, if not regulated, simply become a form of *over-analysis* which, far from being useful, is sadly just another mental ritual. The line between healthy examination of the evidence and fixation with finding the *truth* (and thereby certainty) is not always an easy one to draw. Often it can raise only further uncertainty which, frankly, is no good for an OCDer at all. It has invariably been my own experience that if a treatment plan does not sound simplistic on paper it will rarely ever work. That is not to say that treatment itself is ever easy, just that complicated solutions to complex over-thinking is counter-intuitive to say the least.

For me, recognising the 'faulty beliefs' inherent in my OCD was empowering but not liberating. I found that the rituals and the thoughts did not go away. Temporarily it might bring my obsessions briefly into question but it was seemingly never enough to stop me hurtling down the same ritualistic pathways again and again and again. '*What happens if this time it is actually not just OCD?*' was a frequent concern. '*What if on this occasion the OCD and reality just so happen to coincide in a display of beautiful synchronicity*?' The problem with evidence-gathering for a legal mind is that one will always find (and be able to dig-up) some justification for whichever premise or argument they wish to support.

Treatment is often what one makes of it. The trick is not to adulterate it or to bend it to a particular agenda (usually an *OCD* agenda). Instead, it must be followed diligently and painstakingly and in the spirit with which it is intended. Often for this to work, one must be well-supported and inundated with copious expert supervision. At the very least a patient must have a practised and effectual therapist at hand to answer their questions and help them back up when they fall off the wagon. Unfortunately for me, I knew through my own personal experiences with Joseph, that I would not be able to rely on such expert supervision. That working through my problems would invariably be a *solo* endeavour. And it is for that very reason that my commitment to treatment, and in particular to CBT, was only ever at best half-hearted. At its worst it was almost totally non-existent.

"On a journey of a hundred miles, ninety is but half way." For me, CBT, and in particular ERP, on its own and inexpertly applied did not constitute an adequate arsenal. Unfortunately for all concerned, neither did Joseph constitute an adequate therapist.

It is a warm summer's afternoon in August whilst on my lunch break at work when I ring Joseph to let him know that I will not be re-attending our sessions together. We have been through eleven hours all in (so just over half of the dedicated or allotted time) and it feels like now we have perhaps come as far as we can. Unsurprisingly, as I speak candidly about how I have found my sessions with him, the limitations on treatment etc, he does not try and talk me out of leaving. Nor does he offer me an alternative course of action. Instead he seems almost relieved at the news that I will not be coming back.

"Thank you for letting me know Aron," he says earnestly. "I suspect though that you will be just fine from now on anyway."

He tells me that he thinks that I already have a "firm grasp" on the main tenets of CBT and that I have made plenty of progress since joining back in March. He also offers to phone me in a few months time to see how I am and, should I need it, organise a follow-up session. "We will definitely stay in touch," he tells me with what the two of us know to be more comity than truth.

I thank him for his time and he wishes me well, once again, for the future.

I know I will not hear from him again.

Chapter 16
"WHATEVER WORKS"

"Do not fight the thing in detail: turn from it. Look ONLY at your Lord. Sing. Read. Work."
Amy Carmichael, *Gold by Moonlight*

And so it was, in the months following my discharge from therapy, I had resolved to get better on my own. In many ways it seemed like the only option. Sometimes it still feels that way. After all, only *we* can make a difference to the way we think and feel; only *we* are able to take the necessary steps, to place one foot in front of the other on the road towards true and meaningful change. Nonetheless, I knew it would not be easy. I also knew it would not just be a case of reading and re-reading the same old material over and over (which, at any rate, runs the risk of becoming, well, a tad OCD). Getting from poorly to well, from A to B takes *action*; "If you're not prepared to do the work," says Margo, "then all the understanding and analyses, all the thinking and theory in the world will not help you recover."

There is a quirky, up-beat little phrase by Henry Ford that sums up the situation handsomely: "If you always do what you've always done, then you'll always get what you've always got."

The same is undoubtedly true for OCD. If you always respond to anxiety in the same way, by giving in to it or engaging in endless compulsions or mental rituals, then chances are you will only ever get the same results back out again - namely, shit loads more anxiety with a nice side dolloping of guilt and shame for good measure.

Changing how we *think* requires changing what we *do*.

And so, over the following weeks and months, I tried making small but significant changes to my life; I tried brand new things that I thought would help. In fact, I even tried things I did not think would help. Sometimes, it is worth just trying *everything*. It never ceases to surprise me how often it turns out to be the case that what on the surface seems to be a little *OTT* or even darn right bizarre ends up providing that missing golden nugget, the next step on the ladder towards revitalization.

Some things worked whilst others did not. I guess that is only to be expected; one man's meat is another man's poison and all that. But, as it happens, *nothing* was a complete disaster. My efforts had given me renewed hope and I saw each endeavour, however wide of the mark, as merely a step closer to happiness; as one further step towards being able, finally, to jump off that spinning carousel of mental illness.

In the winter of 2010 I decided to join the local gym. I was rather sceptical at first (not having done any proper exercise since realising I had put on a bit of extra 'puppy fat' during year ten and going to extra cross-country practices to remedy the situation) but now it seemed like literally everyone was doing it. "Maybe you should just give it a try," said a friend one afternoon, after I had driven them mad pondering the issue aloud. "Yes," I concluded eventually, "I think you are probably right."

As it turned out, it was one of the best decisions I have ever made.

According to the authors of a recent pilot study looking into the effects of moderate-intensity aerobic exercise for obsessive compulsive disorder, the role of exercise as an adjunct to other more conventional OCD treatments should not be overlooked and may even play a vital role in reducing OCD symptomology. The authors conclude that:

"OCD patients in this study were highly adherent to the exercise intervention and demonstrated and maintained cardiorespiratory fitness improvements 6 months after the intervention. They also reported that exercise was helpful in reducing their OCD symptoms and that it was not likely to trigger obsessions or compulsions. The findings of this study suggest a rather robust effect of a 12-week moderate intensity, aerobic exercise intervention on reduction in OCD symptom severity. Furthermore, reductions in OCD symptom severity seem to persist 6 months later. Lastly, a significant improvement in overall sense of well-being was observed following participation in the 12-week intervention."

The article goes on to suggest some of the reasons why this might be the case. One line of thought put forward by the authors of the study is that exercise increases brain serotonin levels. If OCD, as it has been suggested by many exponents in the field of research, is caused by an imbalance in the neurotransmitter serotonin, then it stands to reason that exercise would have a positive effect in that regard. In fact, it is even suggested further on in the study, that exercise may have a very similar effect to that of selective serotonin reuptake inhibitors (SSRIs), the group of drugs specifically targeted to reduce OCD symptomology. I have often, over the years, tormented myself over my decision not to take drugs. By not taking them, I feared it meant I wasn't committed to getting better or to alleviating my own - and thereby my family's - suffering. Now, I felt better about my resolution to take on the illness without the help of chemical substances with names like sertraline, fluvoxamine or escitalopram (although, please be clear, I am not for one moment decrying the use of drugs; for some, SSRIs in conjunction with traditional CBT is a vital combination).

As the weeks and months went by, I used the gym more and more frequently until eventually I got into a steady routine of thrice weekly (which I still do to this day). The effects for me were almost instantaneous. Straightaway, I felt stronger both physically and mentally. I had more energy during the day and found I could concentrate much better whilst at work. I felt more resilient, less lethargic. My attention span grew so that I could now read on average two books a week. Meanwhile, my ability to relax in the evenings (something I struggled with, particularly during the worst of my OCD) now posed no issue at all. I seemed for some reason to get far less colds and other irksome little health complaints and, perhaps best of all, the spikes of anxiety and guilt became far less frequent and severe.

Though it would perhaps be incautious of me to assert that gym membership, unregulated, is *always* such a positive and worthwhile experience. As with pretty much anything that gives us pleasure or *reward*, too much of it can be quite bad for you. In some people, it can actually become like an obsessive compulsive cycle all of its own. Although this is, at present, a controversial issue. Whilst some regular gym goers claim that it is possible to get a 'kick' out of the rush of endorphins following exercise, and that this can indeed be addictive, most scientists snub the idea that exercise in itself, without what are known as 'psychoactive substances' to create feelings of withdrawal, can ever truly constitute a *real* addiction.

Personally, I do not think it is that simple. Exercise is often seen, both scientifically and culturally, as a gateway over fitness, body shape, body size and even over mood. For those of us with a propensity to take excessive control over personal things in our lives, such as what we look like (I am thinking, in particular, those of us living with OCD, BDD or the various eating disorders), I can certainly see how exercise might, in some circumstances and after certain conditions are met, become something of an unhealthy preoccupation.

If I can offer one pieces of advice when it comes to exercise or gym membership then it is this: When one feels guilty if they miss so much as a single session or are constantly consumed by the feeling that they are never quite doing 'enough', then this should not be ignored. Exercising under this sort of pressure can be dangerous to both physical and mental well-being. It is important to recognise when exercise is part of the solution and when it is actually simply just a larger part of the overall problem.

Fortunately for me, I can safely say that - at least so far as I am consciously aware - I have not replaced any of my pre-existing obsessions (such as fears of being morally bad) with obsessions related to the gym. I do not run marathons with shin splints or lift weights with torn ligaments. I do not gaze in the mirror for hours at a time or avoid food if I haven't worked out (this, despite having always been concerned about my weight and losing the so-called 'puppy fat'). I like to think I have a balanced and healthy relationship when it comes to exercise and the gym. Though, that is not to say that it did not ever come close to obsessive for me. It certainly has not always been that easy to keep a level head.

For me, it was the intricate nature of fitness as opposed to any crises over my bodily appearance that posed the greatest risk to my obsessional tendencies. I found, when I first started especially, that there was so much information out there on keeping fit that one needed an almost obsessive interest just to keep up with all the literature. It's not a case of just *exercising*. Or so I was repeatedly told by gym enthusiasts and nosey well-wishers alike. In order to make the most of any fitness oriented activity, one must apparently consider the various types of exercise very carefully first and then tailor it to individual, specific goals (weight loss, weight gain, fat burning and reconditioning). There is no one universally accepted approach to how one might optimise their energy expenditure.

I certainly had not expected, upon starting out, how difficult it might be to get it right. In fact, it was only after a few weeks of going to the gym that some kid told me that I was actually doing it all wrong (in reality there is no such thing; there is merely safe and unsafe). "You need to focus solely on the cardio," the strapping nineteen year old told me, looking at the small tyre around my belly and watching as I attempted the 12.5 kilogram dumbbells for the second set. "Then when you have lost the extra pounds you can start using the dumbbells and building the muscle." His reasoning was to do with a number of studies he had read up on showing that cardiovascular activities burn off fat much more effectively than weightlifting which should, he told me finally, be used chiefly or even solely for *bulking up*.

Though a few weeks later and a Polish bodybuilder at the same gym had sworn blind to me the very opposite; that it was strength training exercise that was the key to weight loss due to muscle having a much higher metabolic rate. *"The higher is muscle,"* said the husky, stalwart Warszawianin one session as he attempted to bicep curl over two hundred kilograms on the cable machine, *"the greater is fat burn."*

Ultimately, it was a mixture of common sense and guesswork that, over the coming weeks and months, saw me eventually raise my general level of fitness and lose over two stone of fat. (In fact, since first attending the gym almost three years ago, I have gone from almost thirteen stone right down to ten stone eleven pounds - which means I am now actually slightly *underweight* according to my BMI.) I did not hold on to any highly scientific or specifically tailored programme. I just did what felt good and what I felt safely challenged me. I never pushed myself to ridiculous levels. I certainly never exercised or dieted obsessively.

To this day, I hold firmly to those same principles. And I can honestly say, it works very well for me. Most crucially, the gym is still one of my greatest allies in the defence against the dark and debilitating symptoms of OCD. Whenever I am feeling particularly low or anxious, I go for a run. If I have had a particularly stressful day at the office, the first thing I will do is hit the gym. I can almost guarantee that I will come out feeling better than when I went in. At the gym, I can be simultaneously focused and distracted (from OCD). I can be functional and resilient, poised both physically and mentally.

Perhaps unsurprisingly, and at the time of writing this chapter, I have no plans to stop regularly attending any time soon.

I started going out more. As the summer approached, the atmosphere somewhat lifted, I resolved to make a concerted effort to bolster my social life. I looked good (or at least, I had got into better shape), I felt much more physically robust and, perhaps most importantly of all, my mind was starting to function correctly; a refreshing, delightful synchronicity with the world that gave me a greatly renewed zest for life.

One afternoon, a good friend of mine, Rich, asked me out to a summer garden party at a pub on the river close to where I lived. The event was being hosted by a local yet well-known singer-song writer - I forget now his name - who had spent considerable time putting together a litany of local talent and who had suitably prepared a large acoustic set outside on the terrace.

"There'll be plenty of *girls* going," Richard had explained to me somewhat keenly a few weeks prior to the event over the phone, "and, you never know, we might even get to chat to some of the performers."

And true enough, as had been so fanatically proponed, the garden party had been full of young, attractive girls. Not to mention teems of festival-going, flannel, plaid-wearing indie kids; a veritable 'melting pot' of postmodern Norfolk subculture. Though for me the crowds had triggered an unexpected rush of OCD, a sudden and sharp rise in both guilt and anxiety which had totally taken me by surprise; *What if I brush against someone with my crotch?* I began panicking to myself, tiny droplets of sweat fast gathering on my forehead. *How will I know I'm not trying 'on purpose' to rub my penis on them?* And with each and every cerebral chicanery, I shuddered at the mental image of me doing this, my apprehension sliding steadily up the base-ten logarithmic Richter scale.

Finally, as people started collecting in the garden like molluscs on a damp garden wall, I told Rich that I did not feel sure I would be able to cope.

"*Cope*. Course you will *cope*!" Richard responded rather brusquely. "Don't be such a *pussy*!"

Richard, somewhat lacking in empathy (in case that much wasn't already apparent), has had very little time for my OCD over the few years that I have known him. He would laugh at most of it or else unflinchingly tell me to *fuck off* when he couldn't be bothered to hear anymore. There was scarcely ever a more temperate or middling response. Certainly nothing ever resembling true *sympathy*. Though, in many ways, I have come to appreciate such brutal honesty. Sometimes, this sort of hard-line riposte, this rather uncongenial interdiction can actually be exactly what the OCDer needs to hear; the rather glib and candid dismissal of obsessions giving OCD the attention it truly deserves.

And so it was, that evening, with a small kick into touch from Rich plus an even more forceful attack of will-power from me, I managed to resist the urge to avoid or to ritualise. Instead I resolved simply to throw myself into the party atmosphere. If my decision sounds flip, then you misunderstand me. Resistance, as they say, is never easy. Sometimes it can feel close to impossible. Often the best way through is *distraction*. The bigger the distraction, the easier to shift gears. And with each manual permutation or translocation, the easier it becomes to substitute OCD for something else. *Anything* else.

Fortunately for me, on this occasion, there were opportunities for distraction seemingly everywhere. Minor celebrities, music, alcohol, *girls*. Indeed, it wasn't long before my big break came when one of the female performers, a bodacious and striking young musician from Suffolk, sashayed right passed me following her bristling five-song debut out on set. Not feeling at all deterred by nerves or embarrassment (my OCD creating an almost devil-may-care demeanour with regards anything else outside of my own pattern of intrusive thoughts) I had decided to accost her at the bar and introduce myself, resulting in a conversation that would, unbelievably, last almost twenty whole minutes straight. In that time, my anxiety went down to almost nil, replaced with what can only be described as genuine excitement.

"I can't believe you're actually talking to Ria Richie," Richard later whispered stridently into my left year. "*Ria Richie*. She's the main act! How on earth did you manage to pull off something like that?"

Of course, normally, I *wouldn't* have been able to pull of 'something like that'. Ordinarily, it would be Richard and not me to pave the way in situations such as this; acquainting himself (often intimately) with all the ladies, especially the ones as beautiful and successful as Ria undoubtedly was. He would chat, charm, beguile and inveigle. He would be cheeky, rude, funny and often darn right arrogant. Nine times out of ten, it would work well for him. When he didn't get a snog or a phone number, he would nearly always receive, at the very least, a most prodigious reception. Now, by some small miracle, plus a few glasses of double vodka coke, *I* had been the one to inveigle and charm. In fact, I had made perhaps the most impressive inroads of either of us to date.

"You'll have to come and see me at some of my other gigs around Norfolk," said Ria quite sincerely.

It was an invitation that neither Richard nor I could refuse.

And so it was that the two of us attended many of Ria's gigs following that first garden party in Norwich. We got to know Ria and her friends (including her beautiful cousin Jasmine and her infamous brother Reece) and, on one occasion, were even invited to a pool party at her home in Suffolk though had to turn it down because it was getting late and there was no way of either of us getting back home again. As the months went on, I continued to make Ria laugh and she, in turn, impressed me with her amazing song writing and singing talent (one evening, for a laugh, we even sang a duet together of Wet Wet Wet's '*Love is all around*' in front of a crowd of her friends; even she had to agree that my Marti Pellow impression was actually pretty 'top notch'). Now, almost three years on from our first ever encounter, Ria has made it big time. She has been signed up with an independent musician management company, has played live gigs with the likes of Plan B and very recently, has even had one of her very own new world exclusives '*Something About You*' play on BBC Radio 1xtra.

In many ways perhaps my biggest claim to fame of all time is a photo of Ria and I on a garden patio at one of my local pubs just by the River Yare; she is wearing a cool Persian orange jumper and a stylish rectangular-patterned bandana and I am adorned in a newly purchased light brown T-shirt from Tesco in a size *small*. In the photo we are both smiling. Sometimes, when I feel I am about to hit a bit of a low (hey, it still happens from time to time), I like to look at this photo to help bolster my mood. It is a reminder of how good and exciting things can be; how lucid my life is without the disruptive presence of OCD.

Without a doubt, my new celebrity camaraderie with Ria not to mention the opportunities for partying and socialising this generated, had had a most positive influence on my OCD. It had given me something to look forward to and provided me with an exciting distraction. Though the credit cannot, of course, begin and end with Ria. She is certainly not the only friend to have had such an affirming effect (although she is, by far, the most famous of all my friends). My acquaintances, if my own online social networking service is to be believed, actually go into the hundreds, with at least twenty people whom I can call 'close'. Unfortunately, due to the nature of this book, I am unable to venture into every friendship, to talk about each and every individual who has touched my life, who has made my journey with OCD that much more bearable. But that is by no means to diminish their influence. I love them all.

Friends, in many ways, are perhaps one of life's great tonics against the weighty sense of isolation. They are a lifeline when all around seems cold and black. They are there for us and they divert us; they make us realise that we are part of something much bigger than simply ourselves. These days, my social life is extremely active with friends from all spheres; from work colleagues to old school mates to fellow OCD sufferers. I am never short of an offer or an invitation and I try where possible not to take this for granted. I do not always want to go out but the gesture is always very well received; I am always very grateful to have so many people in my life that want to spend time with me.

One line from Hilaire Belloc's *'Dedicatory Ode'* particularly comes to mind here as I write this passage and maybe sums it up the best:

'From quiet homes and first beginnings, out to the undiscovered ends, there's nothing worth the wear of winning but laughter and the love of friends.'

Of course good friends are important. Though to a large extent they are perhaps only *part* of the picture. Despite the best social life I had experienced in months, arguably years even, I still could not help but conclude that friends alone were not the only or even the main fillip against the chronic symptoms of lonesomeness and seclusion that OCD induces. In fact, with only a moment's contemplation, I could think of something perhaps far more exclusionary, far more perfervid and *impassioned*. So impassioned in fact that, despite such a full and happy social life, loyal friends and a loving family, I knew I could not be truly contented without it.

"What does a *relationship* mean to you?" This was a question posed to me one session by one of my therapists. She came a few years after Joseph and remains to this day one of the best therapists I have ever had the pleasure of working with. She asked me to write free-style for thirty minutes on the subject.

"Just write whatever pops into your mind," she told me. "Do not stop, do not worry about your grammar, just keep on writing." And so I did. This is an extract of what I came up with (unedited):

Relationships to me are a means by which a person may feel like they are complete. A life outside of a relationship can be lonely and sequestered and isolated. I have felt often a sense of isolation and loneliness at being outside of this framework which, increasingly over the years, I have associated with happiness.

Actually, I know that a relationship does not equate to happiness. A good relationship might equate to happiness. A bad one is as bad as being single, worse sometimes. Conversely, I think that some singletons may feel that their lives are perfectly complete without a partner and that their lives are perfectly happy.

I think that, aside from the loneliness (most of which can be quelled from friends and family) is the sense of feeling profoundly unappealing. If I am single and my friends are not, then I am somehow deficient. Unfortunately, when you look at those people that are single on a long term basis (not out of choice*) they are often the ugly ones or the stupid ones or the weak ones or the short ones or the fat ones or something equally as socially maligned.*

Then, of course, there is the sexual frustration. I want to be with a girl and enjoy something physical. I fancy girls quite powerfully and my yearning is often too much to bear when it comes to my feelings for the opposite sex. For whilst I enjoy female company immensely, I also crave girls physically too.

I also tend to be able to become deeply infatuated with some girls. In the case of Loretta, so powerful were my feelings towards her, the rejection which followed was devastating. These feelings, right from the very start, were anything but merely companionable; they were fierce and intrusive and indomitable and powerful and other-worldly.

In truth, the girl for me may very well be a sensible 'plain' looking girl (see - I'm fixated on looks - which I hate because I find it so shallow when girls base their decisions not to go out with me based on equally superficial criteria - I am a perpetrator and victim of the same crime). The girl of my dreams may also be someone who is simply a friend first; who I grow to love over time. Sometimes I think this will be better. I would not get the highs but I certainly would not suffer the lows.

And so I guess it boils down to this; I am unsure entirely about what I want. My heart and head pull in different directions. I want to feel loved and to love but am not sure how I want to love, with whom I should form a relationship and when I should ultimately decide to commit.

My counsellor passed me a wry smile; "It all sounds like a bit of an entanglement," she pointed out almost quite patronisingly. "I can see why it makes you so anxious."

In fact, my thoughts and feelings regarding relationships didn't just make me anxious, they made me feel bitter, angry, frustrated and jealous too. So much negativity; it was perhaps no wonder my OCD was able to take such a vehement hold. OCD thrives on negative thinking - or *stinking thinking* as Julia in the group likes to call it. In many ways, my attitude towards women and my apprehension surrounding relationships or lack thereof provided perhaps the perfect pretext for the rather downbeat and impugning voices now unleashed and unbidden inside my head.

"Perhaps your OCD exists to keep you out of a relationship," my counsellor offered out of the blue one afternoon. I didn't agree with her and still don't. But it was certainly food for thought. Indeed, my general disquietude surrounding sex (i.e. 'questions of potency'), the fear of *rejection*, as well as the constant uncertainty over whether or not I may ever one day find the 'right' person, was anxiety inducing to say the least.

OCD, in its most simple classification, is nothing more than a way of processing and dealing with surplus anxiety. Like drinking or smoking, it exists simply to numb out the uncomfortable effects brought on through feelings of insecurity and foreboding. Without the anxiety, there would arguably be no need for the OCD. And if, as indeed I had now started to conclude, my anxiety pivoted around more general concerns surrounding *relationships* then it stood to reason that a girlfriend might, just *might*, be the answer to all my OCD problems.

But where on earth to find one?

*

In August, I decided to try my hand at online dating. In part this had been inspired by the above, though I had actually toyed with the idea before whilst I had been practicing as a trainee solicitor down in Essex but had never really gotten round to it. Back then I had literally been so busy with briefs to council and trips to the police station that the prospect of actually meeting someone outside the confines of courtrooms and local cop shops had been perhaps as likely as winning all six numbers on the National Lottery. Yet now, with a new relatively light work commitment (most of my free time I spent out with friends anyway) plus a little more confidence (courtesy of the gym) I found, finally, I had both the time and the inclination.

But was online dating really the best way of filling the void? Of meeting a suitable partner. At first, it had felt like a bit of a no brainer: over eighty pages of female contenders aged from between eighteen to 35 all within fifty miles of my own bedroom! In many ways, I had felt a bit like a kid at Hamley's megastore on Regent Street. So much to choose from; I was almost bound to find exactly what I was looking for.

In practice, the opposite could not have been truer. Unfortunately, I was about to learn this the hard way: that where there is choice, there is rejection. Enough rejection to shake a shitty stick at in fact. To put it into context, the average girl receives between twenty to fifty impromptu emails from men every night (my own estimations, though based on a bit of research). Chances are, if they are attractive and you haven't sent them a message first, they won't even have viewed your profile page. Alas, most evenings, my inbox remained empty. Worse still, most girls who I did email, never wrote back. Some were polite enough to tell me in no uncertain terms where to go.

"I'm sorry but you're just not what I'm looking for," said one girl, only 5 ft 2, looking for someone six foot and above. "I'm sure you're a lovely guy though." (It would seem that height in particular is a very important thing to get right with women online. One girl, 5 ft 9 had written on her profile: *"Looking for someone taller than me but that's not hard"*. The words had left me speechless. *Well it is hard*, I felt like writing back, *if you're only 5ft 8*. Perhaps I should have invested in some stacked leather heels.)

Though, despite these initial failings (frustrating as they were), eventually and with some perseverance, my luck did start to ever-so-slightly change. After a few months of so-called *spray-and-pray* emailing (winking at no less than 106 girls), I eventually started going on dates. In fact, by the end, I had actually been on as many as six or seven. Unfortunately, I cannot say that I met anyone special during that time. I certainly did not fall in love. Though each one had been satisfying and significant in its own way. Now looking back, I certainly do not regret meeting any of the girls I dated. On a personal note, they have all gone some way in helping to tackle my profound issues of low self-esteem. As well as, latterly, in dealing with a number of OCD fixations I had surrounding sex and intimacy.

It would be perhaps out of context to go through and list each date/relationship in succession and so I will perhaps just stick to my very last encounter which was, arguably, the longest and most meaningful. Her name was Samantha, 24 years old and studying nursing at the University of East Anglia. Samantha was originally from Boston in America and had a rather cute American accent which, having gone there only a few months prior, I found to be an endearing quality. However, I was never overwhelmingly in lust with Samantha. Nor did I find her irresistibly attractive. But...*but*...there was something about her which I did definitely like; we got on intellectually and shared many of the same interests and values; everything from favourite movies (*Manhattan*, *Deconstructing Harry*, *Vera Drake*) to the role of religion in society (we were both quite scathing). On our first date we had gone to a small bohemian pub in Norwich; we shared a selection of tapas and I had a few pints of real ale. That evening, we both got tipsy and, jokingly, I carved our names with my key into our vintage butcher block table. At the end of the night, we kissed.

Over the following weeks, Samantha and I went on a number of interesting and enjoyable assignations. We saw Lars Von Trier's new film *Melancholia* at the local *indie* cinema, had an all-you-can-eat Chinese on the river and, one evening, signed ourselves up for an educative, though perhaps fairly unconvincing, ghost walk round Norwich. Yet, despite the frolics and the rapidly evolving friendship, I couldn't help thinking there was still something missing from our burgeoning companionship; a piece of her personality or maybe even something about the way she looked that had stopped my being fully beguiled. Though what exactly it was that was missing, indeed whether those shortcomings could somehow be surmounted, I could not say.

The two of us ended up sleeping together. It was not something that I had planned but that seemed just to materialise. For the first time in my life, I understood how one thing really could just lead to another. By this time, my OCD surrounding STIs had almost disappeared from sight (mainly as a result of encounters from previous dates) and my hang-ups surrounding the morality of one night stands (so long as they were conducted safely) slowly began to wither and wilt like a Christmas cactus in dampened or sodden earth.

And it felt good to finally feel free. It also felt liberating to at last be able to indulge in and even enjoy the kind of recreational goings-on common to even the most autogenetic of individuals. Though unfortunately, as is often the case in matters of this kind, the exultation was not to last. After a while of what can only be described as vainglorious rapture, I soon started to worry that I had simply used Samantha for sex. And the thought of this being the case made me feel incredibly guilty.

For days, weeks, I worried about whether I had been a bad person for sleeping with Samantha whilst simultaneously not being sure I wanted to remain with her long term. So many individuals, it struck me, seemed quite casually to elect having sex with people they barely knew, in relationships they had only just entered. Were all these individuals just *using* each other for one thing? How certain does one have to be about the longevity of any given relationship before they can say for sure that they are not simply using somebody else for sex?

Eventually, the fear that I really was leading Samantha on and that this might seriously come to affect her mental wellbeing came to a head one warm summer's evening when I decided to end our liaison once and for all via text. "I'm sorry," I told her, genuinely quite upset and still very much in two minds. "Though I think it's probably for the best."

"I see," she wrote back quickly and casually. "Wasn't expecting that. You're a lovely guy though. All the best for the future."

Much is the format or indeed *protocol* of online dating, Samantha and I have not seen nor spoken to each other since. I guess in many ways, when it came to my dealings with Samantha, my OCD fear of being a bad person had perhaps been the biggest contributor in ending a potential relationship before it had even been given a chance to get off the ground. Or at least, this is what some of my friends have since told me. In many ways they are right of course; our liaison had actually shown a great deal of promise. We had got on well and clearly had fancied each other enough to initiate sex. Nevertheless and OCD aside, I still couldn't help but shake the feeling that something just wasn't *right*. Both regarding the type of girls one might ultimately procure online as well as the rather more passionless and arbitrary process of selection that such a platform tended to espouse. In many ways, online dating is profoundly unromantic. Unromantic love, in my eyes anyway, is *imperfect* love. It was an impasse that I just could not get my head around.

Here is part two of my section on *relationships*:

Girls I've actually dated (and not just fantasised over) are, in many ways, too close for comfort. I am certainly a lot fussier than I ever thought I would be. Though I cannot help but think my problem might simply be a variation of ROCD (Relationship OCD) whereby I have simply become compulsive about whether or not I fancy someone, concluding that if I am unsure then I should probably steer well clear (the consequence of not steering clear in such circumstances, of course, meaning I run the risk of 'using' somebody and thereby being a bad person). And yet, I am, at the same time, painfully aware that you cannot always love someone upfront (at least, from experience, I know this is not always a very good idea). Love can often grow which is why arranged marriages for example often have quite high success rates.

In conclusion, the whole 'relationship' question seems to me to be a bit of a bloody minefield! Unlike most of my OCD, it is perhaps this manifestation which is hardest to appropriately label and dismiss as irrational. Where does OCD end and real life begin? Who do I fancy enough to sleep with? How will I know if or when I've met the right girl? I genuinely hope that I will someday work it all out as the alternative might be a life of endless loneliness and seclusion. Not to mention, many more frustrating years of sexlessness!

They say that before you can be happy with another, you must first learn to be happy with yourself. It took me a long time for this message to truly sink in. Though it has, without doubt, been one of the best life lessons I could have possibly learned.

"The most important part of recovery," Margo once told us all, "is being kind to yourself." It was a concept I had had trouble grasping until someone told me one day about something called *'acceptance'*. 'Acceptance and Commitment Therapy' or ACT, as with the more traditional methods of ERP, is a form of dialectical behavioural therapy that states simply that, rather than trying to reduce the *frequency* of bouts of anxiety, we must instead concentrate on lessening the experiential discomfort when the anxiety does come. Thus, by accepting that the anxiety will hit us at some point, as well as the rather scarier notion that we do not ever know for certain whether we are good or bad, safe or unsafe, we allay some of the worst of our pain simply by refusing to resist.

"What we resist persists," warns Sonia Johnson, American writer and activist.

Eventually I decided to stop pursuing a career in law. The relief was tremendous. For whilst I did love elements of the legal profession, I never managed to quite see it as a vocation, one which I might willingly allow to occupy so much of my free time. That is not to say that I thought that work in general was too much. Quite the opposite in fact: I knew that work would probably do the world of good for my OCD. '*The devil makes work for idle hands,'* warns Chaucer; for no group is this truer than the OCD sufferer with an impish and over-active mind.

And it is for precisely this reason that, from the time of coming back from America to eventually finding the job I currently occupy, I forced myself into a number of second-rate jobs, some of which, ironically, with the very worst of moral reputations. Although none of them seemed very much to bother me. I worked in a call center selling charity lotteries (perfectly ethical save for when it came to bullying and guilt-tripping ninety year-old women over the phone to donate to Age UK - ironically all Age UK literature warned elderly people *never* to give bank details over the phone under any circumstances); I became a dodgy phone salesmen, manipulating parents to put their spoilt fourteen year-old daughters on contract phone (where they would inevitably run up bills of hundreds, sometimes thousands of pounds) and even had a job selling broadband door-to-door.

The latter was by far the worst. In fact, this is possibly one of the lowest jobs anyone can ever be employed to do; ranking duly alongside debt collectors, tax inspectors and even the rich, heavily-bonused bankers.

I am ashamed to say that during my time as a first-rate con-man (unfortunately, I was actually quite good; often awarded 'top salesman' status), I switched more broadband users than I care to remember. "We're halfway through a contract with our current supplier," aporetic householders would decry. "Oh that's fine," I would counter. "I'm simply just reserving you a spot at the telephone exchange so you don't miss out [lie]. If your current suppliers do contact you, then you can simply just cancel the reservation [lie]."

Though there was perhaps one main perk to my job as a door-to-door salesman; a veritable sweetener which meant that, day after day, for a good few weeks longer than I should have, I pounded the streets, harassed innocent inhabitants and worked sometimes until the early hours of the morning. Her name was Rosina.

Rosina started as a door knocker about two weeks after me. She was funny, sweet and *extremely* beautiful. In fact, so striking was Rosina that, following her first day in the office, a warning to all the male staff had been issued by the bosses higher up the chain to, as it were, *steer bloody clear*. Relationships at work were, after all, forbidden. Though I for one had taken little notice. My own rules, invariably emanating from my OCD, bound me tightly like a corselet; by contrast, other people's edicts, short of infringing the actual laws of the land, were scarcely ever acknowledged.

Looking back now, I am glad I had not listened.

Rosina and I had what might be described these days as 'a connection'. At only twenty years old, Rosina was a good few years younger than me but was, despite a rather put-on coltishness, actually rather mature. Certainly more grown-up than I, four years her senior, could ever have hoped to be. Her social background was also very different to my own, having left home as young as fourteen and living, for some time, alone and quite independently on an estate in Norwich. Often I would rib her for being, as I described it, "from the ghetto"; a friendly jibe that would so often make her laugh and which had, somewhat ironically, brought us closer together.

One evening, out of the blue, Rosina texted me for the very first time, proudly claiming that she had obtained my number from a mutual colleague and that here, contained within her rather upbeat message, were her very own set of personal contact details. And for days, the communication had left me reeling with elation (after a dry spell longer than the list of names on the Washington Memorial, it was a relief to finally have some female attention). When eventually I decided only a few weeks later to quit my job as a morally dubious salesman (I knew it was fast becoming untenable), I simply could not resist the urge to finally tell Rosina how much I fancied her. I had not for a moment expected that she might actually have been even just slightly interested in me too. I certainly did not expect that she might be up for meeting up with me. Nevertheless, a few weeks after my departure, Rosina and I went on what might very loosely be termed a date. Already out with a few of my own friends at the time, I had sent Rosina an impromptu invitation to join me and she had responded instantly by catching the bus into the city to come and meet me out:

"Haha of course I'll come out, I'd already be tapin my foot waitinggg."

That evening, we both spent almost exclusively in each other's company; laughing, joking, occasionally huddling together in the cold. At the end of the night, following a fair few drinks and plenty more jesting and light-hearted raillery, we shared a taxi back to hers and from hers I walked home triumphantly in the rain. It had been, even in retrospect, one of the best evenings of my life.

Though, alas, my success with the dazzling, angelic Rosina was not to last. In the weeks following our trip out, the two of us continued to text; me quite keenly, her more reservedly, until eventually it became quite apparent to me that Rosina had in fact met somebody else. "Please stay in touch," she said to me finally, genuinely remorseful and seemingly unable - or perhaps even *unwilling* - to cut off all ties completely. "Promise me you will stay in touch."

As I write this chapter, I am not 'over' Rosina. That is not to say that I still have any residual *feelings* left just that, unlike with Loretta or even Isabel, my friendship with Rosina still remains to this day. That a girl as beautiful as Ros could ever have seen me as more than just a friend has been a great confidence booster over the years. It has made me see that an average guy like me, albeit abnormally preoccupied with mental refuse (itself inspirited by low self-esteem), might still nonetheless be an attractive proposition to somebody. In this instance somebody quite beautiful.

“A beautiful girl", says Paul in the 1996 movie, *Beautiful Girls*, "can make you dizzy, like you been drinkin jack and coke all morning. She can make you feel high, for the single greatest commodity known to man - promise. Promise of a better day, promise of a greater hope, promise of a new tomorrow.”

Often, when our thinking is flawed or unhelpful, we must attempt to change our *behaviour*. At least, this is what behavioural therapists tells us we must do. In CBT, for example, distorted cognitions and maladaptive beliefs are classically addressed by means of *behavioural* experimentation, focusing primarily on concepts such as exposure and habituation. Similar such behavioural modification is also used to treat post traumatic stress disorder (PTSD) as well as depression and other social phobias. But what of the *cognitive* element in all of this? Is it not possible to challenge and indeed, alter, the way we think by attacking our existing thought patterns directly?

In late 2012, I decided to try out hypnotherapy. In fact, I had not deliberately sought this form of psychotherapy, instead stumbling across it quite per chance when the fairly elegant woman with a nice house at the end of our road told us that she was a practicing hypnotherapist with over twenty years' experience and that the condition of OCD could, in fact, be treated quite successfully in this rather uncustomary manner. "Not only can hypnotherapy change your conscious thinking," she explained to me, after I had confessed my mental frailty one evening on the stretch of road outside my house (returning, as it happened, from more conventional therapy), "but it can speak to the subconscious mind too. It's like a double whammy - think of it, if you will, as a bit like *unconscious CBT*."

Unconscious CBT – it sounded pretty, well...*effortless*. In many other ways though, it sounded almost too good to be true.

"You do know it won't work," said Jake a few evenings prior to my first session. It was during another one of our random drives; this time to Wroxham, a town not more than eight miles north east of Norwich.

"It *might*," I said indignantly. "Why do you always have to be so negative...stop engaging me in *stinking thinking*!"

"Stinking *what?"*

As it happened, neither of us was qualified to form a valid opinion. A few months later and after six sessions of suggestion - based hypnosis, my OCD remained almost as it was. Though it was not, as Jake had bemoaned, a complete waste of time. Firstly, and perhaps more relevantly than even I had first acknowledged, I found it had relaxed me. Although the slow, anodyne speaking often did nothing but make me want to giggle inappropriately, I did find that, afterwards, I would feel much, much calmer. In fact often I would come away feeling so soporific that I would manage to avoid having a single OCD all evening; enjoying a good night sleep with very little anxiety by the next morning. It was a respite that, though only ephemeral, was nonetheless a welcomed reprieve.

Secondly, hypnotherapy had somehow bolstered my self-esteem. During the sessions I would be directed into progressive relaxation and guided imagery. Any negative self-talk was redirected and my mind was entreated to see each situation afresh. I stopped judging myself negatively. I stopped feeling inadequate. I stopped carrying past rejections around on my shoulders like a capuchin monkey and saw new hope and opportunity in all things; accepting that I, along with everyone else - and as much as everybody else - *deserved* to find someone and be happy.

In many ways, self-esteem, or rather *low* self-esteem, has an extremely large part to play in the onset and perpetuation of OCD. It feeds into our NATS, helps shape out negative biases or cognitive distortions and, ultimately, sets a pretext for our own sense of worthlessness (which extinguishes our outrage and indignation at the prospect of years of meaningless and unnecessary suffering).

Finally, by the winter of 2012, I decided I no longer wanted to be the martyr to such an empty cause. For the first time since my OCD had begun all the way back to my days at university, I came to the realisation that, actually, I did not *deserve* it. That contrary to almost a decade's worth of entrenched thinking, I was not the bad, horrific person I had so imagined myself to be.

"I am a good person," I said in the mirror one evening not long after my last course of hypnotherapy. "No scrap that! I am *me*. I am me and my true values will always shine through. I am me and I accept myself for it, the good and the bad. In its limited place, I even accept the OCD."

I re-started my diary. As the anxiety and guilt abated, so the quality of my life improved. And as life became worth living again so too did it once more become worth writing about. I worried far less about utilising tragedy in my prose, accepting instead that all writers do this and that my own intrusive thoughts were simply just that. I knew that I did not want my family to suffer any more than I wanted to eat dangerous wild mushrooms or allow the rather hideous orange-kneed tarantula to lollygag across my face. The small kick I did admittedly receive over any new storyline - explosions, illness, conflict, *sex* - was simply just a contradiction in my nature – or maybe that should just be a contradiction in *human* nature - that I would simply need to accept without modulation; without compulsion or avoidance.

And there were certainly a number of writers and diarists that were on hand to help me overcome such literary guilt. There was Alan Bennett who wrote frequently about his mother's depression, James Lees Milne who, in the penultimate volume of his diaries in particular, speaks candidly of the death of old friends and, perhaps most influential of all, Christopher Hitchens who not only wrote candidly on mortality but indeed on his *own* mortality (having written a collection of essays on the subject in *Vanity Fair* before his untimely death from oesophageal cancer in early 2011). As it happens, Christopher Hitchens had also written, perhaps unwittingly, about the very strange yet, again, very *human* phenomena of wanting and not wanting a thing all at the very same time. In his description of witnessing an IRA bomb explosion in his memoire *Hitch 22*, he writes the following: "I had that terrible inward feeling that I have since had at bullfights and executions and war scenes, of wanting this to stop while simultaneously wishing it to go on, and wanting to look away while needing to look more closely."

"The test of a first-rate intelligence," says Scott Fitzgerald, "is the ability to hold two opposed ideas in the mind at the same time, and still retain the ability to function."

One thing that OCD cannot deal with well is ambiguity and contradiction. It demands certainty and is unyielding in its endeavours to secure it by whatever means possible. It stands to reason that perhaps the best way, if not the *only* way to tackle it must be to live in uncertainty, even to embrace it. Writing in my diary was one very obvious way of achieving this aim and, as the months went on, together with an active social life and plenty of cardiovascular exercise to stave off the worst of my anxiety, I had begun to find living in doubt easier and easier.

Now of course I live in doubt all the time. I actually quite like it here. No anchor, no restriction, no stagnation. Most of all, I have learned, through various techniques, some of which mentioned in this very chapter, to habituate the fear and the anxiety that so often accompany living in uncertainty. A creature of habit by nature, I am never at my freest or most able than when living in wonder. It is a place I hope to become more and more at home with as each day passes. It is a place I hope I have visited on more than a few occasions in this book. And finally, it is a place I sincerely hope that you, dear reader, will venture into with a degree of aplomb.

Chapter 17
A NEW JOURNEY

So what have I learned about OCD in my time as a sufferer? And what have I learned, if anything, about what it takes to get through. Well, the first thing without a shadow of a doubt (bold coming from a pathological doubter) is that OCD doesn't go away by itself. It is the dark, sulphur dioxide-infused smoke clouds of Guandong or the thick black smog which hangs menacingly over Mexico City. It is not, by contrast, the more innocently formed rain clouds of, say, Henderson Lake which, by turns of nature, will ebb and flow. OCD, in all material ways, is the absolute opposite of fleeting or transitory; it is a life-time affliction. That is, if you allow it to be.

Finding a decent strategy or strategies, as you can imagine, is therefore of vital importance. So too is good old fashioned valour. Though it is the latter that is often missed from all the manuals and text books. Facing down your OCD takes *guts*. "Like a person confronting their fear of heights by bungee jumping off a tall building," says Margo, "OCD is scary because it involves facing up to that which you are most afraid."

Actually, in my opinion, it is much more than this. OCD is not just about facing down fears but about challenging dyed-in-the-wool beliefs. People with the dreaded *O* aren't just afraid of what might happen if they throw themselves into some bizarre, insane activity such as jumping out of a plane or eating a living earthworm, they are deeply disturbed with what they believe to be a genuine threat which they must face up to every single day of their lives. Crucially, they are rarely ever afraid of the danger they pose to themselves. They are, by stark contrast, much more concerned over the danger they may present to others, their main apprehension always being orientated towards those around them or those to whom they believe they owe or may owe a degree, however small, of responsibility.

Which is exactly why OCD should not ever be dealt with alone. Anomic and self-sacrificing by nature, we are often not the best people to help ourselves constructively through the pain. "By itself OCD is a tremendous and burdensome affliction," says Margo. "Faced alone, it is almost insurmountable." Hiding symptoms of OCD, I hope I have managed to successfully impart throughout this book, is often the very worst thing we can do.

In many ways, nothing has been more valuable to me and my recovery than friends, family and my OCD group. They are a support and a lifeline. They are there when I am at my lowest or even when I need, as is often the case when I am with Rich, just a very small kick up the backside. How could I have known that outside of my own little microenvironment, outside my local stomping ground where fellow sufferers, by and large, are pretty darn hard to come by, there would be a whole *community* of OCDers just waiting to be discovered.

In November 2011, I attended my first ever OCD Conference. It was a full day event, hosted by *OCD Action* (one of the UK's leading National OCD charities) and intended to enable OCDers from around the country the opportunity to meet up as well as to hear from leading experts on current treatments and research. "You ought to go," said Margo, handing me over the flyer which had been sent to her in the post. "It's a bit far for me but I'm sure you would get a lot out of it."

And in more ways than even I had bargained for, she was right.

That year, the year I attended, the event was being held at the New Academic Building at the London School of Economics and I had travelled all the way down by train to be there (risking, as it were, transport-induced OCD along the way). Though, as it turned out, it had certainly been worth all the effort. Throughout the day (which actually started as early as 9.30 a.m. and didn't end until 4 p.m. that afternoon, following which there was an annual GM for the members), I got the chance to meet a plethora of thoroughly inspirational people: members and facilitators of groups up and down the country (I was surprised to learn that there were literally *hundreds* of groups) as well as clinical experts and not to mention some rather thought-provoking guest speakers.

The first of these inspirational people perhaps worth mentioning here was author of *'The Essential Guide to OCD'*, Helen Poskiitt, who had been asked by the charity to open up the conference with something stirring and light-hearted (and whom had used the event as an opportunity to plug her new novel, *'Rising to the Surface'*). During her rather doctiloquent speech, Helen talked humorlessly about her own OCD as well as on the new book, a story of a young woman with OCD and her rather risqué encounters with a less-than scrupulous therapist. Later on that afternoon, I got a chance to speak face-to-face with Helen following a lunch time creative writing workshop that she had laid on for those interested in putting down their OCD experiences into poetry or prose. It is worth noting here that, at the time, writing about my own OCD had perhaps been only latent in mind. I certainly did not have plans to transform any of my page-a-day scribblings into a full blown *memoire*. Nonetheless, Helen, noticing my flare (or, at the very least, my interest) in writing, opted to give me some further words of encouragement: “What could be more rewarding,” Helen said to me, after the workshop was over, “than putting down your own quirky internal experiences onto paper. Such a rich, rich source of material.”

It had certainly been food for thought.

As well as speaking with Helen that day, I was also afforded the opportunity of meeting renowned consultant psychiatrist and senior lecturer at the Institute of Psychiatry, Dr David Veale as well as clinical expert on OCD and co-author of *'Overcoming Obsessive-Compulsive Disorder'* Dr Rob Wilson. In the afternoon lecture on 'Keeping on top of OCD' given by the latter, Rob highlighted some of the things we could all do - promoting a sort of ready-made OCD survival pack if you will - to help make sure we did not relapse. "It is very important not to forget the journey you have all been on to get where you are today." It was an aspect of my recovery that I perhaps had, thus far, not given anywhere enough attention to. It is an aspect of recovery I fear that no one ever gives enough attention to.

Finally that day, and possibly most meaningfully for me, I had the pleasure of being introduced to 35 year-old Keira Bartlett, a rather attractive lady and fellow sufferer from none other than my own home county of Norfolk. Unbeknown to me at the time, Keira had been facilitating a group not forty miles from our own group which I had found to be, if nothing else, a tremendous ice-breaker; setting the scene, as it turned out, for a long and fruitful friendship. That afternoon, Keira gave the closing inspirational speech. In many ways - and despite her chronic nerves that afternoon - it had quite simply been a case of saving the best until last. Her own story, much like my own, has been one of constant struggle through relentless thought-based OCD. And yet, remarkably, *inspirationally*, she had not only come out the other end but had also dedicated her time to helping others with this wretched condition. So much so in fact that, aside from facilitating the Norfolk group, Keira was also working with OCD Action directly to improve the effectiveness of the charity in reaching out to as many carers and sufferers as possible.

It had all been enough to alter my perspective on my own suffering almost irrevocably.

That my illness might actually be *worthwhile* to someone gave my life, as well as my often deleterious experiences, a new sort of meaning. It would be a major shift in my thinking, not to mention a vital reagent, the final step on that ladder towards that all-important transmutation from a depressed and encumbered adolescent back into a vibrant and functioning young *man*.

It would be a more than welcomed change.

*

It happens that I do not wear my OCD on my sleeve nor, indeed, as a badge of honor. But nor am I ashamed by it either. It is a part of me, it is a part of so many I know and care so deeply about. It isn't anyone's *fault*. It is not indicative of a weak or feeble mind. Nor should it be treated as an illness reserved primarily for those lacking percipience and insight or even moral decency. It can happen to anyone and tends to happen to those with only the desire in life to do good (although, as I say, this is no justification for subscribing to its lies or nurturing its presence).

Following the conference in London, I became convinced that what I really wanted, above all else, was to end the generational shame surrounding the disorder. To end the stigma, the judgment and the widespread ignorance. I wanted to help people understand the true nature of their affliction as well as to help educate those on the outside constantly looking in, never seeing anything more than the often outlandish behavior which will, from time to time, invariably spill into the observable world. It was the *inner* narrative, warts and all, that I somehow wanted to convey.

One evening Margo called me up and asked me if I wanted to help her run the group in a more formal capacity. "How would you feel about being co-facilitator," she asked me one evening over the phone. "You are so good at explaining things, I think you would be brilliant."

"Yes," I said, genuinely flattered, "I'd be delighted."

In fact, my appointment could not have come at a better time. Our group had just launched with its own website and had been granted funding from the National Lottery which meant, for the first time ever, we could afford to rent a proper room, pay for advertising and even have a Christmas meal for all the attendees. Slowly the group evolved from being primarily about 'tea and sympathy' to being a fully functional *support* group with elements of "constructive empathy" and psycho-education.

We changed our slogan. Our mission statement was now *"to provide empathy and constructive support to those with OCD and their carers"*. In fact, I had been the one to come up with the term 'constructive empathy'; I liked and still like the way it encapsulates both the need for compassion as well as that all-important push towards positive *action*.

In group sessions, we discussed CBT, mindfulness and many other psychotherapeutic techniques. We discussed the practical elements of OCD such as where to go for help, how to get onto the NHS waiting list as well as the more academic topics on OCD such as the role of the caudate nucleus, the benefits of SSRIs and the tenuous link between OCD and various childhood illnesses. My specialty was my overly simplistic but arguably quite effective brain diagram. From my copious reading on the subject, I tried to show sufferers where in the brain OCD lived. How it worked from a bio-chemical point of view and how such a circuit could be broken. I used the diagram to help people see how their OCD was almost entirely separate from their true selves. How it was no more than a kink, a bow, a hook in the flow of neurotransmitters or maybe a microscopic lesion somewhere inside of the orbito-fronto striatal cortex in the brain.

Sometimes I felt guilty passing myself off as someone who knew what they were talking about. I did not have any qualifications in psychology or CBT nor had I conversed, at least on a regular basis, with those that had. "Sometimes we are our own best experts," Margo would say. And to a large extent, I agreed. Though, for sure, I knew I did not want to inadvertently do more harm than good by imparting the wrong information or offering otherwise correct advice in a clumsy or ineffective way.

Now, I try, where possible, to relate all the advice I give to my own personal experiences. I do not pass anything off as fact or scientific or conclusive. The problem with OCD is that there is scarcely anything *conclusive* about it. There is still so much work to be done in uncovering the secrets of OCD; what causes it as well as how best to treat it. As an OCDer, one must invariably learn to avoid conclusions as a means of dealing with anything.

A few months later, I found the inspiration to write this book. By this time my diary had been re-invoked but it no longer seemed to hold the same appeal. Diary entries were cathartic but samey. They were also, to my mind at least, excessively private. I found that expending energy purely for my own isolated and sequestered pleasure now seemed something of a waste of, if not my talent, then of my slowly developing literary skills. Why not try to write for a much larger audience, I started to consider? Why not open up my struggling to the rest of the world? It seemed like the perfect way of blending both my need to write (perhaps spurred on by meeting Helen at the Conference) together with my newfound desire to spread the word on OCD; to end some of that *generational shame*.

And so, over the next few weeks and months, I set about converting notes and diary entries into passages and chapters. I found it, at first, to be most enjoyable. And much more of a challenge than merely chronicling the prosaic, run-of-the-mill events of daily life. Now I had a *message* to convey. Like the disciples of the Christian New Testament or the supra-national Muslim ummah, I felt a great sense of overwhelming pride in spreading the news. *But how best to do it,* I thought to myself over and over? How does one even begin to explain such a complex condition? Unfortunately for me, the answers were not so forthcoming.

To a large extent we can blame this literary block on the good old British media. The way that it is both glamorised and censored simultaneously means that OCD is possibly one of the most publicly misunderstood illnesses in the field of mental health. OCD, often portrayed as an endearing quirk or an amusing caricature, has a much more serious side indeed. It is not simply the small and harmless idiosyncrasies that help make up an eccentric best friend or an adoring but outlandish great aunt.

Nor is OCD contagious or hazardous either. Sufferers are neither mad, bad nor dangerous. I hope that by being excessively honest over the last eight or so chapters, particularly regarding subject matters that more naturally do not form a part of everyday parlance, I have managed to go at least some way in helping to set the record straight. I also hope more than anything that I have helped to dispel the myths surrounding what is otherwise a dreadfully serious, though, in the most part, conquerable, illness.

In 2012 I emailed a journalist. It was National OCD Week - an awareness event first launched back in 2011 (again, through OCD Action) and suddenly I had this abiding urge to contact someone, *anyone,* who might be willing to hear the truth about OCD. Not to mention help spread the word.

"We owe it to the group," I told Margo, a few days after I had hastily fired over the mail, "to explain this wretched condition to the world; to *make* people understand."

A week or so later, off the back of my correspondence, I got a call from the local health correspondent, Kim Bassett. "Thank you very much for your email," said the rather sweet but professional-sounding female voice at the other end of the line. "We've carefully considered your proposal for a story and, well, we would very much like to do a piece on OCD. How do you feel about perhaps meeting up next week so we can interview you further?"

"That sounds absolutely splendid," I said, with only modest enthusiasm. Though the truth of it was that this had been the most exciting thing to happen to me, indeed to the whole group, for a very long time and I reeled with elation.

The night of the interview was a dry and mild evening in April. Margo and I met Kim and her small camera crew just outside Norwich City Forum and I couldn't have felt more pumped up; buzzing, as it were, from the prospects of this rather luminary convocation. Against the backdrop of the splendid Gothic Cathedral of St John the Baptist, Margo and I had our photos taken outside the amphitheatre before, finally, making our way inside the forum for a cup of coffee and what had been designated by Kim, 'a small informal chat'.

In many ways and quite unbeknown to Kim or the team, the city's forum had been a fitting locale for the interview. Back in the early days, before we had received any form of funding, our small little group would routinely meet here on the first Thursday of every month. To protect people's confidentiality, we would speak in hushed tones and would refer to OCD simply as 'O' so as not to arouse any outside suspicion. It wasn't perfect but, at the time, it had most certainly been preferable to having no group at all.

Now, of course, we spoke quite openly.

"So," said Kim, settling down onto one of the leather couches in the al fresco café seating area by the window; she wore a long brown skirt that rode up slightly as she shuffled around to make herself comfortable. "I guess my first question to both of you should be: What influenced you to set up and run an OCD group? Why is OCD so important to you?" Margo and I looked at each hesitantly. It was certainly, if nothing else, a rather personal opener.

"Well," said Margo anticipatively, being the first of us to speak, "we both have it if that's what you mean." Margo passed me a stringy, rather drawn-out look, as if to slightly apologise for speaking on my behalf (and thereby very slightly breaching her duty of confidentiality). Margo, quite rightly, was always worried about accidently saying *too much* (hence the religious use of 'O' instead of 'OCD' whenever out in public). "As long as you don't give names," I would say, "you're absolutely fine." And I should have known, I had read the rules pertaining to legal confidentiality possibly more times than anyone in the whole of Norfolk. (Sadly, I had read *all* the rules pertaining to the legal profession in the same forensic detail.)

"OK brilliant," said Kim, scribbling down some notes into her small A5 pad. "In that case, would either of you mind telling me a little more about your own particular experiences…that is, if you are comfortable with that?"

Margo again, looked over to me and then back to Kim. "I wouldn't be comfortable with that," she said honestly. Margo was part of the generation where OCD was still extremely taboo. Her parents who were both now in their eighties had always been incredibly hard and unsympathetic with Margo over her OCD. They refused to believe that such things as OCD or depression even really existed. For them, OCD was no more real than mermaids or unicorns or the mythical characters of bronze-age Mesopotamia. By contrast, I have always been blessed with very understanding friends and family. Even my employer has been overwhelmingly accommodating over the years. During the second year of my employment at my current work place, for example, my bosses had actively encouraged me to take every Thursday afternoon off for therapy. I hadn't even been required to work through my lunch to make up the hours.

All this, of course, had gone towards a much more enlightened view of my condition.

"I don't mind saying a few words," I eventually came out with, exuding perhaps a little too much willingness to speak up. In truth, I actually quite liked talking about my own OCD. I was, and still am, an egomaniac at heart. In the world of social media and confessional literature I guess we are all great *egocasters*.

"That's great," said Kim, smiling quite emulously. "Please go on."

And so I told Kim as much about my early experiences of OCD as I could remember. I told her of the tap checking when I was ten and the subsequent fear of germs. I told her about my current aversion to even the slightest snippet of bad or immoral behaviour (leaving out perhaps some of the sex-related finer details - possibly evidence in itself that, even in today's progressive society, this illness is still enveloped in shame) and mentioned plenty about my time with OCD during university as well as the highly deleterious effects of being away from home.

After I finished talking about me and my own personal experiences, both Margo and I talked at length about the group. We discussed how OCD affected people more generally, the various treatment methods utilised and the importance of never feeling like you are alone.

"This is all such great material," said Kim, finally looking up from her notepad. "You have both given me so much. I think I can put something really good together here."

Margo and I smiled at each other. Seemingly, we had achieved exactly what we had set out to. We had raised awareness and had done our bit, albeit only a small part, to end the shame. At the end of the interview, Kim gave us both her card and wished us well with everything. "The article will probably appear in next Tuesday's edition. Look out for it," she said on her way out, adjusting her skirt once more as she departed the large glass doors of the forum entrance, held open by one of the much taller camera men, himself encumbered with a tripod and a hefty black canvas shoulder bag.

That evening, I walked home in the rain. It was a fine rain that fell from the sky gracefully, nevertheless soaking me through to the bone. Though, in such a positive state of mind, I might just as well have been floating through sunbeams. I had not felt the discomfort of my clothes sticking to my newly toned chassis or even the feeling of cold drips down the small of my neck.

Quite crucially, I had not seen the looming puddle in my horizon; the final cold *plash* along the journey towards full and meaningful recovery.

Chapter 18
THE WORRIED WELL

"I wanted every novel I have ever read to end with a true beginning."
Adalet Ağaoğlu, *Curfew*

"Worries cured," read the pithy sub-headline a few weeks later in the local paper. It was a mini-section in the article all about me. "Mr. Bennett," it went on to say, "from Norwich, Norfolk has successfully managed to overcome most of his OCD symptoms and now actually lives a relatively care-free life." And at once the editorial made me jolt back with unease; a revulsion that shot through me, shot through my body, like a cardiac catheter direct to the heart. Worries *cured*? I read the title again in disbelief. Somehow it didn't seem possible.

And yet, there it was, in black and white. Laid out in front of me like a picnic blanket in the throes of a hot summer's day. And as I attempted again to read the article for the third, fourth and even fifth time, I couldn't help but question its rather heartening and, to my mind, rather too consolatory content. Had I *lied* to the reporter that fervent afternoon at the forum? Perhaps I had reported back on someone else's life; the life I longed for but perhaps would never quite attain? Maybe, in my overenthusiasm to spread awareness, to show how conquerable OCD could really be, I had simply just got *carried away*?

"You have a pathological aversion to dishonesty," one therapist had actually told me not long after my return from university. And at the time, I had not really known what to make of it; of what it meant about me or about my OCD. Now, it seemed all too obvious. It was, if not unlikely then highly improbable, that I would ever be able simply just to *slip into* deceitfulness. Certainly I could not have ever lied *intentionally*. And on that basis, there had to be another reason for the article's bubbly, rather sanguine headline which was, I now couldn't help but think, that the piece did in fact quite accurately represent the *truth*. That, yes, I really was feeling "relatively carefree". After all, and when I *really* gave it some thought, I simply could not remember the last time I had suffered significantly with intrusive thoughts or debilitating rituals. When and where I did get the odd bout of OCD or *spat* of anxiety, I had seemingly been able to shrug it off with almost effortless resolve.

In many ways, I guess I should not have been overly surprised by such an outwardly fulsome recovery. After all, it hadn't happened overnight. Nor had it occurred without considerable effort from yours truly. There were, I believe, a number of reasons for my slow progression from sick to well; the first undoubtedly had been my trusty *toolkit*.

Following the lecture by Rob Wilson at the National Conference, I had almost at once set about creating my very own medi-pack. This veritable bag of tricks contained everything from my favorite hobbies (such as reading and writing or looking up random facts on Wikipedia) to strategies such as 'shelving' and mindfulness. It even included, dare I say it, ERP. Yes, that's right, you haven't misheard me; even classical CBT had something to offer me in eventually finding my way to recovery. Though I could not have implemented it successfully alone. Which leads us neatly on to the second and perhaps *main* reason for my recovery.

In late 2013, I stumbled across one of the best therapists I have ever had the pleasure of working with. Her name was Meghan. She was a tall, robust woman with long Bantu-style dreadlocks who also just so happened to be senior clinical tutor at the local college. "Leave the therapy to me," she had told me quite early on in our treatments. "You think far too much. You must simply concentrate on what I tell you."

Meghan's mantra was simply this; that the strategy for combating my OCD should be left to her whilst I dutifully, though mindfully, did what I was told. As far as Meghan was concerned, thinking for myself was perhaps the very biggest threat to my recovery. Worse than 'flooding', worse even than total, unadulterated ignorance.

One session I remember coming into the therapy room excitedly with a piece of paper in my hand. "Look!" I exclaimed with glee and feeling somewhat positive. "I had an OCD this week but I was quickly able to push my thoughts to one side by making a list of all the evidence for and all the evidence against." I handed over the list to Meghan, grinning like a cat that had not only got the cream, but swilled down a whole 410 gram tin of carnation milk whilst they were at it.

Meghan did not, however, seem so impressed. She read what was on the page and instantly looked back up again. "Did I *ask* you to do this?" she said, in her rather primary school teacher tone. The piece of paper held loosely between her thumb and index finger was filled with scribblings on both sides, each line full to the brim, with further notes crammed like sardines into the entire available margin. Clearly, it had taken me a good few hours to produce.

"No," I said, looking slightly crestfallen, "no you didn't."

"Then maybe, rather than always going lone ranger, you should just try doing what I ask from now on."

Meghan's point was that my OCD was so entrenched and my mind so over-active that analysis on any level was probably not a very good idea. Apt only in creating a whole new OCD sub-type.

Instead, and perhaps rather uncomfortably at first, Meghan had got me doing full-blown ERP (I know, even I have trouble believing it)! I would be asked each week to perform a specifically tailor-made task. Sometimes the tasks seemed directly relevant to my OCD (e.g. watch an online video of a baby's nappy being changed and allow myself to *look* fully at the genitalia) whilst others seemed to be more about distraction and uplifting my mood. One week, Meghan asked me to look out for the number four on my journey to and from work. "It'll be a good distraction from thinking constantly about looking at people's crotches," she had said. And so I looked out for *four* wherever I went. I was surprised at how many times I saw it on my way each morning to Norwich station:

Number **4** Bus via Ravenswood, Number **4**, 1**4** and 2**4** on front doors and wheelie bins, a **4** on car registration plates, an Audi A**4** 1.8SE **4**dr parked outside a kebab shop, a Clarksteel en12**4** CATV man-hole cover on one street corner and Waterway D**4**00 gully gratings dotted all along Thorpe Road.

At no point in any of my therapy tasks was *thinking* involved. "We are going to take your OCD apart one block a time; trial and error. Like a game of Jenga; one day we will pull out a block and the whole structure will collapse."

In fact, my OCD did not collapse; rather it slowly, often jarringly, began steadily to weaken and crumble, my OCD castle eventually resembling the ruins of the once magnificent Acropolis. Or Hadleigh Castle if you live anywhere near Southend-on-Sea. The top-up therapy, the handy toolkit, the acceptance and commitment, these had all seemingly worked wonders. I had not only strategies in place but fully blown roadmaps to keep me in a permanent state of recovery. Moreover, I had friends, family and a wide network of fellow OCDers to make sure my OCD never lead me, unchallenged, down another long and winding journey, away from emotional stability and well-being. In a nutshell, I had, finally and after so many years of quite desperate searching, a winning formulation.

* * *

So where am I now? One year on and it is now the summer of 2014. I am sat here writing at my computer, looking out the window at the beautiful plants and flowers planted by my dad; at the red-winged blackbirds gliding over our tiny bird table and at the vibrant staghorn sumac positioned near the back fence, its velvety carnelian stems prominent against the evergreen backdrop. The sun is shining brightly and the purple delphiniums are almost aglow in the light. And so too, believe it or not, am I. In fact, I haven't felt this light and carefree for almost as long as I can remember. It seems unbelievable to think that only twelve months previously, still struggling in the darkness of my own overgrown garden, I had gone *mano a mano* with one of the greatest enemies of peace, of harmony, of life itself.

Who would have thought that, just a short time later, I might ultimately have emerged triumphant.

As with any worthwhile research study, follow-up is often essential. At least it is if the results contained within are to be believed fully. Yet this is not a *research* study. This is a story, albeit a true one. It is a story of doubt, of hope, of great learning and even greater turmoil and frustration. It is, above all, a story of journeying through suffering and arriving at the other end. I have a mental illness. It will never go away. It cannot be *cured*. But it is no reason to give up either. I am still *me*. I have a life that I wish to live, to make every second count. I have places to see, people to meet, things I want to do. *Egosyntonic* things like finding a girlfriend, travelling the world; like *helping* people.

A little while ago now I received a call from Keira. Following a general catch-up about this, that and the other she told me that she had recently accepted a new role at OCD Action. She was now going to be in charge of a brand new project, entitled 'Better Together' designed, in the main, to help out independent OCD support groups up and down the country with everything from funding to advice on how to work more closely with local services. She asked me whether I would be interested in getting involved.

"We need about five regional volunteers. With your experience running the Norwich group, you would be a perfect RV for the South East."

"Yes!" I said, not taking any longer than a few seconds to decide. "I would love very much to get involved."

My enthusiasm was probably just as well. All these weeks later, it seems like I have simply not stopped getting involved. Last month, for example, I had travelled up to Birmingham (yes – *by train!*) for a one day training course to help with my new role. There, I met the other volunteers on the project and, together, we worked through, from scratch - and, of course, under the guidance of Keira - our three year strategy. "The importance of this project," announced Keira at the beginning of the session, "is to be available at all times as a national resource; to provide worthwhile support to the wider OCD community both practically and emotionally."

Following that very useful training in Birmingham, I have since spoken to over twenty facilitators in my region. We have opened up countless new groups, some in remote towns and villages otherwise cut-off from most of the rest of the outside world. We have helped groups with everything from finding venues, to accessing funding to advice even on policy documents (Vulnerable Adults, Data Protection etc). Next month we have our first ever Facilitator Day which, again, will be hosted in Birmingham. We are inviting over fifty groups across the UK to attend. It demonstrates an unprecedented level of proactivity and the start of what I now consider to be a united war against this otherwise abstract and intangible enemy. This minatory, contusing anathema known as OCD.

And I for one simply cannot wait. *Bring it on!*

Back at my computer desk, the sun is now beginning to shine even more brightly, sheets of light coming in through the recently erected skylight. It is not the longest day of the year but it's around mid-June so it's pretty close. The birds are singing away in the trees and, as clichéd as it sounds, my heart is abundant with, well, *love*. Not the love of a woman perhaps but a much more nuanced passion for *existence*, incorporating both a sense of self-worth as well as hope for a brighter future.

In so many ways, my life now seems so much more fulfilled. I feel like at long last there really is now true direction and *purpose*. Who'd have ever thought back during the days of heart-stopping anxiety and guilt that my journey with OCD might actually have turned out to be so rewarding. That my illness would actually be useful or even provide me with truer, deeper meaning.

Who'd have ever thought that I'd be, in my own unique way, blissfully happy.

Lightning Source UK Ltd.
Milton Keynes UK
UKOW02f0103111116
287404UK00001B/10/P